M000290422

The Death Café Movement

Jack Fong

The Death Café Movement

Exploring the Horizons of Mortality

Jack Fong
Associate Professor of Sociology
Department of Psychology & Sociology
California State Polytechnic University
Pomona CA, USA

ISBN 978-3-319-54255-3   ISBN 978-3-319-54256-0 (eBook)
DOI 10.1007/978-3-319-54256-0

Library of Congress Control Number: 2017939703

Cover design by Fatima Jamadar

Printed on acid-free paper

This Palgrave Macmillan imprint is published by Springer Nature
The registered company is Springer International Publishing AG
The registered company address is: Gewerbestrasse 11, 6330 Cham, Switzerland

I died for beauty, but was scarce
Adjusted in the tomb,
When one who died for truth was lain
In an adjoining room.

He questioned softly why I failed?
"For beauty," I replied.
"And I for truth, the two are one;
We brethren are," he said.

And so, as kinsmen met a night,
We talked between the rooms,
Until the moss had reached our lips,
And covered up our names.

—Emily Dickinson

For my son, Pattarakorn "Darius" Bhumichuchit

PREFACE

A few years ago I realized that I was attending more funerals than weddings. This book is a product of the transformation that continues from such a realization.

Not until I was complete with my doctorate and well into my career at my university did a variety of death circumstances compel me to reflect more critically about death and dying. However, even during graduate school the theme of mortality continued to be an unexplored topic of interest. The concepts behind mortality were somewhat made operative through my research on the Karen Revolution. In early 2004, I had the privilege of access to the Karen National Liberation Army (KNLA) and the Karen National Union (KNU) as they prosecuted their revolution against Burmese military rule. During my association with the KNLA 202 Battalion at Mu Aye Pu and my stay at the Thai border town of Mae Sot, I documented their struggle. Access to the inner workings of people engaged in revolution was made possible by a wonderful childhood friend who, in her capacity as a journalist, had contact with the rebels. My stay with the Karen gave me the raw reality checks people experiencing systemic crisis and death must contend with.

The Karen had repulsed different brutal military regimes that had governed Burma for decades. Not until Aung Sa Suu Kyi's rise and Thein Sein's exit can we now say that the country is slowly healing, although a myriad of unresolved political issues remain. At the time of my stay with the KNLA's 202 Battalion, political developments were exponentially less hopeful. In spite of their dystopia, the Karen managed to love, smile, dance, and raise their families. Many Karen also got very sick, starved, fought, and died together.

One important insight I was able to glean from the Karen struggle is how people in survival mode exhibit much lucidity about their wants, their lives, and their deaths. From their experiences, I attempted to understand society when it actually breaks down. It became clear that systemic crisis drastically alters social relationships in ways where a "new" sociology of sorts can be discerned. Indeed, much of sociology does not examine systems that break down; the concept of a "failed state" and its sociological consequences simply did not generate the bulk of findings comparable to, say, the examination of racism within states that have yet to fail. Again, this pointed to the hubris that many intellectuals harbor within their fortress of cultural capital: they induce and deduce from primarily "stable" systemic contexts to draw their conclusions. In this regard, sociologist Kurt Wolff, one of the many iconic sociologists whose ideas will be discussed in this work, was correct in observing how sociology has not been effective in confronting evil.

By the time my teaching career was launched, changes to my network of friends and kin who died began to take place. Their deaths synchronized with my role of caring for my ailing parents, a bonding process that allowed them to divulge many historical narratives of surviving wars and civil catastrophe. My father survived the Japanese invasion of China's eastern seaboard during World War II only to later, as a Kuomintang pilot, participate in the Chinese Civil War before beginning the Nationalist exodus to the Republic of China. My mother spent her young adult life in French Indochina only to later witness South Vietnam and North Vietnam embark on their epic war of attrition that compelled both my parents to depart for Laos, where I was born, and to Thailand, where I was raised. Both my parents lost many members in their respective families due to state-related affairs. Thus, the narratives of mortality flowing from this core of governance required epics, heroes, and glorious deaths. Self-authorship of mortality could not withstand how the tides of wars, failed states, and systemic and institutional failure of societies meted out mortality. Both my parents attributed the loss of family and individuals to the hope and collapse of nations.

Death informs epics and tragedies. It informed my dad's nationalism that in later life he acknowledged was misplaced, and it informed my pragmatist and sanguine mom's hatred of war. Yet their accounts of people's experiences with systemic crises through wars were rarely contextualized at the community level even though *communities*—not only families, individual, and warriors—*are destroyed during conflict.* In this context, the state expropriates death from the self and tosses it into the winds of war. In the process, there is the victimizing, glorifying, and demonizing all who have died or will die in ways that varied with political climate and revanchist orientations within and without the state.

It was this period in my life that I felt was the right time to immerse myself into new literature about mortality. This turn away from my urban and political sociology writings allowed me to appreciate a more existential approach toward life and living, as well as thanatology in general. Indeed, in the context of mortality, life and death are highly unstable systems in their own right. After reading about and attending my first Death Café where strangers gather to discuss all issues related to mortality, I realized that there was a monograph ready to be written about its unique participants and their concerns. Why? Because community via the Death Café remains intact and kept intact by, of all people, strangers. Just as importantly, there was also a need to illuminate how society at large distorts these concerns if not hide them. Moreover, after cautiously extrapolating from my exploratory study's data on Baby Boomers—the demographic that primarily attends Death Cafés—I felt that the public needed to consider the concerns and contemplations they are bringing into the discussion of healthcare *and* deathcare, and of mortality in general. Because Baby Boomers are no strangers to antisystemic struggles given that many were witness to if not participants in the Civil Rights struggles that began during the 1960s, they are now ready to make some important demands upon if not challenge a healthcare system that will soon be attending to them in sizeable numbers.

At Death Cafés, the state and its organs that can quickly expropriate from us our biographies of living and dying are contested during "death talk." In this regard, Death Café participants—and in our case, the 40 attendees whose voices on mortality constitute the core of communicative data for this exploratory study—have unwittingly become activists against aspects of our social system that deny them their authorship or personalization of mortality. Thus, the content of Death Café talk presented herein offers a refreshingly new twist on life and living and on death and dying, freed from framing by politicians and bureaucrats, freed from the paeans provided by nationalists and hawks, freed from corporate and institutional dictates, freed from war. Like nesting figurines, the voices of our grassroots participants emerge out of their differing yet concentric life contexts, informed by cultural, secular, or religious environments, only to arrive at the destination of our shared humanity as a whole.

Since time immemorial, people have conceptualized and articulated mortality in ways that have rarely been heard. For thinkers like Erich Fromm and Anthony Giddens, to name but a few, the wake of industrial societies saw mortality's sequestration. Death talk violated the optimistic drive of modernization and was rendered taboo outside of religious sensibilities, a sentiment shared by Death Café participants. Yet where death can be seen as glorious and romantic, even agapic, pride of place is then given to heroes and warriors, to poets and sages. The two diverging antipodes—especially in individualistic cultures such as the United States—reveal how unnecessarily extremist our understanding of mortality can be. However, the vast expanse between these two antipodes still constitutes a dynamic lifeworld, for the lifeworld serves as a repository of the human condition, one that frames our daily experiences since time immemorial. Although the death experience conveyed herein adopts a "Western" lens, it is my view that such a lens is useful for observing how death talk and Death Café practices can still be inflected with diverse cultural textures gathered from all over the world. The history of how life and death are tied to social life and social change, then, cannot simply be framed by conflagrations or natural disasters. Indeed, it can be framed by death talk engaged with strangers, who in our case, have unfettered themselves from manufactured narratives of mortality provided to us by macro-level social institutions.

In spite of attempts throughout this work to remind readers that the Death Café is actually a very enlightening, and in many instances, a lively environment, I concede that it does open up many fearsome themes. Indeed, getting to know the self that will die in an age cluttered by information and misinformation is a fearsome process. Nonetheless, it is thus hoped that the themes illuminated in this work will strip readers of their veneer of finer and finer discernments about the self, which under capitalism, are shaped by material culture of comfort and denial, and rarely by epiphanic transcendence. But alas, how else can we grow unless we stop deluding and marking ourselves with the diacritica of titles, materiality, and conspicuous consumption? With the ubiquity of narcissistic egos made possible by late capitalism, we might need to realize that we are the emperors with no clothes, dressed by powerful social institutions that require a captive, not emancipated audience to keep the machine of capitalism in operation.

I hope that my work will display cues that inspire us toward some form of transformation, one that can only come from an immersion within our communities that desire to view death and dying together, without the adamancy of cultural scripts or rituals. The Death Café participants introduced in this work have conveyed to us that we are not resigned to being isolated individuals trapped in impenetrable existential fears until our moment of death. Instead, as part and parcel to community and society, we can employ our encounters with mortality in ways that are collectively life-affirming. It is a dialectic that Heraclitus, Hegel, and Marx never employed. They are, however, bygone thinkers of emancipation while we are still thriving authors of our mortality.

ACKNOWLEDGMENTS

This work would not have been possible without the assistance of the following wonderful people: at the level of logistics, my wonderful research assistants, Joanna Sarinas and Deena Wahba, sat through many hours of Death Café recordings to transcribe people's recorded discussions. Each Death Café event presented herein would not have been possible without their diligent transcription efforts over a one-year period.

I also thank Dr. David Horner, who in his capacity as department chair, worked with me to get appropriate course releases that would provide the most writing time. Without the efficiency of David, Joanna, and Deena, the progress of this research would have slowed. I would also like to thank Dr. David Adams and Dr. Michael Cholbi. Their interest in issues of mortality assisted me in establishing the trajectory of this work. Additionally, I am indebted to Dr. Elbert Chang, MD, for providing insight about mortality issues. In his capacity as a pulmonary specialist, I was given valuable insight into the blind spots inherent in how healthcare is experienced in American life. I also am grateful to Dr. John Brown Childs who provided important cues for how to "unpack" death talk. I am delighted to have evolved from being his student so many years ago to being his colleague and good friend.

My gratitude also goes to the great Death Café facilitators who have been very generous to accommodate my data collection visits. Betsy Trapasso, MSW, Lisa S. Delong, RN, Dr. Karen Wyatt, MD, Lizzy Miles, MSW, and Jon Underwood are wonderful people doing important work by their hosting of Death Cafés. It would be a gross understatement to note that my interactions with Betsy, Lisa, Karen, Lizzy, and Jon have transformed my views on life and death. In a world of much stimuli, they showed me how one can carve an uncluttered path through them and emerge rather unscathed. It has been a pleasure to communicate and associate with all of you.

I am also eternally grateful to all the Death Café participants I have met. All of you are people with such big hearts and I feel very fortunate to have listened to your rich "death talk." Each one of you inspired me in more ways than one. My only regret is how textual exposition of dialog cannot capture the tone and rhythm of verbal discourse, attributes of communication that all of you exhibited dynamically during death talk, one that was frequently interspersed with wisdom, deep insights, healing, humor, and transcendence.

Finally, I owe much of my inspiration and gratitude to my wife, Thasanee. Employed in the healthcare industry, Thasanee has much insight and wisdom about the human condition in our current age. Indeed, Thasanee's compassionate views on how encounters and confrontations with life *and* death can foster a shared humanity are but the same views conveyed at Death Cafés as participants embark on their journeys toward different horizons of mortality.

CONTENTS

LIST OF FIGURES

LIST OF TABLES

CHAPTER 1

Coffee and Death

Michael Wolgemut's *Dance of Death* (1493).

© The Author(s) 2017
J. Fong, *The Death Café Movement*,
DOI 10.1007/978-3-319-54256-0_1

As one reads this work, somewhere in numerous urban pockets of the United States, as well as in many parts of the globe, strangers are regularly gathering to talk about death and dying. Soothed by good foods, pastries, and beverages such as coffee and tea, participants of the Death Café community gather respectfully with one another to confront the numerous permutations emanating from the theme of death and dying. At their favorite haunts, and depending on location or organization, in restaurants or homes that have been open to the public in ways that evoke a small café-like environment, Death Café participants engage in "death talk," a dynamic that will be explored throughout this work. By informally gathering with strangers to talk about all issues pertaining to death and dying, from the most challenging and personal to ideals and convivial speculations of what constitutes a good life and death, Death Café attendees appear to be personalizing, if not authoring, their own crucial narratives and expectations regarding end-of-life issues. Café attendees are essentially preparing for death by exploring cues that will allow them to live at their fullest expression, be they inspired by pain or profundity. They sense their individual life stories when compiled possess a formidable momentum that can contest the stigma around death talk. Indeed, this theme is frequently emphasized by Betsy Trapasso, MSW and Lisa S. Delong, RN, Los Angeles's earliest Death Café hosts/facilitators, as well as Karen Wyatt, MD, all of whom were so kind to grant me access to their events for my research.

Death Cafés, of which my work conceptualizes as an existential and transformative social movement, aim to create communicative space where discussions about mortality can be made to promote a healthier outlook on one's life *and* death. At these gatherings of primarily non-terminally ill Baby Boomers, attendees unpack their orientations toward mortality over a healthy meal, drinks, and deserts. Enjoying one another's company with unpretentious energies, a variety of mortality considerations are discussed. Conversational topics include the logistics, services, and finances of attending to death, medical care at end of life, and if a good death can be had. Atmospheric themes that blur the line between the metaphysical and physical are also an integral part of their dialog. Considerations about the afterlife, what near-death experiences mean, whether the deceased are still "there," and what it is like to be with a dying person are voiced, as are the realizations that death experiences have had in positively transforming Café participants. Café attendees that are bereaved are welcomed into a warm environment even while grieving or mourning, as are those who have failed in their attempts to die by suicide. They sit alongside other unique Café participants and tell their stories, ask for advice, offer support, and provide wisdoms for one another. Thus, Café attendees are not employing Café venues to enchant a disenchanted world, a tendency seen in an increasingly secularized society as argued by Ritzer in his eponymous 2010 work. Café attendees are aware that such a process would require a copious amount of consumption of services as a means to sustain their explorations into mortality. As such, Café participants have opted for what can only be described as a transcendence from their disenchanted worlds, one that could be considered as post-material in orientation (Inglehart 2008).

Many Café attendees are enthusiastic about encountering cues they are on the verge of understanding. In regard to the sample of this exploratory study, Café attendees, among strangers, confront death and dying outside of everyone's cultural scripts: chaplains sit across from shamans, near-death survivors sit across from a member of the Baha'i faith and a former Christian Scientist, moms still grieving the loss of their children sit across from widows and a psychic; all unpack in ways that seek and achieve intersubjective agreement if not mutual consensus on a variety of death and dying topics. Because Death Cafés have "no ideology or agenda for the gathering" according to thanatologist Lizzy Miles who started the United State's first Death Café in Ohio with her associate Maria Johnson in 2012, attendees have the privilege of seeing a unique cross section of society on their own terms as they focus on that final facticity of life: our mortality (Miles and Corr 2017).

Even though Café attendees are not sociologists trained to identify the influence of social institutions, they nevertheless have a sense that something is amiss from the medical system insofar as understanding key existential and metaphysical issues related to mortality are concerned. Bill Thomas, MD, a gerontologist profiled in the poignant documentary *Alive Inside* (2014) captures this sentiment. He candidly notes how "the real business" of medicine "is in the pill bottle." He continues:

Our healthcare system imagines the human being to be a very complicated machine and we've figured out how to turn the dials. "Blood pressure? Oh, turn that down!" You know? "Blood sugar? Oh, turn that down!" We have medicines that can adjust the dials. We haven't done anything—medically speaking—to touch the heart and soul of a patient (2014).

Although attending Death Cafés appears to be an unpleasant undertaking, attendees actually leave meetings with new cues for affirming life. This is undoubtedly due to how Death Cafés are actually introspective and healing environments. In such environments, solidarity and even humor permeate the interpersonal atmosphere. However, in spite of the richness of differing intellectual, cultural, and spiritual views, in spite of the differing demographics, all Death Café attendees seek a deeper rendering and personalization of their mortality. They are in the process of reassembling and personalizing their own narratives on living and dying from cues provided by other Café attendees.

My work thus illuminates a variety of existential themes that have been conveyed at Café gatherings, themes that are important for sociology to examine so as to document how society and community provide different cues for persons as they travel toward end of life. It should also be emphasized that my work is exploratory in nature, one that that gives pride of place to intersubjectivity between members within community. It is a work of sociological observations and cautious extrapolations of strangers that temporarily establish a communicative community to attend to our existential human condition. Correspondingly, I make visible how Café participants communicatively engage the market, media, and medicine's rendering of death, unfettered from institutional control. I have adopted these approaches because most Americans do not die with sovereignty. Instead, many die logistically and technologically, with contraptions and chemicals, lawyers, document pushers, and the acumen of business people employed in deathcare industries (Mitford 1963, Smith 1996; Slocum and Carlson 2011; Butler 2013).

The goals of my study are thus fourfold: (1) The first goal will be to make visible how macro-level institutions have constrained the ability for us to openly and culturally engage in conversations about death and dying, providing for the population instead extremist views on death and dying from the media, market, and medicine. To accomplish this, I will be making operative important concepts by sociologist Jürgen Habermas drawn from his seminal two-volume work *The Theory of Communicative Action* (Habermas 1984, 1987) along with his other important works. Where theoretical blind spots surface in Habermas's theory, I bring in additional thinkers that are able to enhance our Habermasian analyses of Death Café dynamics. Most importantly for this particular goal is that whenever this study encounters material consequences that are able to ground many of

Habermas's abstruse and atmospheric concepts, I will employ the concepts from those particular scholars to anchor Habermas's contentions.

(2) The second goal of this monograph is to examine how Death Café attendees confront their mortality in ways that can inform others about a nascent "death identity," one that encourages a self-authoring of one's own mortality in ways that provide wisdoms for living and dying. As a noun, the term "death" often denotes a cessation of vital functions. Yet a death identity reappropriates the term, potentially evolving it into a greater signifier of a philosophical or existential orientation of one fully mindful of the finitude of life. In this regard, the Death Café advancement of death talk as an ethos able to contest its taboo status renders the Death Café a social movement in its ideational and formative phase.

(3) The third goal of this work attempts to make visible existential themes and social critiques that underlie death talk in our sample of Death Café attendees: their transcriptions from attending Death Cafes have been inputted into the Wordle meta-data program, a word or "tag" cloud generator to be discussed in greater detail in Chapter 4, so as to capture the most frequently mentioned themes that orbit death and dying. It will be argued that these themes have a degree of profundity that the market, media, and medicine do not articulate for attendees. Indeed, the "trinity" of the market, media, and medicine may only serve to maximize people's fear, anxiety, and despondency when they confront mortality issues due to the neglect of existential themes in the systemic discourse.

(4) Finally, I intend to describe how the Death Café is a bona fide transformative and existential social movement. Toward the conclusion of the text, I remind readers about the purpose of researching the Death Café movement: to remove our understanding of death and dying from its technocratic and vulgarized connotations seen in the trinity, so that we can all have agency authoring our own trajectories toward our mortality, and in ways that create a shared humanity. These four major centers of gravity will be addressed in different degrees throughout the work.

THE DEATH CAFÉ VIBE

The Death Café in its most current form harks back to 2004 in Neuchâtel, Switzerland, when Swiss sociologist and anthropologist Bernard Crettaz held the first Death Café, or Café Mortels. By the time Crettaz had achieved his run of facilitating over 40 Death Cafés, which by 2010, saw its first gathering in Paris, France, the United Kingdom's Jon Underwood, a British web designer and later a globally important figure in the Death Café movement, had read about Crettaz's exploits and launched London's first Death Café in September 2011. With his associate psychotherapist Sue Barsky Reid, and his mother, the UK's first event welcomed six attendees. In spite of its smaller size, the synergy was apparent for Jon:

> We had our first pop-up Death Café yesterday. It was a powerful and moving experience. It was attended by a diverse group including a grief specialist Kristie West, a Buddhist nun, a management consultant and a council strategist. It was expertly facilitated by Sue Barsky Reid, a qualified psychotherapist. We are energized by this and are planning more (Miles and Corr 2017: 153–154).

Four months later, Jon's Death Cafés were filling beyond capacity. In his January 2012 blog Jon notes:

> Forty-nine people attended the Death Café over the weekend and unfortunately a number left frustrated due to lack of space. The sessions I facilitated were powerful and moving, especially on Saturday. Consistently we see a real hunger to talk about death from those who attend. In some cases it seems to make a huge difference as people get time to say things they've rarely or never been able to say before (Miles and Corr 2017: 154).

Jon continues to see in the movement an ability to function as an unexplored repository of wisdoms and critiques on issues related to death and dying (see the Death Café website promulgated by Underwood at www.deathcafe.com). In an online interview given to Karen Wyatt, MD, July 2015, Jon explains his vision of the Death Café:

> *Jon:*   So, the Death Café is a pop-up event. And at that event people come together and have a conversation about death and dying over tea and cake. There are no inputs, there are no objectives or directions we have to get to, or ground that we particularly have to cover. Really it's a space for people to talk about where they're at with this subject and sort of air it out a bit, because there aren't too many places where people can talk about these subjects, in my experience. And because people don't have that opportunity so much, when they come to Death Café on their own volition

because they want to talk about this, what they say is really rich. It's a kind of thing that makes me feel privileged to hear. So it makes for a wonderful conversation.

Karen: Yes, I've attended some Death Cafés and I have to agree with you. It's so rich and it's really interesting this synergy that happens when strangers come together who've never seen one another before, but have something in common, which is the desire to talk about death. And I agree with you: every Death Café I've attended has been totally different. The conversation has always gone so many different directions but always very, very rich and heartfelt.

Jon: The format for me never gets tired at all. It's very easy to facilitate. We do have the role of facilitator at Death Cafés and their primary function is to make sure ethics and principles are observed. But the people who've come forward, like yourself, to play that role, are from my perspective such an incredible group of people, with so much to offer to society and it's wonderful that Death Cafés have been a vehicle for people to do that.

As a bona fide grass-roots movement, Death Cafés are not venues to promote businesses and one "should never decide to offer a Death Café for this reason" as noted on its website. Additionally noted is that Death Cafés will "never accept sponsorship from or associate with" private organizations involved in provisioning health care in the death and dying sector, political organizations, or "campaign groups whose remit includes contentious issues involving death such as right to die, abortion, or vivisection."

By the time the first Death Café was launched in the United States in July 2012 under the facilitation of Lizzy Miles and Maria Johnston in a suburb of Columbus, Ohio, the gatherings were conceptualized as "a pop-up event where people get together to talk about death and have tea and delicious cake" (Miles and Corr 2017: 152). For Miles and Corr, the description that a Death Café is a pop-up event is meant to remind visitors that the Death Café need not be a literal restaurant or coffee house. In contrast, the terms "pop-up event" was meant to "convey that the events are not planned or scheduled on a regular basis" (Miles and Corr 2017: 152). Moreover, so as to discern its unique community presence and cultural orientations, Miles and Corr further adds that "the concept of *tea and delicious cake* was meant to impart that these events are warm and inviting, and not goth gatherings of teenagers with black t-shirts and black eyeliner" (Miles and Corr 2017: 152).

During one of my discussions with Southern California's pioneer Death Café host Betsy Trapasso, the Death Café is seen not as a support group;

"it is not a therapy group, so you know it is sort of a social movement. So people come to Cafés for multiple reasons whether you know they had been sick or you know someone in their family had been sick, or someone has Alzheimer's" (February 18, 2014). She continues:

> New ones are popping up every day. They're in Poland, Italy, South America, New Zealand... And it's really just a social gathering. There's no agenda. The meetings are confidential. Normally it's in a home and we do a potluck. Everyone here is just supportive of each other and it's a non-profit. You're not here to listen to me. We want to know what's important to you. My role is just to sit back and let you all just talk. It's time for you to talk about what you want to talk about. This is why I don't have questions or tell you what to say (April 22, 2014).

According to Betsy, attendees at Death Cafés often "form close bonds" afterward because "their kids died, their spouses died, and they continued" (interview conducted on January 18, 2014). Miles and Corr add to Betsy's sentiments that Death Cafés are "not an educational session, a lecture, or a source for information on end of life topics. [A] Death Café is simply an event where people talk about whatever is on their minds related to death, dying, and bereavement" (Miles and Corr 2017: 153).

Betsy is delighted with the progress of Death Cafés seen in the case of the United States, noting how "we have one coming to every city. Almost every week there is a new Death Café. So the US is completely catching onto it, which is amazing" (interview conducted on January 18, 2014). However, due to the immense popularity of Café events, some attendees simply are unable to attend due to space issues. As notes Betsy during our discussions regarding the popularity of the Death Cafés, "I sometimes have to turn people away for a year, and I feel so terrible that I sometimes have to turn people away." In such instances, Betsy advises them to "go start your own. My whole goal is to get people talking about it. If you want to start your own Death Café, it's totally cool." Such freedoms afforded Café participants in the United States have anecdotally surfaced as positive feedback, with the Cafés described as "safe and interesting" according to Miles and Corr (2017: 153).

When France's first gathering was promulgated by Crettaz in Paris in late 2010, what entailed was a dozen of strangers that gathered to talk about death and dying for but a few precious hours. Crettaz laments in an interview published on November 1, 2010 about a dearth of dialogic confrontations with death in French culture (a statement that likely describes the condition of attending to death and dying in many cultures around the world as well). For Crettaz, "French people find it very difficult to talk about death" and that it had to be liberated from its "tyrannical secrecy." Crettaz continues by noting in a manner that would have made Sartre proud, that he was "never so in tune with the truth as during one of these soirées . . . and . . . the assembled company for a moment, and thanks to death, is born into authenticity" (Guinness 2010: 1).

At the time of this writing, there are close to 4,000 Death Cafés across 37 countries, on every continent except Antarctica. The top five countries with the largest number of Death Café events are the United States of America (1,178 Death Cafés), the United Kingdom (350), Canada (126), Australia (103), Italy, and Taiwan (both with 29 Death Cafés). The numbers are sure to change. The United States currently hosts Death Café events in over 100 cities such as New York, Atlanta, and Los Angeles (www.deathcafe.com, Miles and Corr 2017). Smaller urban centers have seen a spread of Death Cafés as well "including St. Joseph, Missouri, and Gig Harbor, Washington" (Miles and Corr 2017: 154). Moreover, other scholars such as Western Oregon University's Paula Baldwin and University of Glasgow's Naomi Richards are current enthusiasts of such venues and are themselves involved examining Death Cafés.

During this research period, the two most popular venues in Southern California where my research took place were based out of Santa Clarita and headed by Lisa Delong, R.N., author of *Blood Brothers*, while the other was out of Topanga Canyon through the efforts of Betsy Trapasso (although Betsy frequently changes and travels to different locales to host her Café events). However, bona fide Death Café communities exist online as well. End-of-life-care activists like Dr. Karen Wyatt hosts an innovative monthly online Death Café where callers chime in and discuss all matters related to death and dying. Jon notes that if an average of 10 persons attended each event, the Death Café experience would have touched close to 20,000 individuals in a globally decentralized yet thematically cohesive community experience. With the spread of Death Cafés in the United States, the news and lifestyle media took notice, finding coverage in the *USA Today, NPR, Huffington Post, The New York Times,* and *The Los Angeles Times* (Miles and Corr 2017: 154).

It was during 2013 when I was exposed to the phenomenon of Death Cafés through a *Los Angeles Times* article. I came across a report by Nita

Lelyveld almost too casually one morning while enjoying my customary cup of coffee. After contemplating the article's implications and cues, I realized how important its themes were for sociology to make its entry into examining mortality issues. At the time I felt that my sociology was taking a very existential turn—a process that I found comfort in after realizing that one of the greats of sociology, Kurt Wolff, also experienced a similar transition when he tried to examine how members of society develop sociological insight.

Seeing the architecture of a transformative social movement being assembled at these gathering, I felt compelled to contact our two Southern California Death Café organizers, Betsy and Lisa, in late 2013 regarding the possibility of conducting research at their gatherings. After receiving the approval from my university's Institutional Review Board, both Betsy and Lisa welcomed me to their Death Cafés between 2014 and 2015. Through Betsy and Lisa, I was connected to London's Jon Underwood. I scheduled a long distance call and in short order was able to have a wonderful dialog with what our compatriot across the pond had to say about importance of Death Café events. Indeed, the solidarity was not only experienced between Jon and me. By 2015, Karen had scheduled Jon to be interviewed on her online Death Café. She graciously accommodated my request to hear how her online Death Café proceeded.

Betsy's links to the Death Café are historical. She recounted her immersion in "death work" during one of our January Café sessions:

Just briefly my history and how I got into the end of life work: The first hospice in the country was in my hometown, in Branford, Connecticut. It's called Connecticut Hospice. My grandfather helped bring hospice to the US; so the first one was in my hometown. So I watch this thing called hospice as a young kid come to the US; he was mayor of my town which is right outside Yale University. So I went to these meetings about the hospice.

My grandfather was mayor for many years; bringing hospice over was one of the things he was most proud of in his life, so I always say it's in my blood, it's in my family. I wanted to do advocacy so I became a psychotherapist, worked with every type of population, became a hospice social worker and now I work on my own through advocacy and am trying to get the word out on how we view and do death. I love how we're connecting people around the world so that they can share with each other; I love what comes out because every group is so different.

Well, I found out about Death Café. My friend Lizzy Miles hosted the very first Death Café in the United States in Columbus Ohio. And so I heard Lizzy was doing something called Death Café and it originated in England through Jon Underwood in 2011. So she had heard of him on the internet and then she hosted a Death Café and I thought "Oh I'm going to do that too!" But Jon Underwood got the idea from Bernard Crettaz. He's a sociologist and he would have these "Café Mortels" at a motel over in Paris, so he would gather people together in cafés and talk about death. So Jon said he wanted to start a movement, and now it's happening all over the world and it's a growing movement.

By the conclusion of 2015, I had the privilege of gathering data from five Café events that yielded transcriptions derived from face-to-face meetings. These meetings were headed by Betsy Trapasso and Lisa S. Delong. Two of the Death Café transcriptions were derived from online call-in formats where callers communicated with the Death Café facilitator and with one another. The call-in formats were administered by Karen Wyatt's End of Life University that included a Death Café portal.

The panoply of diverse life themes atmospherically nurturing all communicative attendees is what makes Death Cafés unique community environments. They are not only a bellwether of community health but serve a vital function in establishing community solidarity. As noted by Betsy and other Death Café organizers, the gatherings are not environments for dogma or therapy (although participants cite their therapeutic qualities). Even the most dogmatic attendees empathetically give pride of place to members whose turn it is to enter a focused state so as to convey their sentiments on mortality. They come from all walks of life and from different spiritual, cultural, and political sensibilities. Yet these are subdued identities. During my data collection, what struck me as a wonderful was how all Café attendees are punctilious. Death Café attendees have cast aside their differences so that they can better appreciate the different nuances in how people, their cultures, genders, and religiosities approach the issue of death and dying. Death Cafés allow participants to communicate freely their anxieties *and* sense of liberation when attending to end-of-life issues in ways that point to our shared humanity: that the end of our lives and the uncertainty of when that end is nigh, for most of us, are irreconcilable and frightening inevitabilities. Such dynamics at Death Cafés behooves us to consider the many rationales for Café attendances, all of which were illuminated by Miles and Corr (2017) in their excellent account of the Death Café movement.

Miles and Corr had queried some of the attendees as to their intentions for attending the Death Café and found that participation is due to six main motivations: (1) to process loss as it relates to one's own mortality, (2) to process loss as it relates to a metaphysical experience, (3) to examine mortality of loved ones, (4) academic/philosophical reasons, (5) to fulfill a desire to help others, and (6) for professional reasons. In the first condition of attending a Café to reflect upon one's loss and how this informs one's trajectory toward death and dying, Miles and Corr (2017) provide an attendee's reasoning:

> My brother-in-law died this past April and my husband and I have been thinking a lot about his life and how it had not been a fulfilling one for him. How his brother did not actually do the things he said he wanted to do. Which, in turn, has made us think a lot about our own lives and plans. We have both worked in hospice and would very much like to attend the next meeting (Miles and Corr 2017: 156).

An attendee that visited a Death Café to attend to loss as it relates to a metaphysical experience conveyed:

> I read the article in the paper and found the thought of this gathering intriguing. I have only lost a few people in my life so far and of those losses I have had interesting experiences with two of them that have made me feel confident that there is something else for us after we pass away. I would be interested to hear what other people have to say about their experiences and acceptance of death. While I can at least think about my loved ones that have since now passed without crying, their loss still saddens me and I would like to see if others may have found better and or different ways to cope. I did not find traditional grief counseling very helpful, and thought this opportunity might help me cope in some way. I have a tendency to observe more than share in a group setting, but if the group tends to be animated I would probably share what I consider unusual experiences (Miles and Corr 2017: 156–157).

Another Café attendee was motivated to attend a Café gathering due to the felt need to prepare for death and dying by examining the mortality of loved ones:

> Hi there! I'm interested in attending this event because I'm an only child, technically speaking (I don't speak with my biological father or his other children). My mom and step-dad are all I have, and they are

both getting older and live on the East Coast. My step-dad in particular has a family history of heart attacks and strokes, and just last year there was a major scare when a tree came down just a few feet from their home during a hurricane. I realized then that I wouldn't know how to handle the inevitable, and both my parents are unwilling to discuss it. So, perhaps something like this will get me comfortable with it and, in turn, help them get comfortable with it! (Miles and Corr 2017: 157).

Other Café participants approached mortality issues intellectually and philosophically, a popular recourse:

I'm very intrigued and would be very enthusiastic about attending the first Death Café here in Columbus. My interest in death and attending is largely academic, but also philosophical. The oft-repeated phrase about nothing staying the same except for death and taxes is really quite an apt description. I find it bizarre for such a universal experience to not be shared more openly. I also would like to challenge my own preconceptions of death, and hopefully expand the meaning and scope of my life by having a better understanding of death and dying. My schedule is clear for that evening, and I hope my presence would make the event more enriched. I hope to hear more as the event draws near (Miles and Corr 2017: 157).

Still others attend Cafés for the purpose of refining their ability to cope so that they may, in turn, help others to cope.

I am 50 years old and have been widowed twice. Both of my husbands passed away via suicide. The first time in 1983 when I was 20 and the second time in 2007 when I was 45. Grieving and learning to live again is something that I know well. If I can, I would like to come to listen and offer my perspective. I look forward to hearing from you! (Miles and Corr 2017: 157).

Finally, some participants attend Death Cafés for professional development, such as Miles and Corr's last example where a hospice nurse noted, "I've been at it for 25 years. I would love to come and visit with people. I'm obviously a strong advocate for early intervention" (2017: 157).

For the Death Café community, a quality death need not be defined solely by a milieu of doctors, nurses, and health specialists equipped with medical technology, anesthesia, feeding tubes, and respirators, but with loved ones whose emotive and metaphysical connections with the individual have given meaning and depth to that person's existence. To be able to emphasize this aspect of death and dying freely shows how the Death Café movement, according to Miles and Corr is *"meeting a felt need* among individuals in our society [for] both…who are moved to arrange and host a Death Café, as well as those who decide to participate in one of these events" (Miles and Corr 2017: 159). As noted by two classic scholars on the topic, Philippe Ariès, author of *Western Attitudes Toward Death* (1974) and the *Hour of Our Death* (1981), and Ivan Illich, author of *Medical Nemesis* (1976), in the Western tradition—at least until hospitals ensconced themselves in communities as large bureaucratic entities—most end-of-life moments took place in the village or in the home, often with the dying individual surrounded by family and close members of the community. Indeed, death and dying as a process has only recently been bureaucratized and systematized. Particularly in the United States and other free-market economies, it has been transformed into a profit-driven process. That many Death Café attendees I have spoken to concerned themselves with these developments point to discontents toward a systemic framing of mortality, one that behooves them to consider the importance of personalizing, if not authoring, their own lives and deaths beyond systems.

Death Café gatherings thus exhibit a visceral sense of collective purpose that is thematically greater than the sum of its individuals' sentiments. However, because of the free-flowing dynamics at Death Cafés, Betsy noted that "no two Death Cafés are ever identical." Jon conveyed similar experiences during his July 2015 online discussion with Karen. However, he concedes that there had been teething issues at the outset of his first Death Café, which prompted him to subsequently pursue a very different orientation.

So the first Death Café was very scripted. There were about six pages of notes about it. It involved people coming and going through a series of exercises and writing things down on pieces of paper and putting them in envelopes. And at the end, the envelopes were burned in a ceremonial burning of some sort. It was very complicated really. In spite of this it was an amazing conversation. I knew most of the people there but the one person I didn't really know just spoke about things she'd never spoken about before, to a group of strangers—really deep and personal things. And afterward she wrote a blog about what a powerful experience it was for her. So it was very beautiful nonetheless. And the afterward I knew I wanted to do more and I debriefed with my mom.

She said that all those envelopes and the writing and the burning, just let people talk. So when we organized our second Death Café it was completely different and because that was integrated into the core of it. Because of that developed the format that is now sort of our core model which is non-group directed discussion of death. And from then on that's what we've done (Interview given to Dr. Karen Wyatt on July 16, 2015).

However, the turn toward a more decentralized orientation for the Death Café initially exhibited problems with its dynamics as well for it potentially caused the movement to lose its center of gravity due to, ironically, the alacrity of its members. As Jon notes:

> As Death Cafés have grown we needed a very clear set of guidelines that enabled people to do something which was relatively consistent. This is very important. At the time it was an issue because people were starting Death Cafés and getting very excited and changing it into something else, saying "Wouldn't it be great if we just had a speaker at the start from the local hospice to tell us about their services which is so fantastic." Someone else would then say "Wouldn't it be great if we showed a film about end of life care at the start of the Death Café?" It became less focused and so we really tried to clarify our model that it's group directed discussion... but in doing that we pushed a lot of amazing work out, you know (Interview given to Dr. Karen Wyatt on July 16, 2015).

Moreover, Jon notes how because "Death Cafés have been completely been run by volunteers... it's hard work." Betsy describes a typical Café venue she hosts:

> Most people have them once a month. Some people have them every third month. We've just had our 500th Death Café. And they're in South America, Australia, New Zealand, Europe, Singapore. We just had Hong Kong. There's one in Orange County [California]. A potential host just spoke to me as there are no Death Cafes in Orange County, so I'm glad about that. Because I think LA is just so vast. That's the thing—the vastness. What I love about LA, however, is all the different cultures, all the different ethnicities (February 18, 2014).

One of the most important aspects of Death Café dynamics is how certain regions make the gatherings rich due to a diversity of peoples. Gatherings can be evocative: there are different aromas, different appearances, different forms of dress, and, frequently, different accents with their unique inflections and lilts. Moreover, an often overlooked benefit of conducting Death Cafés in Southern California is its favorable climate, allowing for more mobility of its attendees to attend different venues as they emerge. During one of our sessions, Betsy celebrates the energy of Los Angeles's diverse populations:

> One thing about hospice, end of life, the green funeral movements, death mid-wives, there are just so many people out there in LA, It's such a huge movement. For example, at one of the Death Cafés there was a participant who signed up for cryogenics! You never know who is going to show up. He's a medical doctor and very sweet. The Death Café was at his house. I had no idea. I had been in contact with him and his wife for months (January 25, 2014).

During another of our January sessions, Betsy notes how there are so many "amazing people…adding to the death movement" and that "we're all working together beautifully. Death people are very forgiving. LA is a huge center for all the changes that are happening. Huge center for green burials, for everything."

Because Los Angeles functions as a large metropolitan hub for the Southwest, many attendees come from great distances. As Betsy highlighted during one of April's Café gatherings:

> It's about sharing knowledge. You know some people say "What was that like?" Sharing knowledge, healing, support, it is home to everyone. And it [Los Angeles] is an amazing place to do it. I mean look at these amazing people over here. You know, they're wonderful, they drove from all over. You know, Sarah came from Colorado, Carla from Big Bear, we got people who want to come and I got a waiting list. People want to come so I want more hosts out there, more Death Cafés, so it can cradle Los Angeles because right now it's two of us doing this. LA is so huge and we need more people.

Betsy's vision for how Death Café can grow in Southern California "is to get every culture, every ethnicity, to really unite this city and to get people talking about death." Betsy notes how in the past most people going to Death Cafes here were White: "Someone in London I spoke to said, 'Oh my God, I never even thought about that'" (February 18, 2014). Indeed, Betsy even travels great distances to hold Death Café events: "I take requests so last time I had six. So I had a request for Thousand Oaks recently. I have a request for Palm Springs and all the way to Joshua Tree. So I travel."

During my data collections at a variety of Death Cafés, all participants on their given day of attendance have never met one another and were strangers at the outset. As people arrive for a Café event, an informal environment surfaces where attendees introduce themselves to one another, engage in some ice-breaking dialog, as well as "sensing" one another with nervous alacrity. Upon finding their preferred seats, an introduction by Death Café organizers follows. At my particular research venues, Lisa and Betsy introduced themselves and explained the reasons for Death Cafés. Café attendees then introduced themselves to one another. One introduction during an April Café hosted by Betsy went as follows:

So welcome everyone to Death Café Los Angeles. Thank you really for bringing food. It means so much to me because, you know, one of the things about the Death Café is that...we don't make any money off of this. We don't charge for anything so it helps that you guys brought food so I appreciate it. I am just the host and I will just talk for a couple of minutes, and then it's really your group so I sit back and listen. Everything we say here is confidential. Because people usually ask "what did you talk about at the Death Café?" and people don't say you know "Bob said this, Julie said this..." you say, "Oh we talked about this or that." People are going to be curious about it. And there is no set topic or speakers and there is no agenda. For everyone, just be really nice to each other. So no one be mean to anyone towards any particular thinking or, you know, argument. Just be supportive to each other. We usually go until 9:30. People can just jump in and talk about whatever they want to talk about (April 22, 2014).

Following everyone's self introductions, I am introduced to the group as a researcher. I then thank all of the attendees for allowing me to be there with them, hand out the consent forms for them to sign, and ready my digital recording device for the session. The dialog then begins in earnest as Café attendees begin to "unpack" and discuss issues and experiences about death and dying.

Even Karen Wyatt's online Death Café exhibits the same solidarity without the corporeal and tactile components of interaction. For example, during Mother's Day in 2014, Karen began her Death Café with poignancy:

Since today is Mother's day I purposely decided to schedule this on Mother's Day knowing some of us have lost our mothers as well as moms who've lost their children, who are actually dealing with a lot of grief on this day when it is generally a day of celebration and celebrating mothers. I was wondering if you have anything to say about this, or if any of you have been thinking of your mom or the loss of your mom (May 10, 2014).

As discussions flow, the hosts of the Cafés tend to defer to emergent themes, group dynamics, and discussions, allowing them to surface with minimal interruption. In many instances when such a communicative flow is established, my role as researcher becomes activated, resulting in proactive questions on my part. In other instances, however, I remain in the background until queried for my views. Depending on the gravity and depth of the attendees' accounts, attendees either synchronize with the narratives and continue the dialog, or they welcome the next speaker to begin a new discussion.

The proliferation of Death Cafés, especially in the United States, implies that Americans are less afraid to talk about death and dying. Indeed, many Americans do engage in death talk. Miles and Corr note how today, the vast majority of universities and colleges in the country offer death and dying and/ or courses on bereavement that found traction decades ago during the 1960s and 1970s. Most surprisingly, many of these courses are popular and well attended according to Corr (2015). Surprisingly, senior citizens, the demographic that is most vulnerable and most proximate to the horizons of their respective mortalities, can be surprisingly frank in their discussions. A 2016 UPI report titled "Many of Oldest Old Say They're at Peace with Dying" notes how Britons in their 90s are "often willing to talk about death, but they're rarely asked about it" (Dallas 2016). Dr. Jane Flemming of Cambridge University's Public Health and Primary Care Department, leader of the study, interviewed several dozen citizens over 95 years old and found that many acknowledged they were living on "borrowed time" yet felt "grateful for each passing day, and didn't worry too much about the future." Flemming's team notes how most interviewees accepted their fate and were prepared to die, citing a subject who noted that "I'm ready to go . . . I just say I'm the lady-in-waiting, waiting to go." The study also hints at what a "good death" is like: many hoped that they would pass away in their sleep, to "slip away quietly." One of her participants noted how "I'd be quite happy if I went suddenly like that." Most enlightening were the responses by those who were unafraid:

When asked if they would prefer lifesaving medical care or treatment to help them remain comfortable, most opted for comfort. Most were also not afraid of dying. For some, witnessing the peaceful death of others helped them manage their fears. One women recalled her parents' deaths, saying, "They were alive, then they were dead, but it all went off as usual. Nothing really dramatic or anything. Why should it be any different for me?" (Dallas 2016).

Miles and Corr believe that Americans exhibit this growing tendency to dialogically confront their mortality as well. However, Miles and Corr concede to the view that we are still an overarchingly death-denying society where people are reluctant to confront or engage with mortality issues. Their observations are not new, for even as early as 1972, Dumont and Foss concluded in their important work *The American View of Death* how Americans "*both* accept *and* deny death, simultaneously" (1972: 95 cited in Miles and Corr (2017)). Dr. Morag Farquhar, Cambridge University's senior research associate in Flemming's department, notes that "having these conversations before it is too late can help ensure that an individual's wishes, rather than going unspoken, can be heard" (Dallas 2016) while for Miles and Corr "failing to speak about death is to give it power and make it fearful, so much so that when we are forced by events to speak of death, we may not be able to do so in any healthful way" (Miles and Corr 2017: 162).

Alluded to earlier in this section is the notion that not all Café death talk is macabre due to its welcome of humor. Observed at my Café data collection was how lighthearted moments do not cheapen dialogic dynamics between attendees. Indeed, perfectly timed quips often punctuate the dynamics of discussion, intermittently lightening up an otherwise heavy dialog. Because humor has an intermittent place in bereavement, grief, and mourning if cultural sensibilities are understood by participants who confront a death episode, it can function as a social lubricant—what DeSpelder and Strickland (2009) describe as the "oil of society." Sensible humor in the context of death generates sentimental cohesiveness for a bereaved community. For DeSpelder and Strickland, humor "defuses" our anxieties toward death situations in four ways:

> First, it raises our consciousness about a taboo subject and gives us a way to talk about it. Second, it presents an opportunity to rise above sadness, providing a release from pain and promoting a sense of control over a traumatic situation, even if we cannot change it. Third, humor is a great leveler; it treats everyone alike and sends the message that there are no exemptions from the human predicament. Thus it binds us together and encourages a sense of intimacy, which helps us face what is unknown or distressing. Humor can be a "social glue" that helps us . . . comfort survivors as they recall the funny as well as painful events of a loved one's life. A sense of humor can moderate the intensity of negative life events (2009: 24).

One example can be seen during one of our January 2014 events when Betsy celebrated the mixing of dining and death talk, to which some attendees responded with humorous banter and group laughter, signified by the "(~)" where it surfaces in dialog in this chapter and elsewhere:

Betsy: Yeah, someone once pointed out that with cake and coffee you're actually killing the people that are coming to your Cafés because cake is unhealthy and coffee is unhealthy. (~)

Trent: Oh stop! Sheesh...(~)

Betsy: And I'm laughing because you know LA people....

Trent: Cake and tea equals death? I mean, I'm sorry people I missed that memo...

Betsy: And I've had the vegan ones, the green juice ones!

Cheyenne: Sigh...(~)

Trent: Oh Jeez!

In another January session, Betsy revisited the theme about the uniqueness of each Death Café because "everyone makes it their own, like someone once proposed a canoe trip down the 'river of life' so to speak," inciting group laughter and prompting one of the participants, Cora, to remark "and it would culminate at a waterfall!" Similes, metaphors, and perfectly timed quips are rich at Death Cafés. During one May 2014 Café session, host Lisa S. Delong commented on the unique dynamics of Café attendees, to which some attendees responded:

Lisa: Yeah there's no wrong way to think about death and dying. It's very courageous to come to a strange group of people attending this thing called the Death Café.

Hera: It's freeing because you're all here by choice and you know what the topic is going to be.

Scott: And there's food! (~)

Humor is not always a result of vertical communication from the Death Café hosts to attendees. Some of the good natured exchanges take place horizontally between attendees as can be seen at a January 2014 Café event:

Pat: The funeral industry is really operated in a very monopolistic fashion and so I like it that there's this new entrepreneurial spirit that's stealing that corner from manipulative people. I don't have a problem with Costco selling coffins.

Stephanie: Like solar energy for death. (~)

Similarly, after being introduced by Betsy on an April 22, 2014 Café event, an attendee to responded in a perfectly timed quip:

Betsy: So we usually go until 9:30. People can just jump in and talk about whatever they want to talk about and I also want to introduce Jack. He's doing research. And he can tell you a little bit about it. He is studying death in the US and the Death Café. So he's been coming to our Death Cafés. He's going to write a great book about it, so, he's also doing research! That's great!

Tim: It's a call from the "other world"! (~)

During a May 2014 Death Café hosted by Lisa, two guests were divulging the degree of work they put in for their own self-development so as to be better equipped to approach the theme of death and dying:

Scott: And I did a lot of therapy. And a lot of books I read (and I might bring you one or two) [gesturing to Leonard] that might help you right now to feel good.

Leonard: I've got a library! (~)

Later during the evening, Scott was concluding what was perceived by his spouse, Hera, to be a lengthy soliloquy:

Scott: I have four grandchildren and I'm trying to think of what could happen in my life that could cause me to ever go back to maybe ending my life. And I don't know but I'm not going to push it with fate where I lose my sons, or my grandchildren, or Hera. This is Hera [gesturing to Hera]! Just checking. (~) But I do value life very much and one of the things I've noticed, introspectively at first, is that I appreciate every day of my life. My heart's beating, I'm relatively healthy, I think. And, uhm, a little bit obsessive. (~)

Hera: Noooo. (~)

Scott: I don't mean to preach, I just...

Hera: That's why we let you go last! (~)

Even Karen Wyatt's online/virtual Death Cafe administered from Colorado included callers enjoying lighthearted moments where humor was employed:

Karen: ...so true, more conversation about anything is good. It's good for us to be talking more and more and representing our ideas and our thoughts about it and putting it out there. It will be interesting to

see how that goes. In my state of Colorado we had a Death With
Dignity law that didn't even make it out of committee in our state
legislature so I know it will be coming back every year. It will be
brought up again.

Molly: And you have legalized marijuana and that's pretty amazing!
Karen: Maybe people think if we have marijuana we don't need death and
dignity. (~)
Molly: And they could be right actually! (~)

In spite of the many lighthearted moments at Café events, the majority
of exchanges are serious and deep due to the varying degrees of death
anxieties exhibited by some Café attendees. Café dialog exudes a level of
depth that draws attendees together, if not in terms of having a meeting of
the minds, then in terms of a total corporeal commitment toward the
speaker's speech utterances (i.e., body language and orientation toward
speaker, eye contact, silence during speech utterances by one who is
communicating). In this process, Death Cafés create a community that
helps attendees cope with bereavement, grief, and mourning. This is
rather extraordinary given that participants are strangers to one another.

The consequential iterations of loss, bereavement, grief, and mourning,
in fact, propel much of the dynamics at Death Cafés. These losses deserve
finer discernment as they are often casually employed interchangeably
(DeSpelder and Strickland 2009). The stage of bereavement is one
where the individual has the experience of loss. However, grief and
mourning do not follow subsequently as stages, as both grief and mourning have overlapping emotional constellations that are both borne from
the experience of loss. Grief is the inner, mental, cognitive state of the
person who is in bereavement, manifested as a psychosocial reaction to
loss, while mourning is the process through which grief is displayed.
Mourning is cultural, determined by cultural scripts and aesthetics. No
consensus exists as to how long one should grieve and mourn, or where
and how to grieve and mourn. In the latter process, culture makes its
entrance, prescribing rituals, prayers, dress, songs, and gatherings to help
cushion the dying person or the community that dies—if only briefly—
with the decedent. The momentum of grieving and mourning during our
periods of bereavement is thus shaped by the personalized dynamics of loss
and by the sociological conditions that frame events leading to the loss and
its ritualized farewells. That is, how our protagonist encounters mortality,
be it through terminal illness, accidents, systemic destruction from wars,

or through calamitous events brought forth by exceptional circumstances, influences how the death-encountering self and the community experience loss.

Café attendees at face-to-face gatherings arrive enthusiastic and intrigued. There are some nervous attendees but the surfeit of warm smiles and sense of community establishes the atmosphere of each gathering. Amid the clanking of silverware on glass, greetings that serve to break the ice, and the eventual sitting down of Café attendees with their plate of finger foods, a subdued excitement sets the mood for the evening. With the Café facilitator introducing the event and the attendees, the conversations often begin with, ironically, silence. This is to be expected of course: some attendees have not yet finished sizing up one another, while others wonder how one can even break the ice to begin death talk. Inevitably, an individual unafraid of this newfound freedom will start the night's conversation. The floodgates then open and death talk is underway.

Alacrity, curiosity, excitement, and solemnity then guide the energy of the gatherings. In my attendances at the Death Cafés, I did not witness any listener invalidate another participant's confrontation of death and dying. The reason for this is obvious for any of us that have attended a Death Café: many may not have ever asked such questions, conveyed such points, or highlighted certain curiosities about death and dying before, let alone to a group of strangers they will likely not see again. Death talk takes practice. Yet Café attendees know that they are in a safe and healing atmosphere as the talk proceeds throughout the session, with respect bestowed by everyone toward everyone. Calhoun accurately captures the public sphere that is the Death Café (1994: 29):

> The ideal of the public sphere calls for social integration to be based on rational-critical discourse. Integration, in other words, is to be based on communication rather than domination. "Communication" in this context means not merely sharing what people already think or know but also a process of potential transformation in which reason is advanced by debate itself.

Café gatherings are approximately two to three hours long. The online/virtual Death Café organized by Karen tends to last approximately one to one and half hours. At the face-to-face Cafés, attendees feel at home due to the dining experience, a wonderful strategy for people who might want to enjoy a few bites and sip their drinks while each of their new friends is in the process of conveying their stories. The social environment is relaxed, often deeply moving, and as noted in the preceding paragraphs, frequently lighthearted. For online attendees, even if callers are unable to physically interact, a supportive atmosphere still exists between callers. It remains an atmosphere with a surfeit of empathy and compassion.

The size of each Death Café is variable. Some events have less than half a dozen participants while most have at least 10. Still, other Death Cafés may have many dozens, requiring attendees to be divided into different groups seated at different tables. A cursory search of Death Cafés images around the world will indicate diversity in event size, table configurations, and venues for Café gatherings. Furthermore, depending on the preferences of the host, Café events can be held repeatedly at one venue or vary in terms of venue location. Betsy notes how:

> Most people will have them in the same place, and hold a Café the first Monday of every month, at the same time. I prefer going out and trying all these different locations—where nothing is set, which is much harder work but I like it. You just don't know what you're going to get. I'm one of the people that limit the attendance to 10. You feel like you get to know each other more (February 18, 2014).

Betsy further adds:

> I never have large but only small groups. There are Death Cafés that have 60 people, some with 40 people. I really like the feel of one small, intimate group, that's why I limit it to 9–10 people otherwise you know that one table and you're looking at another other table and they are laughing and your table is way boring but you are trying to listen to what the other people are saying. But this way it is nice, small, and intimate and everyone can talk before and after over the potluck. So this is just in my opinion, so that you're not distracted with chatter in the background. (April 22, 2014).

In spite of such creative permutations and configurations for each Death Café, Miles and Corr concede that Café gatherings "do not claim to meet the felt needs of everyone, but they do obviously speak to the concerns of those who join in them" (2017:162). In my many attendances, no attendee offends and no attendee was ever offended. Interjections are mindfully timed. Most surprisingly perhaps is that even religious attendees, many of whom hail from the Abrahamic faiths, do not proselytize or sloganeer religious maxims. Death Cafés are a sort of benevolent purgatory of percolating existential cues, some of which could haphazardly abut one another, yet remain tame due to the desire for the community to hear out new cues on living and dying. The vast majority of Death Cafés promote a town-hall or focus group environment where "death talk" is conveyed in mostly an apolitical, non-macabre, even sanguine manner.

Although Café hosts remind guests that Death Cafés are not therapy sessions, the fact remains that all attendees that participate are viscerally aware of the catharses as they leave their events to renter the world of clutter, scripts, and distractions. Talking about death and discussing how to prepare for it can serve as an immense stressor in a person's life. At Death Cafés, the process is relaxed. When the event concludes for the evening, many attendees are in good spirits: some exchange phone numbers and emails, some take photographs with one another, while for some, lingering convivial talk ensues. As the evening winds down, some attendees become poignantly aware that their paths may never cross again. Many others leave politely and quietly. Indeed, how a Death Café concludes is also unique to each facilitator. Betsy concludes her Death Café session by citing the time and reminding attendees about the logistics for keeping in touch:

> I want everyone to keep in touch. I will send out an email to all of your with your respective emails. Keep in touch and ask questions. You know, keep the conversations going about what everyone was saying. So that's why I am so grateful to do this and have this opportunity again. Get people coming so we can get the word out and get more hosts in LA because of how few people including myself are doing this. I feel terrible turning people down which I am doing. So get more people out there to do it, to be a host (April 22, 2014).

Lisa, inspired by the positive energies during one of her May sessions, concluded the evening with parting words of wisdom:

> I'm so thrilled that all of you are here. And I just have to say that in every Death Café we've ever hosted, there is this beauty of what I call God's universe: There's always a person who connects with another person and says exactly what that other person needs to hear. Every single Death Café for this entire year that has happened, happened organically, naturally, and unplanned. That's the greatest joy for me. Really! It's a pleasure to have you here . . . just engages my heart in a way that it just fills me up. And so it's good. It's the goodness of life. This is the good part, when you get to talk about the deep stuff. And that there was so much discussion about suicide

tonight is such a beautiful thing. It's not something to be ashamed of. Look how prevalent it is (May 22, 2014).

Most Death Café attendees avidly seek out coming Death Café venues in nearby cities, counties, and even other states to attend. Regardless of whatever motive drives their curiosities, the possibilities of a shared humanity based on confronting issues of mortality are conveyed. The communicative process about mortality appears to mute the chronology of time so that the timeless wisdoms of those prophets, sages, philosophers, scientists, and ordinary people can be invoked in ways that so many of us fail to appreciate. Indeed, at Death Cafés, those invoked "attend" the gathering with participants.

OVERVIEW OF CHAPTERS

A brief summary of what the remainder of the book entails is in order. In Chapter 2, I discuss the key demographic that attends Death Cafés, the Baby Boomers, that is, those born between 1946 and 1964. I note how by participating in these monthly or bimonthly meetings, Café attendees are in the process of personalizing their own crucial narrative and expectations regarding end-of-life issues. They are preempting technical control by institutionalized medicine and distortions by the media and market, a process that takes place in a supportive community environment. In the chapter, emphasis is also placed on how the Boomers generation witnessed if not participated in the Civil Rights struggle, inculcating in many a rather dauntless orientation toward perceived systemic abuse. They are mindful of this as they are now—in the guise of Death Café attendees—contesting large systems that are attempting to monopolize a discourse that purportedly frames and articulate their curiosities and concerns about mortality.

The chapter discusses a landmark study by the Pew Research Center in 2002 titled "The Civic and Political Health of the Nation," one which explores in greater detail how Boomers continue to show their civic and political engagement in greater degrees than members of Generation X and the Millennials. The participation of Boomers at Death Cafés is significant for another reason: poised to shape how senior citizens are cared for by the medical establishment, their concerns will likely continue to shape public policy for palliative care in the United States, currently ranked ninth globally according to the *Economist*'s "Quality of Death Index: Ranking Palliative Care Across the World" (Economist Intelligence Unit 2015). In the United States, Death Café attendees are part of the demographic that participated in the passage of California's End of Life Option Act, passed in October 2015.

Chapter 3 introduces Jürgen Habermas's concepts that can be made operative when we analyze the themes of Death Café talk in Chapter 4. The concepts are primarily derived from Habermas classic two-volume work, *The Theory of Communicative Action* as well as from his other publications. The chapter discusses Habermas's contention that democracy need not be embodied by macro-level institutional mechanisms that promote elections, a process that is dependent on bureaucratic mechanisms that operate only during election cycles. He contends that attributes of democracy can be unearthed in free communication that exists in the lifeworld, a world of everyday activities, and through its corresponding communication content that facilitates these activities. For Habermas, communicative action is a useful political and deliberative process as it "presupposes the use of language as a medium for... reaching understanding, in the course of which participants, through relating to a world, reciprocally raise validity claims that can be accepted or contested" (Szczelkun 1999: 99).

Habermas also underscores how free lifeworld communication has been "colonized" by macro-bureaucratic forces that shape the content of communication. In the context of the Death Café, critiques by attendees center on how the medical establishment, the market, and the media monopolize the framing of what death and dying *should* be. This condition is reflected in our inability to appreciate how deeply instructive death and dying in our respective lifeworlds can be. As such, the colonization of lifeworld communication as a grievance voiced at Death Cafés suggests that citizens do not have appropriate venues to voice how they conceptualize their own mortality that promote a good life and a good death. That sociology has yet to explore the social contexts where and when such communication takes place, opined Habermas, renders democracy an unfinished project of modernity. For Habermas, democracy is incomplete simply because between elections cycles are the large bureaucracies that speak *at* (not *to*) its citizens, often in a manner that is vertical—that is, top-down—highly technical, overly legalistic, regulatory, and lacking in norms. These institutions, for Habermas, cannot be seen to promote free expressions that build community solidarity, one that requires free horizontal communication. Indeed, his forebears in the Frankfurt School felt the same, describing how even ostensibly neutral social institutions (as in the media and market) can have authoritarian tendencies. Calhoun's edited text about Habermas's notion of the public sphere (a topic that will be enumerated in Chapter 6) notes how Habermas sought "a more transcendental basis for democracy" through "an account of human communicative capacity that stressed the potentials implicit in all speech . . . in a world still torn asunder and subjected to domination by . . . bureaucratic power" (Habermas 1994: 32).

The chapter also highlights key patterns of communication that promote community and solidarity. Different types of arguments that bring parties toward intersubjective agreement or mutual consensus are outlined. How arguments that encounter ruptures are resolved by communicative action are discussed. Finally, the chapter concludes with a discussion of Habermasian blind spots, informing readers that later chapters (specifically chapters 5 and 6) will harness other sociological speakers to attend to the blind spots and smooth out the contours of Habermas's ideas.

Chapter 4 "reads" the Wordle canvases that have been generated for each Café participant *and* each event where data collection was undertaken. The most important aspect of my research appears in this chapter as I employ Jonathan Feinberg's Wordle text analysis program and tag cloud generator to present key themes emphasized during dialog, as well as situate these themes within the framework of participants' utterances. Wordle takes inputted text and subsequently outputs word compilations where a larger word size indicates greater use of that particular word in the text (Viegas et al. 2009). Thus, tag clouds display text data *about* text data: they are outputs of all words presented on a spatial canvas, with larger sized words assumed to be more suggestive than their smaller sized counterparts. From the tag clouds, cautious extrapolations of Wordle outputs will be made so as to make visible key themes and concerns of each participant and of each Death Café.

Following our Wordle analyses, I discuss how Habermas's communicative action manifested during dialog. The chapter also explores the main critiques Café attendees harbor about aspects of their social world, aspects that cluttered their attempts at forging a more lucid trajectory toward life and death for those bereaved, grieving, and mourning, as well as those who desire secular, intellectual, or spiritual renderings of mortality. Due to the cathartic effects of attending a Death Café, I note how narratives shared by attendees are becoming foundational themes for a bona fide death identity, one that generates coping mechanisms for death very much ahead of schedule, one that allows for a degree of the personal in terms of attending to the logistics of the corporeal as well as the metaphysics of the beyond. The diacritica of a death identity is then assembled to reinforce participants' critical appreciation of life and living. Indeed, Café attendees' coping mechanisms and means of empowerment reflect Corr's (1992) four primary dimensions of coping with dying: physical needs, psychological needs, social needs, and spiritual needs.

Café attendees—by simply being able to convey their thoughts on mortality—are thus returning a community and public to death and dying in ways that connect them with all those from time immemorial as well as with all those in the present. More importantly, Café participants are essentially beginning preparations for the bereavement, grieving, and the mourning to come. They are preparing for death early in life, whether viscerally from inspirational sentiments provided by fellow attendees, or from deep within their own experiences with personal loss, in hopes of living their days with deeper purpose. As Death Café events are now systematically accessible around the world, Death Cafés can be seen as a vital organ of civil society, a new iteration of a death system beyond the hospital. In this regard, I conclude Chapter 4 by beginning my conceptualization of the Death Café as an existential and transformative social movement, one where its participants can confront mortality issues while still energized and independent, and in ways that promote a shared humanity.

In Chapter 5, I employ the ideas of Erich Fromm and Kurt Wolff to enhance Habermas's ideas. Erich Fromm's ideas conveyed in *To Have or To Be* (1976) as well as *Escape from Freedom* (1969) remind readers that certain modes of human conduct, such as the incessant need to be satisfied with materialism, distances people from the profundities of being. It also creates a shallow humanity that becomes fixated with commodities and goods that promote what this work refers to as an "immortality complex." Indeed, the profundities of being are what Café attendees are aiming for with existential and mortality cues that they are just on the verge of understanding.

Fromm notes in *Escape* an ironic consequence of democratic systems and/or free societies: that when there is a surfeit of freedom, people will retreat from it. This rather counterintuitive observation explains how a surfeit of freedoms given to social actors also mandates that they engage in the labor of making many important life decisions. It is the overload of decision-making dynamics in democratic societies that compels their retreat. By doing so, they blindly defer to an authoritarian personality and/or institutions that will provide dramatic answers and reassurances, that will make decisions for them, enabling the conditions that allow for authoritarian tendencies to surface in macro-level institutions of society. In Chapter 5 the trinity of the media, market, and medicine is rendered into such an authority that citizens turn to if they escape from their freedoms to accept their mortality. Thus, Fromm argues that many people in free and/or democratic societies are actually unfree. In my research, it has become rather clear that Death Café attendees are not escaping their freedoms to author their own mortality, fully aware of the difficult logistics, cultural demands, and metaphysical uncertainties of death and dying. This is an expression of freedom in a Frommian sense, that is, to use freedom "to" instead of freedom "from" for important decision-making episode.

The ideas of Kurt Wolff will also be harnessed to enhance Habermas and Fromm's ideas. Wolff asserts that the experience of life epiphanies is catalytic in providing a high degree of personal truth for those that experience it. Through his surrender and catch thesis, Wolff argues that exceptionally profound moments in the human condition inspire protagonists to confront the meaning of existence in ways that allow them to self-actualize. The significance and utility of Wolff's surrender and catch thesis cannot be overemphasized: many Café attendees only found their mettle to live well after exceptionally close encounters with dying, encounters that declutter life so as to unearth the lucidity and courage needed to continue living.

I also note in the chapter how death talk allows many attendees the will to find happiness in the aftermath of confronting death, yet they also caution about the responsibilities and logistics that emerge after one experiences existential crises. Many attendees' life courses embody the social and psychical dynamics alluded to by Habermas, Fromm, and Wolff, in that they convey narratives from profound encounters with death and dying that are not cluttered by ideas scripted by medicine, the market, or media. Many Café attendees celebrate the ability to freely personalize and consider their own mortality in ways that are pragmatic and realistic (Habermas), and in ways that are about being, not having (Fromm). However, these dynamics often follow deep moments of epiphanic realizations that cannot be relegated into denial (Wolff). For Wolff, moments of surrender and catches are what ground actors into a *reality with purpose*. His ideas are thus amalgamated with those of Habermas and Fromm so as to give synergy to our analyses of Death Café communicative dynamics.

Chapter 6 attends to Habermas's notion of the public sphere as where communicative action takes place. Habermas takes great pains to outline how the dynamics of communicative action indicate a healthy democratic space for mutual consensus and intersubjective accommodations that build solidarity, but he had little to say about how such venues of communicative action promote a zeitgeist on mortality *in toto*. Although his tracing of the public sphere is historically rich, the process and its historical contextualization remain abstract. Nonetheless, as indicated by Habermasian scholars such as Cohen (1999), Schudson (1994), and Calhoun (1994), Habermas's work *The Structural Transformation of the Public Sphere* (1991) contains all the vital components that had been explicated in his earlier works such as *Legitimation Crisis* (1989) and *Communicative Action*. Containing much utility for Death Café analysis, Habermas actually discusses cafés as public sphere sites where news and information about the economy, trade, finances, and the state intertwine, but at the price of excluding a grass-roots community.

The notion of a public sphere where Habermas's democracy project can be completed renders it useful for conceptualizing death talk as a means of democratic expression, one that can contest narratives from social institutions and the state. I note in the chapter how death talk, a comparatively suppressed form of communication that has been rendered "depressing," now has a community-oriented response that encourages one to love and live with mindful awareness that death will come. However, because of the colonization of the public sphere, technocratic, sensationalized, and vulgarized notions of death are meted to the population.

A more optimistic rendering of a public sphere environment can be seen in Ray Oldenburg's classic work *The Great Good Place* (1999). Oldenburg elaborates in his work what he terms as "third places," an analog—with some inflections—of the public sphere. Third places are constituted as environments such as pubs, coffee shops, bookstores, even hair salons, that function to promote community interaction and civic engagement. That the third place appears so interchangeable with Habermas's public sphere behooves me to amalgamate the two, and I employ both the public sphere and third place concepts interchangeably toward the end of Chapter 6.

As a useful concept for looking at communities that are formed in spite of the presupposed alienation among urban dwellers, Oldenburg distinguishes third places from the first and second places. For Oldenburg, first places are *private* and *informal* environments often embodied by the institution of the family. Second places, are *public* and *formal* environments, embodied by an actor's place of employment. Third places, then, function as a sort of social

glue for generating community because of their *informal* and *public* orientation. Oldenburg emphasizes the importance of environments like pubs, hair
salons, cafés, and book stores—organs of civil society—as vital for community health and democracy. For Oldenburg, the converse is also hauntingly
true: totalitarian systems would never tolerate public and informal gatherings
of citizens critical of the government. Moreover, Oldenburg notes how class
demarcations are blurred at third places, leveling all patrons. Oldenburg
takes his ideas to the same horizons as Habermas's contention that public
spheres are ideal environments for communicative action dynamics. Indeed,
the formulation that will close this chapter is that Death Cafés are primarily
third place or public sphere phenomena.

In Chapter 7, our final chapter, I amalgamate important concepts provided by scholars presented in the monograph for a final reading of the
Death Café phenomenon as a social movement. With pride of place still
given to Habermas's theory of communicative action, I demonstrate how
the amalgamation of communicative action concepts that underpin a death
identity—inflected with the ideas of Fromm, Wolff, and Oldenburg, along
with other scholars—can be as significant for the actor as ethnic, cultural,
religious, and gender identities. I note how a death identity articulates a
shared value system that reminds us that engaging in death talk is not an act
of social subversion. On the contrary, it is vitally important for society to
confront death and dying issues in all its intellectual, metaphysical, emotional, and even legal iterations, in ways that transcend systemic colonization
of their lifeworlds. In this regard, I remind readers that we are witnessing a
decolonizing of the lifeworld through Death Café renderings of death, one
that attempts to return agency to community and grass-roots articulations of
mortality, and ultimately, what a good death might entail. I note how such a
decolonization through Death Cafés serves to articulate our shared humanity in an age of divisive identity politics.

After the amalgamation of the entire work's concepts into an architecture that contains the diacritica of death talk, I forward some views on
why the Death Café has taken on the momentum that it has, fully
accommodating the fact that communities have all had their episodes
where people sat around fires, the fires that bring people together, to talk
about death. Yet the distinction I make between the Death Café community and those that were embodiments of a more sacred, even "deep"
time, is that the former aims to personalize for the actor a trajectory freed
of scripts and dictates from above, be it religion, government, medicine,
or even the market.

The closing sections of our final chapter elaborate on sociologist Anthony Giddens's views about the catalytic aspects of social risk that propel participants toward generating a cultural response to an increasingly precarious society. A discussion of how Giddens further discerns risks into those that are natural and those "manufactured" by society is undertaken to forward the view that social actors and social systems have an obsession with risk calculations. The desire to engage with risk calculations can be seen as a set of factors that motivate Café attendees to mitigate risks by decolonizing their lifeworlds through death talk. To understand their efforts as a movement, a condensed review of social movement literature is undertaken. The main reason for this odd placement of the review is due to my concern that were such a review provided at the outset of this work, readers might be skewed toward assuming *a priori* that the Death Café is already an advanced social movement. Such a conclusion would overlook how the Death Café as social movement is but at its prototypical phase of self-definition and consciousness-raising through communicative action. Additionally, by conducting a review of social movement literature in the last chapter allows the literature to function as a crescendo for the efforts of Café participants, all of whom are framed as bona fide social movement activists in this work. Having identified public spheres and third places as important spatial sites for communicative action, and for Death Café proliferation in general, the successes of the Death Café as social movement are discussed in ways that fill some of the blind spots in the social movement literature.

Some readers might disagree with this work's alacrity toward an experience like the Death Café. For example, Lofland framed such groups as part of a happy death movement in *The Craft of Dying* (1979). The orientation taken in this book reminds readers that the ethos of the Death Café is not about the affective attribute of mortality. This would be too egregiously simplistic a rendering of an overly complex idea about the human condition. Throughout this work, I hope to give voices to those Death Café attendees who directly or indirectly assemble death themes through communication, themes that emphasize existential sovereignty in all its inflections as they, or we, head toward our date with death. The position taken in this monograph is that the exploration of the *whys* is far more vital for understanding society's temperament on mortality than the mechanistic and systematic approaches that generate bureaucratic and institutional discourses on mortality, a process that stifles the voices of the grass roots. The sentiments in my work—not unlike those expressed by the Baby Boomers in my sample—adopt a critical view of our mainstream and consumerist cultures and how they cheapen the sacrality and understanding of living and dying. In the process of attending to these cues, I also intend to highlight other key thinkers I believe will shed light on why participation in the Death Café movement is now percolating in the industrialized and developed world. Only then can the Death Café be celebrated as a much needed social movement for people to freely converse about mortality in ways that allow for a nonsystemic rendering of coping, acceptance, and preparation for end of life.

In the next chapter, we turn our attention to the civic engagement profile of Baby Boomers, the primary demographic that attends and participates at Death Café events. With an impressive history of civic engagement, Boomers and their attendances at Death Cafés are poised to generate new cues and narratives about mortality.

CHAPTER 2

Baby Boomers and the Death Café

Charles Allan Gilbert's *All is Vanity* (1892).

© The Author(s) 2017
J. Fong, *The Death Café Movement*,
DOI 10.1007/978-3-319-54256-0_2

KEEPING IT REAL

The American Baby Boomer generation, those born between 1946 and 1964, is aging. In the process of being forced to confront a more proximate mortality horizon, many in the demographic are attending Death Cafés. They attend for a variety of reasons, but primarily do so because they are entering an opportune period in their life cycle where mortality issues have great influence in shaping their decision-making. Although an unequivocally heterogeneous group with its own intersected identities of gender, ethnicity/race, and religiosity, they nonetheless exhibit one important unifying feature of their generation: that their generational passing will likely register as the largest number of recorded deaths in the annals of American history. However, before diving into demographic data about Baby Boomers' active engagement in political life, we need to explore issues that prompted some of them toward Death Café participation.

Currently, a growing global movement, Jon Underwood organized the first Death Café in London[1] in September 2011 after being inspired by Swiss sociologist Bernard Crettaz's launch of Paris' first Death Café in 2010. As of 2016, there are close to 4,000 Death Cafés located in 37 countries. As noted in Chapter 1, in the United States, venues have been established in Gig Harbor, Washington; Searsport, Maine; Ann Arbor, Michigan, and Cleveland, Ohio, to name but a few. In Southern California, a Santa Clarita venue is headed by Lisa Solis Delong, R.N. and author of *Blood Brothers* (DeLong 2011), the other, by Betsy Trapasso, M.S.W, in Topanga Canyon, to name but a few. For *Los Angeles Times'* Nita Lelyveld who covered the first Death Café gathering in Topanga Canyon on April 15, 2013 in "Passing Thoughts at L.A.'s first Death Cafe," their confrontations exhibit a level of courage, honesty, and lucidity that is impressive. Regardless of locale, all Death Cafés advocate a healthy *and* organic atmosphere of discussion for its attendees.

Lelyveld's observations should hardly be surprising. Death Café attendees are in the company of people that ultimately develop some type of solidarity with one another due to the uniqueness of being in an environment that explores death and dying in the context of living. More importantly, Café attendees reject the flooding of imagery and cues on the *hows* of death and dying, opting to explore the *whys* of death and dying, and by implication, of living. Indeed, for Italian thanatologist Marina Sozzi (2005), Western culture and its technological advances upon understanding the body has contributed to mechanical views that are unable to make "the experience of death fecund; thus, death becomes an impersonal deadline of the body, a fatality inscribed inside it, pure biology" (cited in DeSpelder and Strickland 2009: 43). Not an event that explores the biological finality of life, Death Café conversations instead discuss candidly topics on mortality in a less morbid, but more anti-systemic fashion. We can be grateful to the Baby Boomers for such an orientation. As a demographic group with cohorts that witnessed the Civil Rights, Baby Boomers have again embarked on a new social movement, this time to regain control of the narrative on death and dying, ahead of schedule, and while still independent, proactive, and pre-emptive within the lifeworld.

The lifeworld, a term popularized by philosopher Edmund Husserl and sociologist Alfred Schutz, represents the world of everyday occurrences and social interaction. As an epistemological and ontological site, the lifeworld is that space in social life where interactions take place beyond the scripts and messages dispensed to us by our frequently reified institutions. These institutions then regulate our lives with purposive rationality, rendering such rationality as a force of domination. For Habermas, the lifeworld's significance is how it functions as a site of democratic production and activism that can challenge such domination from above. It is a dynamic horizon that is "always already moving" due to its face-to-face communicative dynamics (1987: 119), one where "communicative action relies on a cooperative process of inter-pretation in which participants relate simultaneously to something in the objective, the social, and the subjective worlds" (Habermas 1987: 120).

By participating in these monthly or bimonthly lifeworld meetings, depending on the time management of Café hosts, Baby Boomers are in the process of authoring their own crucial narrative and expectations regarding end-of-life issues such as the finances of death, medical care toward end of life, how assets are to be handled, whether feeding tubes and ventilators are necessary, how children and/or parents will be cared for, and how one should be allowed to die in the comforts of home rather than in highly bureaucratized and technology-driven settings such as hospitals. Metaphysical and spiritual themes are also discussed, hinting at Boomers' search for a deeper, existential framework to contextualize death and dying.

The Baby Boomers attending Death Cafés in the study are unwilling to surrender their authorship on death and dying to macro-level institutions. Even those who have been indoctrinated since childhood and who remain devoutly religious, secular, or adamantly scientific realize that cross-cul-tural community narratives on death and dying constitute a new grass-roots voice that is, at the very least, interesting and, at most, allows them to become unfettered from large social institutions that aestheticize, vulgarize, or commoditize death. In an age where identity politics have fragmented social relations, especially in the United States, the Death Café movement and its many fans are reinvigorating the view that our shared mortality is our shared humanity.

Humanity remains fearful of death in ways that are foundational, a condition noted by Ernest Becker's *Denial of Death*. Neimeyer et al. (2003) extrapolate from this position to frame how death anxiety permeates eventually all members of society. Consisting of "a cluster of death attitudes characterized by fear, threat, unease, discomfort, and similar negative emotional reactions" (Neimeyer et al. 2003: 46–47), such concerns have compelled much of humanity into ritualizing the worship of personified and idealized immortals. Even those who dare face death with courage will first have to deal with an innate fear of dying, for they might die into the infinitude of eternal night and darkness, or they might experience an infinitude of fire and demons. Some fear absolute extinction of all that is the self yet many are convinced of an eternal euphoria that exists in post-life realms.

In spite of great philosophical and religious texts that describe the afterlife in glowing and radiant terms (for those deemed worthy), institutions of society need to continually reinforce death and dying with righteousness, romance, and glory so as to mitigate our fears of death (Sheets-Johnstone 2002): dying for a loved one, dying for one's country, dying while doing what one loves, or dying for a cause, all of which serve to provide for the dying a sense of purpose and meaning. Society provides rituals and contexts for such practices to have legitimacy, thus giving birth to cultural motifs and narratives about death and dying that differ across the present and across time. Even today, we wear colors of death prescribed for us, while in some cultures, moirologists from yesteryear and today can be compensated to cry and caterwaul for the dead, or to pour libations in ways that amplify the deceased person's importance. We are told that certain religious holidays require the buying of goods and services to honor and/or worship the dead. A free market even extends into the metaphysical realm: Due to my Chinese heritage, I have seen those of my ilk burn paper money for their deceased to spend in the afterlife, not unlike ancient Egyptian practices of placing material culture in the tombs of their pharaohs so that their former rulers can experience prosperity beyond this life.

Yet crucial questions remain about life and living in response to a mindful acceptance or adamant rejection of the inevitability of death and dying. Erich Fromm's *To Have or To Be* (1976) provides arguably the best sequence of questions regarding this topic, one that Boomers at Death Cafés are engaging with:

> But what about the fear of losing life itself—the fear of dying? Is this a fear only of older people or of the sick? Or is everybody afraid of dying? Does the fact that we are bound to die permeate our whole life? Does the fear of dying grow only more intense and more conscious the closer we come to the limits of life by age or sickness? (1976: 108).

Those closest to providing important narratives to potentially respond to Fromm's queries, as highlighted to me by Lisa Delong, are the nurses engaged in hospice and palliative care, one of the most poorly paid medical professionals. Consequentially, the process by which society grants cultural expressions of death and dying allows for an *a priori* conflation of ritual and understanding, of form and content—not pure content as is experienced at Death Cafés. That is, people going through the motions of honoring death or the dead can nonetheless be delinked from a full understanding of the profundity of the human condition experiencing death and dying. Form may hint at existential content, but more often than not, symbolize it through metaphors and allegories, or just as well be devoid of it.

With the advent of the sciences in the post-Enlightenment era and the free market that emerged during the Industrial Revolution, one that remains with us today in different iterations, death and dying was reconceptualized, but not necessarily for the better. The scientists within and without the medical system view the process physiologically, unwilling to formally sanction in their discourse the possibility of a transcending soul. Dying was thus seen as a corporeal process where all organs in the body ultimately shut down. For many who die, the moment is often signaled by the "death rattle" that occurs when body fluids accumulate in the upper chest, as well as the Cheyne-Stokes breathing pattern where apnea becomes progressively longer in duration. The state after death is seen in a raw, unphotogenic manner where different stages of putrefaction occur. Depending on how one dies, the eyes can develop the signature Tache Noire while fluids leak from our noses and mouths, only to be followed by degloving. These attributes of the deceased are easily measureable, verifiable, as are the stages before the living enter death—again easily measurable and verifiable. Whether there is the "other side" is precisely the question that is the bane of science, for even the most resolute of empiricists cannot at this juncture in the human experience conclusively verify the existence of a soul or an afterlife. The scientific industrial complex is not in the belief business. Opting to investigate, measure, and control all dynamics of the natural world, humans thus die with machines inside and beside them.

For sociologist Hugh Willmott, science "represents death in terms of its causes . . . so that we no longer hear or think of people 'dying of mortality'" (Willmott 2000: 652). Sociologist Anthony Giddens notes how colonization of the meaning of death and dying thus paradoxically excludes from "social life . . . fundamental existential issues which raise . . . moral dilemmas for human beings" (1991: 156). Giddens notes how culture sequesters death so that it "becomes a difficult, if not a taboo topic to be approached . . . by reference to something else—such as the causes of illnesses and accidents" (1991: 156). De Spelder and Strickland note this same tendency where death language employs a variety of euphemisms to "depersonalize death" by subjecting it with "a lexicon of substitutions" (2009: 11):

> The words dead and dying tend to be avoided; instead, loved ones "pass away," embalming is "preparation," the deceased is "laid to rest," burial becomes "internment," the corpse is "remains," the tombstone is a "monument," and the undertaker is transformed into a "funeral director . . . [while] sympathy cards represent a way for people to express condolences to the bereaved without directly mentioning death" (DeSpelder and Strickland 2009: 11).

Willmott notes that because "uneasiness surrounds death," its corporeal management is "routinely smoothed and managed by a plethora of . . . specialists" such as physicians, mortuary attendants, funeral directors, and priests, all of whom are "employed to render death invisible or . . . minimally disruptive of normal appearances" (2000: 649). Indeed, society upholds such practices such as embalming where the deceased is rendered "asleep" for perpetuity. Dori Fisher, an attendee at one of Ms. Trapasso's Death Cafés, noted poignantly: "The first person I ever saw dead was my grandmother. She never wore makeup, but she was all made up and she was wearing something she would never wear. I said: 'That's not my grandmother'" (Lelyveld 2013). Fromm's views reinforce such a scenario:

> Perhaps the most significant datum is the deeply engraved desire for immortality that manifests itself in the many rituals and beliefs that aim at preserving the human body. On the other hand, the modern, specifically American denial of death by the "beautification" of the body speaks equally for the repression of the fear of dying by merely camouflaging death (Fromm 1976: 108).

An example can also be seen in the power of a medical technocracy that has influenced society's discourse on health and death. In a September 24, 2013, *Bloomberg* report by Shannon Pettypiece titled "Death Dinners at Boomers' Tables Take on Dying Taboo," the author notes how death and dying are seen in the medical establishment as a "losing battle." In practice, the terminally ill patient reaching end of life is often bereft of metaphysically nurturing environments where sentiments and symbolisms from loved ones can be allowed to satiate the patient's final moments. This condition, according to Willmott, demonstrates how science mediates everyday encounters with potentially life-threatening accidents, disease, and illness. For Giddens, People severed from their mortality thus purchase "ontological security through institutions and routines that protect us from direct contact with...death" (1991: 156).

The media cultures of civil society can just as well be implicated in this regard. Although serving as a crucial mechanism for information dissemination—the televised media specifically—employs shock value and sensationalized deaths to vulgarize mortality: Televised news is infamous for conveying not a peaceful death of one's own authoring, but a death that results from gang-related shootings, police violence, school shootings of children and teachers, homicides, terrorist beheadings and bombings, car, boat, and plane accidents, and suicides, all in the hopes of getting ratings and advertisers. In this regard, any node in the framing of the human condition seen on the televised media, be it the body (through homicides, for example), the city (through crime), the region (through a natural disaster), or an era (where history and historical change are functions of wars), becomes vulgarized and distorted in ways that blur the line between recreation and information. As such, the death of a neighbor or colleague, or the death that most of us will experience, is insignificant in the media universe. For DeSpelder and

Strickland, encounters with death on television are skewed toward the spectacular obscuring the ordinary (2009).

> Death is generally portrayed on television or in movies as coming from the outside, often violently, reinforcing the notion that dying is something that *happens to us*, rather than something we *do*. Death is an accidental rather than a natural process. As our firsthand *experiences* of death and violence have diminished, *representations* of death and violence in the media have increased in sensationalism (DeSpelder and Strickland 2009: 10).

Is it any wonder that death and dying seen through the media influences many to have a "mean world syndrome" where their existential orientations are tied to issues of hopelessness, unceasing malaise, despair, shock, angst, and despondency, compelling many to hand over their ability to author their own mortality to macro-level social institutions, only to reify that authority and perceived unassailability of these institutions in the long term? Media analyst George Gerbner affirms that the mean world syndrome contributes to an "irrational dread of dying and thus to diminished vitality and self-direction in life" (1980: 70).

Finally, in the modern age set upon us by industrialization—one which has created and demanded the generation of goods for incessant consumption—death and dying have become commoditized. One can see this at the largest systemic level in how military industrial complexes operate around the world through direct and proxy wars, selling weaponry that has but one purpose: to eliminate lives. During the Cold War, the Soviet Union engaged in what was known as "MIG Diplomacy" whereby Moscow provided its allies, from China to Vietnam, India, Egypt, the Eastern bloc, and beyond with their feared MIG jet fighters so that these countries, slated for socialist liberation, could repulse US and Western imperialism. In US civil society, citizens can go shopping at large superstores like some Costcos where coffins are sold in nicely decorated dioramas that are placed—perhaps with an intended pun—near the checkout lines. Attending to death at many funeral homes is almost akin to buying an automobile: different models of coffins are available and upgrades create a better presentation aesthetic for the decedent, not to mention a variety of other services that are possible if additional fees can be paid. The free market is complicit in the process of death denial as it staves off the implications of aging and death with lotions, creams, botox, facelifts, hair replacement, and the like. Certain practices in the deathcare industry reinforce such a denial through practices such as embalming where the deceased are rendered to appear asleep for perpetuity. Many cemeteries have what are essentially "ethnic enclaves" for the deceased, an idealized simulacrum and dreamscape of an ethnic suburb for the dead.

The media often provides an extremist yet grotesque compilation of death and dying through shock value and sensationalism, as well as through the worship and glorification of eternal youth. Medicine aims to view death as a defeat of their aims and life must prolonged if possible, even if it means subjecting patients to regimens of painful treatment. The market economy through deathcare services sees death and dying as a means for profit, often securing such profits from people who have lost loved ones, people who are at their most vulnerable and impressionable periods. The aforementioned institutions thus overwhelm the dying with their own logistics and procedural stimuli: Should one continue expensive chemotherapy or purchase alternative medicine? Should one be buried or go the more affordable route of cremation? And how do advance directives fit into all of the above? The overwhelming stimuli on death and dying in the United States and developed countries have thus generated some coping mechanisms that take us ironically *further* from the understanding death and dying. Death Café attendees of the Boomers generation are thus decluttering their narrative on mortality by acknowledging these aforementioned factors through death talk. Thus, the raison d'être of Death Cafés: a venue that allows death narratives to address the discontents of modernity, one that is embodied in the statement captured by Los Angeles Times reporter Nita Lelyveld regarding an attendee's feelings on death:

> We all want to make a good death. If you ask somebody, "How do you want to die?" they'll say, "In the bosom of my family, with my friends around." They don't say, "In a hospital bed with tubes coming out of my nose and ears, in a semi-coma—that's my perfect death" (Lelyveld 2013).

Social institutions, from the most bureaucratized to the most communal village council, have made death and dying beautiful, gory, and theatrical, absolving individuals and groups from forging ahead on their own sovereign, existential trajectories. Macro-level social institutions have the financial wherewithal to vulgarize, romanticize, or package death in ways that the individual cannot. Even in the most heinous expression of dying seen on television, movies, and other outlets of the mass media, there is the default obfuscation of how our bodies ultimately appear days, weeks, and months after being deceased.

In many developed countries—and the United States is no exception—the authoring and discussion of one's mortality have been appropriated by media, medicine, and market discourses in ways that have allowed them to colonize our lifeworld, an observation noted by one of the most important sociologists of our time, Frankfurt School sociologist Jürgen Habermas. For Habermas, the *colonization of the lifeworld*—a world of communication and discourse that build community—exacerbates the pull of community away from a grass-roots discourse that could potentially shape public policy. Although Habermas never directly dealt with the topic of sociological death, his illumination of how rational and deliberative grass-roots communication can be infiltrated by macro-level institutions of society is highly relevant for the critiques conveyed in this work.

The ideas of Habermas, other Frankfurt School thinkers, as well as other prominent sociological thinkers will be made to "orbit" our examination of the Death Café movement in ways where a plethora of concepts will be made operative to explain *why* such a movement, particularly in our Western culture, sloganeers the need for "death talk." Such an undertaking is vital for understanding the depth of the human experience since the community that has emerged around Death Café gatherings is essentially about reminding us that there is much more to living than waking up at 4:00 AM to shop at Black Friday venues, getting validation from *Facebook* "Likes," playing video games, and taking selfies. Indeed, as Erich Fromm noted in *To Have or To Be*, materialism leaves us in a hollowed and agitated state of existence, one devoid of meaning. And as prophets, sages, philosophers, and social scientists of yesteryear have already explicitly noted or intimated: understanding mortality allows us to have a shared humanity based on living and loving, a sorely needed task lest we remain confused, distracted, unable to self-actualize, and rendered vulnerable to nihilism. Death Café attendees, therefore, are anti-nihilist activists who seek to author their own meaning and employ coping mechanisms in the context of our greatest existential crisis: the passing of our loved ones and ultimately our own passing.

Modern societies make little room for contemplative and introspective renderings of death and dying even though all humans at one time or another will be taken by existential matters, requiring precisely the need for introspection and contemplation. Without metaphysical and philosophical cues, individuals rarely nor explicitly generate personal narratives on death and dying. Even when the rituals honoring the dead come to pass, most return to the minutiae that define their lives and forget whatever wisdoms were disclosed during memorial services, until the time arises again for those institutions to return to frame death and dying. We want death and dying conveyed to us at a time of our choosing but are reluctant or unwilling to author a timeless approach toward death and dying ourselves. Such is the nature of living in what the great *fin-de-siècle* sociologist Ferdinand Tönnies described as an age of *gesellschaft*, an age that emphasizes opportunism, self-entitlement, and self-advancement. Baby Boomers, because of their current position in the life cycle, are poised to redefine mortality in light of the aforementioned social and personal dynamics that surface when we attempt to confront our own mortality.

BABY BOOMERS

The key demographic that has nourished the Death Café movement behooves social scientists to explore how American Baby Boomers embark on their own trajectory of mortality as they enter the healthcare system in large numbers. However, many do not live sclerotic lives as passive individuals hidden inside communities. A landmark study by the Pew Research Center in 2002 titled "The Civic and Political Health of the Nation," one which we will now be exploring, notes how even today Boomers continue to show their civic and political engagement in greater degrees than members of Generation X and the Millennials. The participation of Boomers at Death Cafés is significant for another reason: poised to shape how senior citizens are attended to by the medical establishment, they may be able to ultimately improve the state of palliative and hospice care in the United States, currently ranked ninth globally according to the *Economist*'s 2015 "Quality of Death Index: Ranking Palliative Care Across the World." Additionally, the participants in my Death Café study are vocal proponents of California's End of Life Option Act that was passed in October, 2015. Yet in spite of its nascent political orientation, the vast majority of Boomers at Death Cafés promote a town-hall or focus group environment where "death talk" is conveyed in an apolitical and non-morbid, even sanguine manner.

Candid about their views on mortality and frustrated with the inadequacies and perceived inhumanity of systemic authority to solely define their destinies, Boomers are now employing this movement to control their narrative and management of death. At this point in US history, they number close to 80 million residents, or close to a quarter of the US population, all of whom will have to contend with the medical, media, and economistic narratives surrounding their mortality, sooner than later. Attendees from this generation are thus trying to bring back and/or resurrect a discourse on death and dying that reveals its uncluttered sacrality. As noted by Betsy Trapasso who launched the first Death Café in Southern California, "Boomers are coming of age and books are being written and that's why there's this shift happening, because Boomers always make noise" (1–25).

And perhaps they should. Pettypiece (2013) notes how by 2030, 3.3 million Americans will die per year. This figure will be up 32% "from the current death rate as baby boomers age." For Carole Fisher, chief executive director of the Nathan Adelson Hospice in Nevada: Boomers will have to "call a lot of their own shots and make decisions and see those decisions through." For Pettypiece, the generation that was catalytic in the Civil Rights, the antiwar movement, and the sexual revolution is now "trying . . . to have it their way right to the very end." For this generation, a quality death need not be framed within the much hackneyed milieu where doctors and nurses equipped with feeding tubes and respirators ply their trade, but with loved ones whose significant connections with individuals have given meaning and immeasurable depth to their existence. Boomers believe that due to the tendency for many to offer up their bodies to technical micromanagement near end of life, the role of culture, community, and family as crucial components in ensuring a "good death" is muted. Patients with terminal illness are thus bereft of nurturing, organic environments where sentiments and symbolisms from loved ones, expressed in physically comforting settings, can be allowed to satiate the moment as the individual prepares to pass on.

Another key reason for the importance of focusing on Boomers as potential movement actors in the Death Café experience is due to their consistency with civic engagement, a trend that continues in the present. In the 2002 study on American civic and political engagement across generations by the Pew Research Center, it was found that Boomers frequently out-participated the Millennials generation (those born after 1976) as well as those from Generation X (born between 1964 and 1976) in community and political activities and engagements (Keeter et al. 2002).[2] From this important study, the tables to be presented in the following pages have been adapted in ways that amalgamate the Baby Boomers with the proliferation of Death Cafés.

Millennials are unable to match the Boomers on key indicators of community and political engagement while many members of Generation X are a distant third in most indicators of community and political engagement. Having been shaped by politicized experiences such as the Civil Rights movement, Vietnam and Watergate, gender-based and ethnic/racial and indigenous movements, and the "sexual revolution," the Boomer cohort "has always been big enough to force the culture to adapt to them" (Keeter et al. 2002: 6). This resulted in a demographic that tends toward free expression, experimentation, and social involvement. These indicators deserve further mention because it illuminates how Boomers' are in the process of transforming the Death Café into a bona fide transformative social movement, one that will definitively inform public policies related to death and dying in the near future.

The Pew study sampled 3,246 respondents regarding their electoral and civic engagement activities, ranging from volunteering to signing petitions (and most other activities in between). Keeter et al. found that the Boomers are still able to maintain attentiveness to both electoral *and* civic affairs, whereas the Generation X and Millennials' participation activities tended to revolve around civic, not electoral matters. For Keeter et al., there is a civic-political divide that is characterized by generational differences. Table 2.1 displays the

Table 2.1   Percent of registered voters by generation

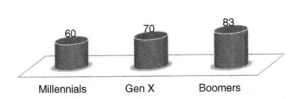

Table 2.2 Additional political activities by generation

Activities	Millennials	Gen X	Boomers
Displays campaign button/sticker/sign (%)	20	18	28
Contributes money to political group (%)	4	11	17
Volunteers for political groups (%)	6	14	22

percent of members of different generations that are registered voters. We see that 83% of Boomers noted they were registered to vote compared to 70% and 60% for Generation X and the Millennials, respectively (Keeter et al. 2002: 10).

Table 2.2 indicates that 28% of Boomers have displayed campaign button/stickers/signs, 17% have ever contributed money to political groups, and 22% indicated that they had volunteered for political groups. Data for these three indicators are higher than other groups. For the same three indicators, members of Generation X exhibited figures of 18%, 11%, and 14%, respectively, while Millennials exhibited figures of 20%, 4%, and 6%, respectively (Keeter et al. 2002: 11).

Table 2.3 reveals that 21% of Boomers had ever contacted a public official compared to 15% and 9% for Generation X and Millennials, respectively. Among those who contacted a public official in the last year only, again Boomers led the way at 20% compared to 16% and 10% for members of the Generation X and Millennials category, respectively (2002: 14). Keeter et al. note that "Older generations have an edge in contacting public officials. Perhaps feeling more confident and with more under-

Table 2.3 Percent having contacted public officials by generation

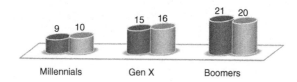

■ % Having ever contacted public officials

■ % Contacted public officials last year only

standing of paths to power, Baby Boomers...are more likely to have contacted or visited a public official at some level of government" (2002: 14).

As can be seen in Table 2.4 regarding discussions about politics and government with family members, again Boomers led the way, with 38% indicating that they frequently did so compared to only 28% and 22% exhibited by members of Generation X and Millennials, respectively. On measures of attentiveness to politics, 50% of Boomers indicated that they followed government and public affairs "very often" while, respectively, only 37% and 24% of Generation X and Millennials indicated so. In a measure that bodes well for cautiously extrapolating about the communicative richness of Death Café gatherings, 63% of Boomers noted that they "talk very often with family and friends" about current events in general while 58% of Generation X and 51% of Millennials indicated so (2002: 15). Boomers again ranked higher than members of Generation X and the Millennials in Table 2.4's three

Table 2.4 Percent indicating frequency of talking about (1) politics and government, (2) government and public affairs, as well as (3) current events by generation

	Millennials	Gen X	Boomers
■ % Talks very often with family and friends about politics and government	22	28	38
▨ % Follows government and Public affairs very often	24	37	50
■ % Talks very often with family and friends about current events in general	51	58	63

indicators of talking about politics and government, government and public affairs, and current events.

In terms of various forms of civic engagement (see Table 2.5), Boomers exhibited the highest value at 24% while Generation X and Millennials registered 23% and 20%, respectively, for in-person community petitioning (not email petitioning) in the last 12 months (2002: 14). As for community problem solving, Boomers are most active: 25% of them indicated they were engaged with some of the aforementioned activities while Generation X and the Millennials exhibited only 22% and 21% rates of engagement, respectively. They also volunteer more regularly (26%) than members of Generation X (25%) and Millennials (22%). Boomers also indicated that in the last 12 months they participated in a run or walk for charity more often (37%) than members of Generation X (29%) and Millennials (28%). Similarly, Boomers were more active in non-electoral group activities (40%) than members of Generation X (29%) and Millennials (22%).

Table 2.5   Additional indicators of civic engagement by generation

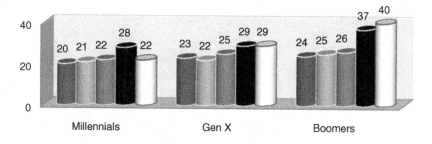

■ In-person community petitioning (%)

▨ Frequency of community problem solving (%)

▨ Volunteer frequently (%)

■ Participated in run or walk for charity last 12 months (%)

☐ Group participation in non-electoral activities (%)

Table 2.6 Source of news by generation

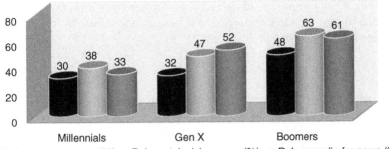

Millennials   Gen X   Boomers

■ Rely on newspapers (%)   ▪ Rely on television news (%)   ■ Rely on radio for news (%)

Findings also point to how Boomers are an informed group, drawing on regular newspapers, televised news, and radio for information. However, being informed from the aforementioned media outlets also suggest that Boomers, Generation X members, and those from the Millennials generations are exposed to the shock value and sensationalism that vulgarizes death and dying. As for relying on television for news, 63% of Boomers did so compared to only 47% and 38% for Generation X and Millennials, respectively (see Table 2.6). Insofar are employing radio broadcasts to acquire information, 61% of Boomers, 52% of members from Generation X, and 33% of Millennials relied on this medium for news. Boomers showed the highest degree of employing newspapers for information, scoring at 48% while only 32% of Generation X members and 30% of Millennials indicated so.

The data suggest how Baby Boomers attending Death Cafés can effectively generate the momentum needed for a social movement. Moreover, at over 80 million in the United States alone, their sheer numbers will likely result in greater Death Café attendance and growth. As will be seen through the voices in many of our Boomers and some non-Boomers' personalities, Death Café attendees approach the issue in perhaps the most compassionate and healthy manner, an approach that is sorely needed in an age where many members of society appear to be lost in a matrix of clutter that, nonetheless, aim to dictate living and dying for us. Herein lies the point of the Death Café movement: to appropriate the terms death and dying from its negative connotations so that we can all have agency in discussing and ultimately authoring our own trajectories toward end of life. In the next chapter, we examine the key theoretical assertions by Jürgen Habermas that will be employed throughout my work. Only by understanding Habermas' communicative action theory in Chapter 3 can we later appreciate the sentiments shared by many Baby Boomers as they engage in death talk.

NOTES

1. The official Death Café webpage is at http://deathcafe.com
2. The "Matures" Generation was also examined (those born before 1946). However, due to every Death Café attendee being from the Boomer generation with three Generation X members, I am only comparing Boomer civic participation with Generation X and Millennials' degrees of participation.

CHAPTER 3

Habermas's Theory of Communicative Action and the Colonization of the Lifeworld

José Guadalupe Posada's *Gran Calavera Eléctrica* (1900–1913).

Attending to Death Café participants' premise that a taboo surrounds death talk, this chapter explores how such ideational constraints are established as well as how actors contest their effects communicatively. Jürgen Habermas's concepts drawn from his classic two-volume work, the *Theory of Communicative Action* (Habermas 1984, 1987), are ideal for such an effort. Habermas's contention that the "practices of communication contain normative potentials of social rationality" is a vital and highly relevant assertion that

© The Author(s) 2017
J. Fong, *The Death Café Movement*,
DOI 10.1007/978-3-319-54256-0_3

is, as we shall see, supported by our attendees' diverse narratives expressed in death talk. Thus, scholars' contentions that can further enrich a Habermasian reading of the Death Café will be made to orbit around Habermas's concepts, if only for the purpose of generating more comprehensibility and tangibility for some of his more atmospheric propositions, many of which have been conveyed in a turgid manner, an unfortunate hallmark of Frankfurt School writers (with the exception of, perhaps, writings by Erich Fromm).

It should be noted, however, that the goal of the monograph is not to engage in an exegesis of Habermas's theoretical assertions, but more rather, to make visible how Death Café attendees make operative Habermasian concepts during their communicative exchanges. The process will allow me to traverse into immanent critique when deemed necessary so as to identify the blind spots in some of Habermas's assertions. I hope to remedy some of Habermas's blind spots by amalgamating his concepts with other relevant scholars that can help us understand the Death Café phenomenon more incisively. Thus, this monograph extends its solidarity with other scholars such as Niemi, who notes in a discussion of communicative action that analytical interpretations of Habermas's ideas should not be construed as "arguments put forth by Habermas himself" (2005:230). Indeed, Habermas's theory of communicative action is not without its detractors. However, their critiques are not part of the scope conditions of this study since we are aiming to highlight the *utility* of making operative Habermasian concepts *vis-à-vis* the lifeworld, a social context which exists incontrovertibly. In later chapters and to the degree it can provide a finer contour of Habermas's ideas, other scholars and their theoretical assertions will also be made operative, again for the purpose of grounding key sociological assertions in lifeworld dynamics so as to give our theories more material consequences.

Habermas defines communicative action as interaction between two or more actors that seek to achieve solidarity by reaching interpersonal understanding. For Habermas, such a context spurs participants to not only attain individual successes through deliberation, but in arriving at collective agreement through mutual comprehension and harmonious interpretations of what are at stake (Habermas 1984; Kim and Holter 1995). In such a context an unfolding of communicative action can be made to take place. In theory, one who decides to attend to an issue forwards a validity claim. Then the speaker making the claim selects a comprehensible linguistic expression...in order to come to an understanding... *about* something and thereby to make *himself* understandable. It belongs to the communicative intent of the speaker (a) that he perform a speech act that is right in respect to the given normative context, so that between him and the hearer an intersubjective relation will come about which is recognized as legitimate; (b) that he make a true statement (or correct existential presuppositions), so that the hearer will accept and share the knowledge of the speaker; and (c) that he express truthfully his beliefs, intentions, feelings, desires, and the like, so that the hearer will give credence to what is said (Habermas 1984: 307–308).

Niemi describes the process *in situ* as where the speaker

(1) begins communicative action by referencing the social world in a manner that allows the speaker to establish an interpersonal relationship with an audience;

(2) the speaker then refers to such a world objectively. Niemi notes how it is in these dynamics that the speaker makes "certain existential presuppositions." In this mode of communication, the speaker now uses facticity to establish an *intersubjective* relationship with the audience or listener about the lifeworld "on an epistemic level";

(3) the speaker enhances the process in step 2 by speaking of the lifeworld by expressing "intentions, beliefs, desires, and so on" about it so as to maintain a communicative relationship with the listener (Niemi 2005: 230–231).

Validity claims thus start communicative action that attends to social or community problems. They are as the name implies, an assertion set off as *conventional truths* that remain contestable by the listeners. Within a time frame, there can be many validity claims made. Listeners contest validity claims through the use of different discourses. That is, within a time frame, many discourses can be "activated" to vindicate or refute the validity claims made by the designated speaker. Because the speaker uttering validity claims is either supported or refuted by counter responses during deliberation, a more complete democratic environment emerges, according to Habermas. Warren notes how such a process is an important embodiment of democracy since it expresses a "kind of politics that favors discursively mediated consensus over other ways of making collective decisions, namely by means of coercive authority, the authority of traditional or other nondiscursively created identities, or the authority of markets" (1993: 211). Communicative action thus "makes...full use of language functions relating to objective, social and subjective worlds" (Szczelkun 1999: 3). Café attendees are not communicatively talking *at* but *to* one another so that each may self-actualize through communication (we shall have more to say about the relationship between validity clams and discourses in the final section of this chapter).

Death Cafés as a physical environment and social movement appropriately lend themselves to a Habermasian analysis for the following reasons: (1) participants at Death Cafés frequently emphasize that there is a need for the community to engage in death talk as a means to improve life and living in ways that challenge the taboo surrounding death. However, attendees are of the view that death and death talk's forbidden status continue to maintain its staying power for a variety of reasons to be discussed. Additionally, (2) Death Café organizers and attendees are able to employ communicative action in ways that appear to satisfy the attributes of communicative action theory explicated by Habermas. Through the articulation of validity claims that are, in turn, vetted by listeners through different types of discourses, mutual consensus and intersubjective agreement—ideal outcomes of communicative action—can be reached. In the context of the Death Café, the attributes of different speech utterances, be they based on validity claims or the discourses that emerge to validate or critique them, are vital dynamics of communicative action that allow attendees to get a deeper sense of existential meaning about their mortality—a sense that takes them to a deeper truth—one which they feel can inform life and living. Here, we again invoke Fromm's views in *To Have or To Be* (1976):

> Most people are half-awake, half-dreaming, and are unaware that most of what they hold to be true and self-evident is an illusion produced by the suggestive influence of the social world in which they live. Knowing, then, begins with the shattering of illusions... Knowing means to penetrate through the surface, in order to arrive at the roots and hence the causes; knowing means to "see" reality in its nakedness. Knowing does not mean to be in possession of the truth; it means to penetrate the surface and to strive critically and actively in order to approach truth ever more closely (1976: 35).

Habermas thus configured his theory of communicative action to serve as a process for collective political empowerment through argumentation, a process that insures "that all concerned in principal take part, freely and equally, in a cooperative search for truth, where nothing coerces anyone except the force of the better argument" (Habermas 1990: 198). Its utility for Death Café analysis cannot be denied: strangers gather and, with much alacrity, convey their deepest sentiments, claims, and orientations toward mortality in ways that seek alternative conceptualizations. That the empowerment felt by Café participants may not reflect the very temporal search for political empowerment, the effects upon participants are none-theless liberating and emancipatory at an existential level.

COLONIZING THE LIFEWORLD OF DEATH

A key proposition by Death Café organizers and their attendees is that there is not enough "death talk" in the daily dynamics of social life. Although Miles and Corr (2017) note that there exists a healthy thanato-logical discourse in academic circles, the communicative content of mor-tality is more amorphous as it appears on the ground and in our lifeworld communities. It is not surprising that there is not an urgent need for research in the social sciences to elucidate this aversion. The main reason for this is rather obvious: one's corporeal demise is not a pleasant proposi-tion to consider. Upon one's passing, nature continues its march toward transforming our corporeal existence into non-sentient states as it renders our bodies into macabre shapes, configurations, and odors that can hardly be appreciated, even in highly romantic terms. This might explain why society's artists, sages, and philosophers confronted the finality of the human condition in ways that are ritualistic and symbolic, just to eke in a bit of romance and even beauty to frame the potential extinction or continued journey of what remains of John or Jane Doe. However, such an orientation tends to establish collective coping mechanisms that are highly aestheticized, based on form and not necessarily on the depth of one's desire to find sovereignty in approaching their mortality: attending a funeral and placing flowers on a casket, donning a type of death color for funeral or crematory ceremonies, chanting specific passages in Pali before a Buddhist cremation, burning paper money for ancestors as practiced in some Chinese cultural orientations toward death, are all aspects of insti-tutionalized repetitive behavior that can be seen as independent from a collective and personal understanding of how existential depth on the theme of death can be informative.

What is discourse as Habermas sees it? Thus far we have employed discourse to refer to that body of knowledge where the narratives within underpin its thematic emphases. Habermas is amenable to this employment as well, noting how "discourses take place in particular social contexts" and are "subject to the limitations of time and space" (Habermas 1990: 92). More importantly, Habermas also saw discourse function as a "form of communication that is removed from contexts of experiences," where participants have free rein to test speakers' validity claims in ways where "no force except that of the better argument is exercised," where "all motives except that of the cooperative search for truth are excluded" (Habermas 1975: 107–108). Alternatively, Habermas envisions discourse simply as reason-giving. For Habermas, reason-giving enhances a rational process of empowerment.

Habermas considers individuals in public spheres engaging in communicative action as exhibiting tremendous autonomy and independence. As autonomous individuals, they "make decisions based on critical examination of their needs and interests...and they have the capacity to participate in processes that resolve conflicts between needs and interests by means of discourse" (Warren 1993: 214). More crucially, Warren reminds us that such autonomous individuals have agency "to...create, to bring new ideas, things, and relations into being. Agency implies some amount of control over one's life history" (Warren 1993: 214–215). For Warren, "autonomy is developed in part through the imagination—the ability to think of alternatives—and is part related to others through reason-giving" (1993: 215). Herein lies the utility of Habermas's discourses: they frame how Café participants are indeed refining the authoring and assembling of their own personalized narratives on death and dying.

Mezirow (2003: 59) explains discourse as "the assessment of beliefs, feelings, and values" that heals potential ruptures that surface in the communicative process. For Warren, the employment of differing discourses serves as a means to resolve the problem at hand "through talk rather than coercion, markets, traditional authority, or blind consensus" (1993: 212). Habermas thus envisions conflict resolution to be dependent on discourse dynamics where dialog, diplomacy, and communally empowering content emerge from the grass roots. Discourse from the grass roots can thus monitor many establishments that work off hypothesis testing, replication, and theory generation, dynamics that take place in major social institutions of knowledge production in society. It can also monitor the market and other mediated institutions. Without awareness of how communities can generate a grass-roots discourse through deliberation, people thus subscribe to information and renderings of death and dying from the top-down, unwittingly reifying the macro-level institutions and ensconcing their power to socially construct reality. In the United States, and according to Death Café proponents around the world, a grass-roots discourse on mortality from the bottom-up overall remains elusive and amorphous. The national and international proliferation of Death Cafés may buck this trend.

Discourse also has its own nuances. In his earlier work *Legitimation Crisis* (1975), the deviating trajectories of the social system and the lifeworld were of great concern to Habermas. Habermas envisioned a society as simultaneously a system and lifeworld, synchronizing with each other through discourse dynamics that exist in public spheres. The rupturing of this symbiotic relationship Habermas describes as the uncoupling of the system and lifeworld—and by implication the failure of discourse. In his lesser known work, *Knowledge and Human Interests* (1971), Habermas forwards the assertion—drawing heavily from nineteenth-century pragmatist and empiricist philosophers such as Charles S. Pierce and Wilhelm Dilthey—that empiricism derives information from three interrelated epistemological nodes to comprehend social reality: (1) the technical cognitive interest adopted by the empirical-analytical sciences, (2) the practical cognitive interest adopted by the historical-hermeneutic sciences, and (3) the emancipatory cognitive interest adopted by the critically oriented social sciences.

The technical cognitive orientation toward comprehending reality stems from results of technical control. These emanate from higher elevations within scientific systems and are distributed back to the public as factual information, a top-down process. This information risks reification. As it stands, such information rarely acknowledges the inputs derived from a community's communicative action even though it can just as well sharpen the debate on social issues toward mutual consensus, or at the very least intersubjective understanding. For Habermas, if technocratic policies yield desirable results, people thus accept the results as true. The power of the natural sciences lies in this attribute of communication that can make comparatively accurate predictions between variables even though the outcomes are conveyed from the top-down. A new cyclicity is thus generated in that ideal outcomes from scientific research serve to further expand the human powers of technical control (Kim and Holter 1995), further reinforcing the continued reproduction of technical knowledge (Habermas 1971). For Habermas, even if society conveys the narrative of death and dying as a most natural expression of nature, the scientific and technocratic establishments will still attempt to foster technical control of mortality: "With increased control over outer nature, secular knowledge became independent of worldviews...science eventually established a monopoly on the interpretation of outer nature" (1975: 119). However, in the practical cognitive orientation of people, social reality is comprehended by attempting to understand one another's meanings, "from the inside out rather than outside in" (Kim and Holter 1995: 209), or according to Habermas, "access to the fact is provided by the understanding of meaning, not observation" (Habermas 1971: 309). Kim and Holter continue:

> Whereas the empirical-analytic method encourages objective distance between the investigators and subjects, the hermeneutic method emphasizes the analysis of text and meaning through a subject-subject relationship more amenable to the goal of understanding meaning (1995: 209).

The issue of practical cognitive interests was much engaged with by Dilthey, who desired to situate hermeneutics within an idealized, scientific approach that nonetheless still allowed for the merits of pure description. According to Habermas, Dilthey viewed hermeneutic understanding as a process too dependent on transcendence. For Dilthey, contemplation can function as a methodological process because its practitioners, the "historians, economists, political scientists, and students of religion are immersed in life, they want to influence it" (cited in Habermas 1971: 178). However, Dilthey concedes that corruption of practical cognitive interests occurs because the cultural sciences

> subject historical persons, mass movements, and trends to their judgment, which is conditioned by their individuality, the nation to which they belong, and the time in which they live. Even where they believe themselves to be operating free of presuppositions, they are determined by this horizon (cited in Habermas 1971: 178).

This resolution of the dialectical dilemma of practical cognitive interests— that is, to what degree science can employ interpretation if facts themselves are assumed to contain their own objective status—can be seen in the content of Death Café communicative action. Because Café dialog attends to death and dying as a center of gravity for living that requires meaning for comprehension, it has already confronted the theme as a non-variable that represents the incontrovertible presupposition of our inevitable mortality. This foundational fact nullifies any arguments about the facticity of death and dying as culturally conditioned if we move beyond their pageantry and aesthetic frameworks which *do* contain culturally conditioned responses (Habermas 1971: 177–178).

Habermas, however, critiques both the technical-cognitive and practical-cognitive approaches as tending toward the dogmatic monopolization of facticity while lacking any "critical basis for interpreting the nature of the problematic situation" (Kim and Holter 1995: 209). However, the basis of emancipatory interests serves to welcome knowledge that is "oriented to liberating individuals from the constraint of domination and distorted communication" and thus, "individuals need to be involved in the process of their own emancipation" from a "constrained existence," ultimately furthering "autonomy and responsibility" in the process (Kim and Holter 1995: 209–210). The uncoupling of the system and lifeworld allows the system to appropriate technical and practical cognitive interests in ways that delinked them from the lifeworld where mutual and intersubjective understanding can be secured through deliberation. These dynamics set into motion colonizing tendencies whereby the system dispenses technical and practical narratives for the lifeworld, stifling if not devouring the emancipatory articulation of the grass roots.

Resolving issues with communicative action is an important undertaking because, as argues Calhoun, the "lifeworld is the locus for basic human values ... it needs to be defended against the continual encroachment of systemic media" (1994: 31). Only when self-knowledge and self-reflection dynamics are embedded in communicative action can individuals find emancipation. For Calhoun, "communicative action thus provides an alternative to money and power as a basis for societal integration" (1994:31). Until the lifeworld is decolonized, individuals and their perceptions of situations remain "clouded by values imposed by society" because "social institutions can be repressive, thwarting the individual in the pursuit of true desires" (Kim and Holter 1995: 210). Such a process can be seen in Habermas's view of the social-welfare state, an institution that for Chriss grants so many "rights" on the basis of race, gender, sexual orientation, age, disability, etc., that the actual legal enforcement of such rights encroach further into the lifeworld (1998).

With the uncoupling of system and lifeworld where the former is delinked from the latter, communication and moral attitudes lose their purpose (Jütten 2013: 590). As a result, speakers and listeners lose their ability to relate to (1) something in the objective world (as the totality of entities about which true statements are possible); (2) something in the social world (as the totality of legitimately regulated interpersonal relations); and (3) something in the subjective world (as the totality of experiences to which a speaker has privileged access and which he can express before a public) (Habermas 1987:120). For Krey (2002), the uncoupling of system and lifeworld precedes lifeworld colonization by larger systemic forces.

> Once systems are no longer merely coordinated with communicative patterns but begin to invade and subdue these communicative patterns of the life-world, then the uncoupling of the systems and life-world is converted into the direct "colonization of the life-world." That means the communicative patterns of the lifeworld are subjugated to alien standards of technical control (Krey 2002: 3).

Habermas nonetheless sees the capacity for social change through the interpretative process as seen in certain spheres of the social sciences, a process that is sufficiently distinct from the natural sciences in that the former "seeks to open its objects to comprehension as forms of inter-subjective communication" while the latter seek to "establish technical control over their objects" (Grady and Wells 1985/1986: 40). Habermas provides a caveat, however, and notes:

> If a shared definition of the situation has first to be negotiated, or if efforts to come to some agreement within the framework of shared situation definitions fail, the attainment of consensus, which is normally a condition for pursuing goals, can itself become an end (Habermas 1987: 126).

Herein lies the incisive insights of Habermas's theory of communicative action: that the goal of achieving community consensus can be rendered difficult if not impossible if lifeworld communication is colonized. Indeed, as we shall see, Habermas's best sociology may be seen in his identification and explication of how the lifeworld is colonized by macro-level institutions, a process that results in a human condition where society's participants have lost the ability to deliberate ideas and resolve conflicts. Such a condition paves the way for organs of the state to intervene and author the trajectories of its citizens in ways that do *not* enhance community solidarity. Attendees at Death Cafés are thus clarifying the ambiguity, the ambiguity that surrounds death in our society by uncovering—often with much alacrity *and* trepidation—how everyone else feels about death in ways that seek mutual consensus or intersubjectivity on the understanding of mortality.

For Habermas, the lifeworld context allows participants to "express themselves in situations that they have to define in common so far as they are acting with an orientation to mutual understanding" (1987: 121) since the concept of communicative action "presupposes language as the medium for reaching understanding... the course of which participants, through relating to the world, reciprocally raise validity claims that can be accepted or contested" (Habermas 1984: 99). Frank notes that the lifeworld generates validity claims to serve as catalysts for community communication as it "carries all sorts of assumptions about who we are as people and what we value about ourselves: what we believe, what shocks and offends us, what we aspire to, what we desire, what we are willing to sacrifice to which ends, and so forth," all of which require "constant reaffirmation" (Frank 2000: 3–4). A colonized lifeworld prevents such communicative dynamics from fully surfacing and taking form. Seen another way, a colonized lifeworld prevents communicative action from fully surfacing to reinforce democracy.

In modernity, the colonizing process is undertaken by the state, various iterations of the media, money, law, and power in ways that "distort the communicative practices of persons in their everyday face-to-face interactions" (Chriss 1998: 1). Habermas's position harks back to *Legitimation Crisis* (1975), a position that is central to understanding his concerns about the constraints macro-level institutions have upon the dynamics of culture and its communicative dimension. He notes how "the state cannot simply take over the cultural system, and that expansion of the areas of state planning actually makes problematic matters that were formerly culturally taken for granted" (1975: 73). For Chriss (1998), this top-down dynamic curtails quality communication from below while Frank (2000) similarly argues how advanced capitalist societies exhibiting this dynamic have increasingly disabled communicative action. In its wake, the marketplace runs roughshod over the "academy, basic information... news, entertainment, and government" (Krey 2002: 5). For Stahl, the grass roots are affected as well since the colonization process entails the suppression or undermining of communicative coordination by the invasion of systemic mechanisms into practices, which constitutively depend on communication. Processes of colonization—in which systemic rationality oversteps its proper bounds—not only cause a loss of legitimacy, a fragmentation of everyday consciousness, a loss of freedom and meaning and cultural impoverishment, they also endanger the integrative function of the lifeworld (2013: 539).

An important rendering of this scenario can be seen in Jütten's (2013) research and critique of the United Kingdom's system of public higher education, one experiencing colonization by the market. Not convinced about the view inculcated into British citizens that education should be deemed a private good, Jütten counters with the normative view that education should instead be seen as a collective good that transcends monetary imperatives and private benefits, that it should be seen as "collectively valuable, both in monetary and non-monetary terms" (2013: 597). Collini shares the same sentiment in *What Are Universities For?* (2012) and criticizes how society should not

educate the next generation in order for them to contribute to its economy. It educates them in order that they should extend and deepen their understanding of themselves and the world, acquiring ... kinds of knowledge and skills which will be useful in their eventual employment, but which will no more be the sum of their education than that employment will be the sum of their lives (2012: 91).

Jütten laments, however, about the state of higher education in the United Kingdom as its research and teaching dynamics have slowly been reduced to market, government, and corporate imperatives. As a result, the commodification of public higher education corrupts it as evinced by how competition between universities takes place through tuition fees, leading to an undermining of "the social mission of universities in terms of the democratization of higher education" since it leads to a "division between students from poorer backgrounds, who will seek out cheaper, more vocationally oriented universities and wealthier students, who will seek out prestigious research universities charging higher fees" (2013: 597). Reay (2013) describes this "education apartheid" as one that "excludes the less wealthy sectors of the population from competition for the best jobs" as well as "from the ranks of the informed, critical public, reinforcing the existing 'class apartheid' of British society" (2013: 117–121).

> Governments and universities have addressed the subsequent shortfall of higher education funding through a shift to a consumer model of higher education, whereby students (and their parents) fund their education... indirectly by the state through a complex web of government secured loans and tax credits.... At the same time, universities have sought to insulate themselves from the vagaries of government support by seeking third-party funding for academic research and by seeking to exploit commercial opportunities presented by their research.... As a result, strategic attitudes oriented at market success replace communicative action oriented toward reaching cooperative goals in many areas of university policy, including student recruitment and curriculum planning (Jütten 2013: 598).

In the United States, the phenomenon of massive open online courses (MOOCs) being introduced by information technology personnel in conjunction with venture capitalists reflects how public education is being colonized in another manner. Often embraced with alacrity by universities who rarely consult their faculty about its implementation, likely due to the fact that its implementation is highly market-driven, Burawoy (2005) presciently notes the tendency for universities to engage in "joint ventures with private corporations" through "advertising campaigns to attract students" while "fawning over private donors" and "commodifying education through distance learning" (2005: 7). Proponents of MOOCs thus provide apologias for university dynamics that embrace market solutions (Fong 2017). Furthermore, in their alacrity to embrace MOOCs, there is no mention of how MOOCs will affect the division of labor in universities, especially the "cheap temporary professional labor" that exists in the guise of adjunct faculty (Burawoy 2005: 7). Often the pioneers of MOOCs are erstwhile academics and professional staff that have begun to pursue entrepreneurial goals of their own accord (Slaughter and Rhoades 2004).

As a consequence, the quality of debate and discussion is instilled in a tepid manner as communicatively shortchanged students leave the university and enter civil society, reinforcing the reification of lifeworld colonization for the next generation. And where is the communicative resistance, the uproar, to the dynamics seen in public higher education? For Habermas and Jütten, the fragmented consciousness resulting from the colonization of the lifeworld of higher education stifles emergence of a discontented discourse from the grass roots that can contest (1) the reification of the system and (2) cultural impoverishment as a consequence of it, a process that "drains the lifeworld of the resources that its members need in order to reach understanding over their collective situation" (Jütten 2013: 599). For Habermas, such "economic imperatives trump lifeworld resistance because there are no normative resources on which lifeworld members can draw in order to resist them" (Jütten 2013: 599). Habermas notes how lifeworld colonization and the subsequent cultural impoverishment in communicative action are intertwined as "the imperatives of autonomous subsystems make their way into the lifeworld from the outside—like colonial masters coming into a tribal society—and force a process of assimilation upon it" (1987: 355). For Habermas, actors are unable to respond to such colonization because large institutions overpower individual agency in ways that subject them to the system, a process that "blocks enlightenment by the mechanism of reification" (1987: 355).

Frank notes how only "communicative action . . . has the ability to regenerate influence and value commitments" that can allow the people to reconfigure their lives autonomously (2000: 4). Frank notes how the "quantitative systems of media, for example money and votes, can *express* influence and value-commitments, but they cannot *generate* these qualities—only the communicative action in life can do that" (2000: 4). However, following the colonization of the lifeworld, money and power become reified and develop the means to regulate social relations and communication patterns. Habermas emphasizes that the problematic of late capitalism is that the voices of the people from "below" cannot be heard to the same degree as systemic expressions because communicative activities on the ground have been colonized by institutional language, procedures, and regulations. Habermas reminds us, however, that democracy and agency do not emanate from institutional mechanisms "above," but from the people themselves who grant legitimacy to social systems through "collective will-formation through discourse" (Warren 1993: 211). The fight for a more complete democracy, then, will need to reactivate in the lifeworld *and* conclude in lifeworld.

Habermas sees democracy as emanating from the lifeworld's public spheres, ideal communication communities that serve as arenas of judgment and decision, where the collective autonomy of participants can generate discourses that can evolve and coalesce into narratives for empowerment (we will be discussing the spatiality of public spheres in Chapter 6). In public spheres are sites where communication is "protected from asymmetries of power and differentiated from the organizational requirements of collective action" (Warren 1993: 213). For Habermas, there is untapped potential for democratic articulation in the lifeworld, hence his desire to decolonize the lifeworld so that actors in society can have an emancipatory and transformative social experience (Mezirow 2003). Yet because communication in the lifeworld has been colonized, Habermas famously laments that democracy remains an unfinished project. Such an "incomplete" democracy creates a sort of legitimation crisis for society's social institutions.

The mechanism that allows systemic colonization of the lifeworld is law, or more specifically, legal regulations that impose conditions and contingencies upon the actor. However, Habermas's critical views of regulation in no way imply that he preferred anarchic revolution to "express" a bona fide democracy. Instead, Habermas's concerns gravitate toward how law micromanages people's everyday lives in ways that "replaces the social solidarity of the lifeworld that formerly was forged tacitly through uncodified norms of communicative acts and reason" (Chriss 1998: 3). The manner in which strict regulatory language is imposed upon the lifeworld—a process Habermas terms juridification—all point to how justice has become "colonized by abstract principles of formal law" as it penetrates all areas of life (Frank 2000: 4). Habermas is concerned by how law "develops into an external force, imposed from without, to such an extent that modern compulsory law, sanctioned by the state, becomes an institution detached from the ethical motivations of the legal person and dependent upon abstract obedience to the law" (1987: 174). Similarly, Stahl points to the juridification of the family "through the educational bureaucracy and family law, as well as the neutralization of the citizen role by the consumer role . . . in the private sphere" as a human condition of a colonized lifeworld (2013: 539). Frank's ability to make operative Habermas's assertions of juridification is worth quoting due to its relevance for understanding the concerns voiced by Death Café participants.

In my own study of medicine, the lifeworld relationships of patients and those who care for them—doctors and nurses—are increasingly colonized by the demands of third-party payers, whether these are insurance companies in the U.S. or government in the Commonwealth countries I live in and visit. The legitimacy of medicine is in crisis: the popularity of complementary practitioners is one indication of this, and the prevalence of malpractice suits in the U.S. is another. The discontent I hear constantly in medical groups and illness support groups is loud and clear—and yet medicine becomes more exclusively a "system" that excludes lifeworld communicative action.... When such talk is excluded and patients are simply told what medicine will offer, take it or leave it, medicine creates the conditions for its legitimacy crisis to deepen (Frank 2000: 4).

Insofar as the Death Café is concerned, event participants are essentially contesting their lifeworld colonization by discussing how one should live and die, freeing the themes from their cultural stigma borne from framing by medicine, media, and market dynamics. The physiologies of death and dying aside, the sociological dynamics of death and dying have increasingly become legalistic. A leading pathology of modernity, then, is this gradual infiltration of legal regulations into ever greater expanses of lifeworld activity. As informal understandings of life give way to formal rules codified in law, the lifeworld becomes increasingly impoverished (Chriss 1998). Frank is more forthright, noting how such conditions suggest that "there is no possibility of reaching a common understanding through these media" (2000: 3).

Members of society are implicitly aware during their interactions with macro-social institutions that there is red tape, often unintelligible legal language, and regulatory policies that predictably inspire complaints if not resistances. There is also a spatial articulation that can be added to Habermas's criticism of institutions that face legitimation crises, particularly in how such legitimation crises can be experienced at the corporeal level. A contemporary of Habermas, architect Victor Gruen provides an insightful but not very charitable view of the situation: "Civic centers are concentration camps for bureaucrats, who are thus prevented from mingling with common folks." That, suggests Gruen, "may explain why they lose their touch with and understanding of the problems of the latter" (cited in Oldenburg 1999: 69).

For Habermas, what is normatively significant for democratic practices is that values and laws should be generated from a consensus of deliberative citizens "coming together to decide their fate collectively through representation" (Chriss 1998: 2). However, Habermas notes how the process of colonizing the lifeworld has been successful because money, law, and power, components Habermas believes underpin all institutions and bureaucracies of the state, exist in a context where no norms and ethics are allowed to embed. For Frank (2000), quantitative media such as money and power are "noncommunicative." When money and power do communicate, they do so by communicating—through juridification—*at* the populace, not *to* them.

A relationship between macro-level institutions and the public sphere is thus facilitated through a medium where no common understanding can be reached, only a zero-sum approach where institutions in the social system dictate and steer agendas of the populace by imposing its regulation and language upon the lifeworld. In such a scenario, the lifeworld is bereft of social actors that can, through discursive discourses, reach a common understanding on social problematics. In its place are elites, who through ideological manipulation and hegemony "control the substance of public deliberation and, hence … legislation … that reflect and defend their own interests at the expense of the relatively powerless masses" (Chriss 1998: 2). The rich and discursive character of the public sphere is thus suffocated by lifeworld colonization.

Frank (2000) notes how money and votes are unable to provide existential understanding or political empowerment since these are primarily quantifiable variables. In such a scenario, the actor either overpowers or is overpowered. Similarly, Calhoun views money and power as "non-discursive modes of coordination … they offer no intrinsic openings to the identification of reason and will, and they suffer from tendencies toward domination and reification" (1994: 6). In this regard, Habermas envisions colonizing forces of the lifeworld as being norm-free, a *deleterious systemic condition,* contrasted by a norm-rich condition that is to be found in a non- or decolonized lifeworld. Citizens living under a colonized lifeworld simply do not know that they can still "draw on the 'moral resources' that are available to them in the lifeworld" (Jütten 2013: 594), something Death Café participants are keenly aware of.

Habermas notes that in capitalist societies, the market is the most significant catalyst for system integration. It performs this function through norm-free regulation of cooperative contexts where the "steering of individual decisions is not subjectively coordinated" (1987: 150). This trajectory needs to be contrasted with the ideal Habermasian condition where cooperation is generated by social integration "through consensus formation in language" (Jütten 2013: 589). Habermas warns that system integration can create a variety of social pathologies such as alienation, anomie, loss of collective identity—and in the case of what Death Café attendees have conveyed—a loss in the ability to appreciate a shared humanity derived from the theme of death and dying. My personal emphasis on Habermas's theory of communicative action as having the capacity to inform a shared humanity through the Death Café movement is not an idealized extrapolation; indeed, Habermas notes how the "lifeworld is always constituted in the form of global knowledge inter-subjectively shared by its members" (1987: 355). However, under life-world colonization "*everyday consciousness* is robbed of its power to synthesize; it becomes *fragmented*" (Habermas 1987: 355).

Habermas implicates money for steering "a social intercourse that has been largely disconnected from norms and values." Consequently, the market contains no ethics comparable to those generated at the grass roots. Moreover, in the worst case, the market's lack of values continues to be regularly reproduced through bureaucratic imperatives (Habermas 1987). Yet, in spite of being norm-free, Habermas incisively notes how the medium of money has structure-forming effects due to its capacity to be an "intersystemic medium of exchange" where "the activities of different organizations for the same function and the activities of the same organization for different functions can be clustered together" (Habermas 1987: 171–172). Moreover, the role that money and power play through juridification establishes complex communicative interactions and networks in macro-level institutions for which no one can explicitly be held accountable for.

It is the power of money, conveyed through juridification, and emanating from different interconnected institutions that allow for the dynamics of lifeworld colonization to be realized. Habermas contends that this rationalization of the lifeworld "makes possible a heightening of systemic complexity, which becomes so hypertrophied that it unleashes system imperatives that burst the capacity of the lifeworld they instrumentalize" (Habermas 1987: 155). Frank affirms this condition, noting "as advanced capitalist societies have developed, the core integrative function of communication has been increasingly disabled" (2000: 1). Thus, the colonization of the lifeworld reaches its crescendo when the language of the lifeworld is replaced with norm-free and regulatory language, rewards, and punishments, all of which prevent the lifeworld from coordinating social action. The colonization of the lifeworld by macro-level institutions thus "appears from the lifeworld perspective both   as   reducing   the   costs   and   risks   of   communication...thus...*technicizing*...the   lifeworld" (1987:183). Habermas notes how the trajectory by which technocratic management of social dynamics "robs actors of the meaning of their own action" further underscores his concerns on how technical details and technology, norm-free in nature, are sloganeered as a panacea for all kinds of cultural and economic problems (1987: 302).

DEATH CAFÉ COMMUNICATIVE ACTION: VALIDITY CLAIMS AND DISCOURSES

Successful communicative action in people's lifeworlds, one unfettered from the domination of juridification, entails creating communication dynamics that allow social actors making validity claims to (1) reach intersubjective agreement as a basis for (2) mutual understanding, so as to (3) reach an unforced consensus about what to do in particular situations in which they find themselves (Habermas 1984, 1987; Kemmis and McTaggart 2007). In Habermas's later but nonetheless important work, *Between Facts and Norms* (1996), he adds (4) a fourth attribute of effective communicative action: the opening up of "communicative space" (Kemmis and Robin 2007: 294). This fourth additional feature of effective communicative action is highly relevant for understanding the trajectory of the Death Café in that opening up communicative space allows solidarity and a sense of community between people, even between strangers, to be established, an outcome seen at my Death Café data collection sites. Such opening up of communicative space improves the quality of community since "cooperation…has an intrinsic morality" (Habermas 1981: 116).

Habermas's communicative action's dialogic dynamics is a process of democracy that need not be reliant on institutional mechanisms but instead on public spheres. Public spheres are vital for providing the conditions for communicative action to become salient so that validity claims can be formed. Indeed, that public spheres also allow differing discourses to contest or affirm validity claims already signify the availability of autonomy for the communicative participant. As noted in the earlier sections of this chapter, fora where citizens can launch their communicative action are, for Habermas, important iterations of democracy. However, not all social actors are cognizant of this and thus allow large-scale institutions to infiltrate or colonize these communities and their communicative action, rendering social actors less autonomous or independent, if at all.

Autonomy in the individual is conceptualized as "certain developed capacities of judgment" according to Warren's excellent discussion of participatory democracy (1993), one which we will derive many cues from in this section. Warren's examination of the utility of Habermas reveals how autonomous individuals are able to be critically decisive of their needs and interests. Moreover, such individuals are ideal for conflict resolution. Thus, the autonomous individuals—and in our case, Death Café participants—have agency to "create, to bring new ideas, things, and relations into being" while "agency implies some amount of control over one's life history" (1993: 214–215). Because autonomous individuals are able to delink the self from systemic demands, one replete with "traditions, prevailing opinions, and pressures to conform," the same individuals can thus be made amenable to constructive criticism by the community (1993: 215). In this scenario, autonomous individuals are in a position to engage in reason-giving, "or what Habermas calls discourse" (Warren 1993: 215).

For Habermas, successful communicative action also depends on how questions and discussions attend to three types of validity claims that emerge during communication that, when satisfied, serve to generate a cohesive community that is lucid in how its members analyze and confront problematics (adapted from Habermas 1984: 99; Niemi 2005: 234; Kemmis and Robin 2007: 298).

(1) That the statement made is true (or that the existential presuppositions of the propositional content mentioned are in fact satisfied), that is, whether these understandings are *true* (in the sense of being *accurate* in accordance with what else is known). Listeners can also reject the truthfulness of the utterance through different discourses.

(2) That the speech act is right with respect to the existing normative context (or that the normative context that it is supposed to satisfy is itself legitimate), that is, whether these understandings are *morally right and appropriate* under the circumstances in which they find themselves. Listeners can also reject the morality of the utterance through discourses.

(3) That the manifest intention of the speaker is meant as it is expressed, that is, whether these understandings are *authentic* and *sincerely held and stated*. Listeners can also reject a rendering of a truthful conveyance, or what Niemi (2005) terms as existential presuppositions.

Niemi's (2005) incisive analysis of Habermasian validity claims reveal how such claims can also manifest synergistically, prompting ever deeper exchanges. Niemi emphasizes that through such exchanges, the interests of individuals are revealed and liberated from an institutionally deterministic view of communication, as in how voting is seen as a "voice" of the people. Because public spheres exist *in between* the institutional mechanisms that allow for democratic practices such as voting, it is the town hall, not the polling booth on election day, that one really hears the voices of the grass-roots speak.

Yetim entertains the converse: the significance of raising validity claims can also be appreciated when they break down, that is, when the validity claim becomes problematic. In this scenario, communicators enter a "reflective mode of communication, that is, to a discourse about the controversial validity claim" that require activation of additional modes of dialog for communication resolution (2005: 10). Habermas himself clearly emphasizes this need, noting that "the stabilization of validity claims can succeed only through discourse" (1975: 72). From these validity claims conveyed during communication, listeners then orient their actions by interpreting the validity claims (Habermas 1984: 118). Kemmis and McTaggart note that even with discontents and tensions during public sphere communication, participants allow themselves to be "corrected in light of... careful observation of the processes and consequences of their action as it unfolds" (2007: 300).

Habermas explains that validity claims in communicative action aim to secure a sense of truthfulness and accuracy for a topic in ways where the speaker "makes a statement, asserts, narrates, explains, represents, predicts, discusses something" so as to search for "agreement with the hearer" (Habermas 1984: 308). Truthfulness is determined "in light of their won knowledge (both their individual knowledge and the shared knowledge represented in the discourse used by members)" (Kemmi and McTaggart 2007: 294). As to whether a validity claim is morally sound, Habermas assigns the determination of its status to what listeners and participants themselves "regard as morally right and appropriate in terms of their individual and mutual judgment about what is... proper, and prudent to do under the circumstances in which they find themselves" (Kemmis and Robin 2007: 294). To satisfy the third validity claim for sincerity, speakers need to utter a "first-person experiential sentence" while disclosing in ways where the listeners are able to determine the degree of sincerity. Sincerity is assessed on "what participants themselves regard as sincerely and truthfully stated (individually and in terms of their joint commitment to understanding)" (Kemmis and Robin 2007: 294). Finally, only when the validity claims convey the correct action to take on a problematic, regardless of whether the speaker "makes a promise" or "appoints or warns somebody," can participants then begin to coordinate their action trajectory (Habermas 1984: 308–309). Habermas notes that satisfying these validity claims is vital for communal solidarity and a democratic practice that can thrive outside of institutional mechanisms. Mezirow's (2003) excellent summary explains how, in the final instance, effective communicative action

> refers to understanding what someone means when they communicate with you. This understanding includes becoming aware of the assumptions, intentions and qualifications of the person communicating. When a stranger strikes up a conversation on a bus, one needs to know whether he or she is simply passing the time, intends to proselytize, or is trying to pick you up. When a stranger recommends a new medicine or an investment, one needs to know whether he or she is qualified to make such recommendation or judgment. The process of understanding involves assessing claims to rightness, sincerity, authenticity, and appropriateness (2003: 59).

In their search for more meaningful prompts and cues for life and living, Death Café attendees and their narratives exhibit features of communicative action that orbit around many attendees' validity claims. Yet how does one contest controversial validity claims that are problematic in their expressions? Habermas identifies in *Communicative Action* five main discourse types—alternatively conceptualized by Warren as "reason-giving" types—that can be employed to explicitly attend to validity claims that are deemed problematic by listeners. In alphabetical order, these are (1) the aesthetic discourse and its concerns on the "adequacy of the standards of value," which for Habermas realizes itself in works of art, (2) the explicative discourse which concerns itself with comprehensibility and meaning of one's social ontology, (3) the practical discourse which focuses on the "rightness of norms and actions," (4) the theoretical discourse that orients itself toward the "truth of propositions," and finally (5) the therapeutic discourse which focuses on the degree of sincerity in dialog content (Grady and Wells 1985/1986). In his later 1994 work, *Justification and Application*, Habermas further discerns from the practical discourse three more discourse types: the (6) ethical, (7) moral, and (8) pragmatic discourses (see Table 3.1 for summary). Habermas also weaves in his notion of the legal discourse, one activated to check on the legitimacy and legal norms of community (Yetim 2005). For my work, the legal discourse will not be set off as a distinct form of communicative action. The key reason for this decision is due to how all Café attendees are, in essence, participating in Death Cafés because they already perceive legal norms to have little legitimacy, especially in how the vast majority of end-of-life decision-making is often shaped. As noted by Alexy (1996), contents of the legal discourse are best appreciated when it is used within the institutional framework of a legal system, not public sphere.

Habermas notes how discourse types serve to "thematize contested validity claims and attempt to vindicate or criticize them through arguments" (Habermas 1984: 18). Warren notes that the discourses allow participants engaged in communicative action to "develop principles of judgment" from different vantage points, and in ways that "challenge the interpretations of others" as well as be "motivated to challenge their own" (Warren 1993: 219). Warren further elaborates that:

> Because individuals are unlikely to be able to challenge their own interpretations of needs and interests...they must be challenged by other individuals. When one must explain oneself to others...individuals come to understand why they feel as they do in justifying their needs and interests to others. In doing so, they may alter their need interpretations, finding that their previous need interpretations, often absorbed uncritically from their culture, were inappropriate and perhaps even a source of unhappiness to themselves. Or they may become more convinced of the rightness of their claims (1993: 219).

By resolving a speaker's problematic validity claims through the use of different discourses, Habermas implies their functionality in judging "the rationality of a speaking and acting subject" by how the person "behaves as a participant in argumentation" (Habermas 1984: 18). Thus, *the essence of communicative action is how validity claims are attended to by the activation of different discourse types until there is intersubjective understanding or mutual consensus.* When intersubjective understanding or mutual consensus is ensured, the legitimacy of the speakers, listeners, and the group is also ensured (Kemmis and Robin 2007).

Warren (1993) notes that the need to ensure that group discussions create mutual understanding is not mindfully attended to because of the time and effort needed to secure public spheres (that are free from institutional colonization) for communicative action to take place. Yet, as seen through public spheres such as Death Cafés, communicative areas in society that are institutionally delinked from collective powers of action do exist. Moreover, they actually serve as a "source of direction and legitimacy" for the community

(Warren 1993: 212). Following from this observation, not all discourse types can be activated in every communicative situation, even ideal ones. However, what must be underscored is that when required, discourses as different instruments exist to validate or critique validity claims through the discursive process of community deliberation and dialog. With such a panoply of discourse types, participants are thus able to "reflect on contested validity claims and attempt to vindicate or criticize them through argument" since discourses "provide structure and orientation for disputing controversial validity claims" (Yetim 2005:10–11). Different discourses are activated depending on the sensibilities of listeners in the group and in ways where their individual lifeworlds seek to synchronize with the communicator *and* one another's lifeworlds. This process is what sets into motion communicative action's trajectory toward mutual consensus based on intersubjectivity.

The aesthetic discourse is engaged with to address the performance of the cultural and social systems. That is, the aesthetic discourse seeks to attend to any claim about particular adequacies of value standards in the lifeworld by examining its performance (Kim and Holter 1995: 214, Yetim 2005: 12). It would be a mistake, however, to view Habermas's treatment of aesthetic discourse as only superficially relevant to Death Café communicative action. Habermas views the aesthetic discourse as one where dialog can be made to assess whether a "work or performance" is able to be "perceived as an authentic expression of an exemplary experience" (1984: 20).

Although initially viewed as a means to critique artistic production, the utility of the term makes it transferrable for critiquing other aspects of society's social constructions. That is, to the extent that institutions of the social system organized and configured uniquely from one another is a "work" subject to critique, then the position taken in this monograph is that the aesthetic discourse can conceivably critique the performance of the market, media, and medicine. Thus, if a social institution is being critiqued because it fails to be efficacious in its mandate—for example, if the school system fails to remedy bullying issues for students in spite of the community's expressed concerns—an aesthetic discourse between parents might convey how a school system's performance, after hearing validity claims made by school officials in a discursive dialog, is lacking and inadequate in resolving the problem. In this scenario, that "work" that some *thing* is the performance of the school system. For Habermas (1984: 20) in such instances "a work validated through aesthetic experience can...promote the acceptance of precisely those standards" needed to assess how a social dynamic performs. The aesthetic discourse thus works by "bringing us to see the work or performance which itself demonstrates a value . . . and depend for their force on the consensus achieved" even though it is deemed less conclusive than the practical or theoretical discourses to be discused (Szczelkun 1999: 2).

The explicative discourse attends to problematic validity claims by ensuring that all parties ultimately understand the resolved narrative. A collective understanding requires, however, a process by which the explication of meaning makes finer discernments of expressions that clarify the intentions and orientations of the speakers and listeners. If listeners find the speaker's claims toward comprehensibility problematic, the mode of response from listeners might include seeking interpretations so as to have a greater understanding of what is being explained (Kim and Holter 1995: 214). For Habermas, the process mandates the exclusion of dogmatic expressions so that pride of place can be given to the "comprehensibility, well-formedness, or rule correctness of symbolic expressions," if only for the sake of clearly explaining an issue (Habermas 1984: 22). An example of an explicative discourse that emerges to challenge the validity claim that "spirits are beings who are lost" might take the form of an addressee who asks "what do you mean by 'spirits'—do you mean ghosts, angels, or apparitions since these are all spirits in one form or another?" Should the explicative discourse gather more momentum, challenges from other listeners might be taken on the sentiment that "I am unsure about your assumption that spirits are always lost and in despair. If they are angelic they may return to provide hope for the individual experiencing crisis." The increasing synergy from addressees that challenge the validity claim of the speaker propounding the lost nature of spirits can ultimately invalidate the claim made by the speaker as detractors offer alternative explanations or queries. Or it can just as well affirm the speaker's validity claim, depending on the validity claim being made.

The practical discourse, according to Habermas (1990), is a critical communicative examination of practical, everyday norms that can be employed to set a course of action. That is, it asks of its participants "what course of action do we want to commit ourselves?" (1983: 71). The practical discourse reveals its dynamics when addressing validity claims that are conveyed as problems in need of solutions. The practical discourse is articulated through the process of thematization, or the inclination to approach validity claims by creating categories to formulate counterresponses that may vindicate or further remain critical of the defined problem. However, unlike the theoretical discourse, the practical discourse aims at acquiring mutual consensus in the form of justifying the speaker's norm of action in the process of problem solving, that is, the "rightness of claims are made thematic by the hearer to which justification is the method of response" (Kim and Holter 1995: 213–214). The practical discourse is understood to have successfully resolved validity claims during communicative action when each participant is "convinced that the proposed norm is equally good for all" (Habermas 1983: 71).

For participants seeking to justify a solution or norm during the practical discourse process that is responding to a validity claim—whether the discourse draws from cultural, technical, moral, or legal diacritica—it must be seen as having engaged with practical, everyday norms that leads to affirmation of the validity claim/s made by the speaker. For Yetim (2005), the engagement process must also include assessment as to whether the resolution proposed for the problem is ideal. To accomplish the aforementioned, participants attempt to take the perspective of the speaker as protagonist in hopes of checking on "unavoidable universal presuppositions or argumentation" (Habermas 1994: 50). For Habermas, the justification can proceed if it "secures the impartiality of moral judgment together with universal interchangeability of participant perspectives" (1994: 50).

For Kim and Holter (1995: 217), an example of listeners activating a practical discourse can be seen in the scenario where a patient utters a validity claim to a team of nurses such as "I cannot go for walk. I am afraid that my gut will fall out if I walk." Such a statement might compel the group of nurses to collectively decide on the merits of our patient's validity claim in different categories of consequences in hopes of justifying some sort of practical action to attend to the patient's claim. The decision conveyed to the patient, following a group deliberation, that "*all patients with the kind of operation you had* [a thematization] are required to ambulate as soon as possible" embodies the practical discourse taking its full course after being able to justify the validity claim made by the patient about the discomfort. The wording "kind of operation" serves as a thematized experience that, in the example, contests the validity claim made by the patient.

A theoretical discourse becomes emergent when listeners feel the need to vindicate or dispute any sort of truth claims that stems from a speaker's validity claims (Grady and Wells 1985/1986). In the process where listeners hear out, vindicate, or potentially contest a truth claim, discursive dialog can also take the form of thematization. For Habermas, the theoretical discourse is effective at countering the teleological framing of a speech act's assumed truth and thus is essentially about responding to truths forwarded by a validity claim (1984: 23).

The ability for a theoretical discourse to check on truth claims can be seen in the hypothetical example of, say, a speaker stating that she encountered an apparition at a nearby sanatorium while out jogging. In the process of uttering her account, she teleologically incorporates emphatic phrases while conveying her jogging experience with statements such as "I know that experience means I got a sign from my grandmother who was at that sanatorium!" Habermas describes such a communicative dynamic where emphasis is employed as when an actor tries to attain an end or bring about "the occurrence of a desired state by choosing means that have promise of being successful in the given situation and applying them in a suitable manner" (1984: 85). However, such an approach must still contend with listeners who will, in short order, vindicate or contest the validity claim. Thus, listeners desiring to find mutual consensus or intersubjective agreement about the possibility of apparitions at a nearby sanatorium would be engaging in a theoretical discourse if responses question the reality of apparitions (with a supernatural world thematized) while another group attempts to validate whether there indeed exists a sanatorium nearby (in this situation, the presence of a sanatorium is thematized). This form of discourse, like others according to Habermas, allows "challenges" to be effectively "directed at truth propositions" (1984: 23).

The therapeutic discourse is engaged in the public sphere when participants are "both willing and able to free" the self "from illusions ... that are based not on errors (about facts) but on self-deceptions (about one's own subjective experiences)" (Habermas 1984: 21). Kim and Holter note how in this mode of communication "the expressions of the speaker's own desires and feelings are contested" (1995: 214) for the "sincerity of the validity claim" (Grady and Wells 1985/1986: 38–39). A discourse that shows Habermas's inclination to take communicative action dynamics toward explaining matters of the psyche, its importance stems from how self-revelations can inspire empathy and *verstehen* from other participants in the communicative process if deemed sincere.

Habermas's emphasis for understanding social structure and action through "motives, values, emotions, and thoughts of others—subjectively, sympathetically, from the inside," underscores his preference for employing hermeneutics to ensure the validity of the therapeutic discourse (Grady and Wells 1985/1986:35). A sensitive disclosure from a speaker in a group setting reveals a degree of vulnerability that proclaims to others that the speaker was subject to some sort of duress, and by implication, incriminates some systemic activity or configuration that can serve to warn others about its effects. However, listeners must be convinced of this and will activate a therapeutic discourse to ascertain whether the speaker has, in the case of Death Cafés, experienced a sort of catharsis in the revelatory process, or whether the speaker is deluded. Habermas elaborates that

> We are dealing here with the expressions of one's own desires and inclinations, feelings and moods, which appear with the claim to truthfulness or sincerity. In many situations an actor has good reason to conceal his experiences from others or to mislead someone with whom he is interacting about his "true" experiences. In such cases he is not raising a claim to truthfulness but at most simulating one while behaving strategically. Expressions of this kind cannot be objectively criticized because of their insincerity; they are to be judged... on the basis of their sincerity only in the context of communication aimed at reaching understanding (1984: 21).

Habermas further explains:

> Anyone who systematically deceives himself about himself behaves irrationally. But one who is capable of letting himself be enlightened about his irrationality possesses not only the rationality of a subject who is competent to judge facts and who... is morally judicious and... reliable, who evaluates with sensitivity...(1984: 21).

Although Grady and Wells (1985/1986) note how such a dialogic experience evokes a Freudian dialog between doctor and patient as an ideal communicative situation while Habermas envisions such a dialog to transpire between participants *beyond* the dyad, the aim of a therapeutic discourse remains to "emancipate" the speaker from "systematic but unconscious self-deception" (Grady and Wells 1985/1986: 40).

Alluded to earlier, Habermas's *Justification and Application* (1994) offers new discourse conceptualizations that are finer discernments of the practical discourse: the ethical, moral, and pragmatic discourses, all of which serve to provide a greater nuance to how listeners and audiences can be seen to respond to validity claims. The ethical discourse is often presented to the audience by an addressee who emphasizes how self-reflection can allow the speaker to live an authentic life by contending with justifications of "regulations from a cultural perspective" and how this may or may not be good for the individuals or groups; that is, the ethical discourse focuses on whether the validity claims made are "good for them" (Yetim 2005: 11). Listeners who engage in an ethical discourse with the speaker are seeking to confirm whether the speaker's validity claims are credible enough to promote "rational motives for changes in attitude ... to attain clarity about ... life as a whole" given the social constraints imposed upon listeners by culture (Habermas 1994: 11). Ethical discourse requires all involved to dive in deep, so to speak, to contest validity claims as well as to "cast off the naiveté of everyday knowledge" that culture appropriates and conveys in a manner that is unable to fully paint a specific profile for someone's individual life-world history (1994: 24).

As a means to respond to the speaker's experiences, an example of an ethical discourse might arise when an assertion made by a pro-science speaker is imposed upon an audience through a validity claim such as "there is absolutely no evidence that there is life beyond this one." An ethical discourse is activated when an addressee responds with a statement such as, "I'm not so sure. After my drowning episode and near-death experience where I saw my kin whilst bathed in a warm, radiant glow of love, I feel that you should reconsider such a view *since I'm now a better person because of it.*" In the process of completing this speech act, fellow listeners and perhaps even the speaker will grant validity to the addressee simply because of the profundity that creates the catalyst for personal transformation among all parties in spite of the hegemonic power of the sciences.

A discourse that remains tied to individual self-actualization, Habermas hypothesizes that when the addressee is engaged in an ethical discourse, other listeners—including the protagonist making the validity claim—will not be able to successfully enter the purview of the addressee with any sort of *verstehen*. The speaker will defer to the addressee's discourse response simply because its profundity lies in the transformation experienced by the addressee, one that is appealing to groups seeking some semblance of emancipation from conventional norms espoused by culture. In Habermas's view, the ethical discourse has as its goal "the clarification of a collective identity that must leave room for the pursuit of diverse individual life projects" (1994: 16). The moment thus belongs to the addressee who is drawing from deep reservoirs of experiences (and wisdoms) that have been unpacked to contest a validity claim that is judged from whether life was consciously pursued, and whether the pursuit resulted in the "personal success" of one's "own life" (1994: 15). For Habermas, the ethical discourse presupposes: "on the part of the addressee, a striving to live an authentic life" or through the suffering of a patient who has "become conscious of 'sickness unto death'" (1994: 12).

For Habermas, a moral discourse emerges to seek "agreement concerning the just resolution of a conflict in the realm of norm-regulated action" (1994: 9). Yetim offers a clearer reading, however, noting that the moral discourse is concerned with whether speakers' validity claims can be justified as being good *for all* (2005: 11), as opposed to how the ethical discourse search for whether a validity claim is good for a group of individuals.

To launch a moral discourse against a problematic validity claim made by a speaker, the addressee/s responding to the speaker's validity claim must delink the self from "the contexts of life . . . with which one's identity is inextricably interwoven" (1994: 12) lest the speaker accuse the listener of relativism. Habermas notes that such a delinking is necessary because "cultural values do not count as universal; they are . . . located within the horizon of the lifeworld of a specific group or culture" (1984: 42). The moral discourse premises the view that it is unnecessary to rely on a cultural framework to assess morality if social effects upon an *overall human condition*, or a shared humanity, is of concern. By challenging a speaker's validity claim that is not perceived to benefit all, a moral discourse is sought by participants to "transcend the social and historical context of their particular form of life and particular community and adopt the perspective of all those possibly affected" (Habermas 1994: 24).

The purpose for such a delinking from the self as the addressee employs a moral discourse to address a speaker's validity claims is that moral judgment—if uncritically approached—may emanate from a preexisting community framework that defines what morality means. Because morality for Habermas is but society's framework of values and norms internalized in the self so that each individual essentially communicates "community from within" (1994: 13), to assess how a validity claim affects all of us behooves us to not challenge a validity claim from only our particular cultural orientation. Moreover, only in a context where an addressee articulates "norms . . . that express a common interest of all affected" will there be "justified assent" toward the speaker (1994: 13). That is, resolving a problematic validity claim requires a moral discourse to be a collectively generated dynamic that nonetheless can still compel "self referential reflections on the reasonableness of moral demands" (Habermas 1994: 24). The moral discourse is characterized by the symbiotic relationship of differing perspectives that are constituted by "the communicative presupposition of a universal discourse in which all those possibly affected could take part" (Habermas 1994: 12). Thus, when a moral discourse is activated, "the ethnocentric perspective of a particular group expands into the perspective of an 'unlimited communication community'" (Yetim 2005: 13).

The pragmatic discourse can be discerned from the practical discourse by communicative dynamics that, upon butting into a problematic validity claim, can be checked with empirical knowledge. That is, Habermas (1994) notes how the pragmatic discourse seeks to justify technical and strategic validity claims and as such has a "certain affinity with empirical discourses" (pg. 10). It creates the conditions for informed listeners to "relate empirical knowledge to hypothetical goal determinations and preferences" so as to "assess the consequences of choices in light of underlying maxims" (pg. 11). He further notes how "technical or strategic recommendations ultimately derive their validity from the empirical knowledge on which they rest," that is, their validity is not dependent on whether an addressee decides to adopt the validation for "pragmatic discourses take their orientation from *possible contexts* of application" (pg. 11). Yetim views the function of a pragmatic discourse as one based on justifying, among other things, "strategic recommendations" from information or data that lead to problem solving (2005: 11).

The role of the pragmatic discourse, then, is to see whether a validity claim can be substantiated with informational details. When listeners are provided with a problematic validity claim, the pragmatic discourse includes those that cite what is factually or scientifically known while simultaneously encouraging affirmation from other listeners, thus positioning communicative action closer toward collective resolution based on what the group can agree upon based on facts. Yet because facticity can easily be relativized by listeners, the mutual consensus-building process of the pragmatic discourse points to the "necessity of compromise as soon as one's own interests" are "brought into harmony with those of others" (Habermas 1994: 16). Table 3.1 summarizes all of the major discourse types that constitute much of Habermas's theory of communicative action.

Communicative action could be deemed as successful when community and cooperation are secured after speakers and listeners subject validity claims discursively through the activation of different discourses. In the process of reaching this goal, Warren notes how the discursive dynamics through the activation of different discourses offer challenges and justifications that "simultaneously produce consensus and increase the autonomy of individuals as they come to better understand their own needs, interests, and desires" (1993: 213). Alternatively, communicative action succeeds when reciprocating acknowledgments, incisive questioning on a dialectical basis, and affirmations based on intersubjective agreement lead

Table 3.1   Different discourse responses to validity claims

Discourse types (in alphabetical order)	Approach to VCs
Aesthetic discourse	Concerned with the performance of standards of value in VCs
Ethical discourse	Concerned with whether VCs can benefit individuals or groups
Explicative discourse	Concerned with comprehensibility in the VCs
Moral discourse	Concerned with whether VCs can benefit all
Practical discourse	Concerned with the rightness of norms of action espoused by VCs
Pragmatic discourse	Concerned with the rightness of technical and strategic details of VCs
Theoretical discourse	Concerned with the truth of the VCs
Therapeutic discourse	Concerned with the sincerity of the VCs

VC: Validity claim Adapted from Grady and Wells (1985/1986)

to mutual understanding and unforced consensus on issues. Warren adds that successful communicative action also ensures the autonomy of the individual as one who can "make decisions based on critical examination of needs and interests" as well as participating in "processes that resolve conflicts between needs and interests by means of discourse" (Warren 1993: 214). The importance of intersubjective agreement cannot be over-emphasized as one of the goals of effective communicative action.

For Habermas, a theory of intersubjectivity contrasts with theories which base truth and meaning on individual consciousness. While an individual may arrive at knowledge through a sudden flash of insight, Habermas insists that such knowledge enters the intersubjective sphere only by being trans-lated into rational, accessible discourse. The sphere of intersubjectivity is not the creation of a single individual psyche, but is a medium of communicable knowledge, created and maintained through the interaction of many sub-jectivities (Grady and Wells 1985/1986: 35).

Habermas thus tows the Frankfurt School line, affirming how society is a dense "web of intersubjectivity, created through the actions and interac-tions of subjects who could become the conscious creators of values"

(Grady and Wells 1985/1986: 35). Satisfying the conditions of intersub-jectivity along with attributes of mutual understanding, unforced consensus, and the opening up of communicative space requires communication to take its course until the group reaches some form of acceptable conclusion. In the case of when registered nurses employ communicative action, for example, Kim and Holter note (1995):

> Nursing actions may become ineffective or inefficient when they are not based on mutual understanding concerning their goals. By applying the theoretical, practical, aesthetic, and explicative discourses, nurses can pro-vide opportunities for arriving at mutual understanding with clients so that coordinated nursing actions may eventuate in the situation of patient care... An application of these five forms of argumentation in nursing practice then involves the nurse questioning the validity claims embedded in the client's utterances or responding to the client's criticism about the nurse's claims in order to provide communicative rationality (217).

Regardless of discourse types, their ability to accommodate unique perspectives on mortality conveyed by Death Café attendees is pro-nounced in ways that allow participants to feel a sense of solidarity during death talk. Communicative action by Death Café attendees thus exhibits the promises of a Habermasian intersubjectivity:

> Skills, sensitivities, and insights are relevant to participating in critical-dia-lectical discourse—having an open mind, learning to listen empathetically, "bracketing" premature judgment, and seeking common ground. Qualities of emotional intelligence (self-awareness and impulse control, persistence, zeal and self-motivation, empathy, and social deftness) are obvious assets for developing the ability of adults to assess alternative beliefs and participate fully and freely in critical-dialectical discourse. In communicative learning, emphasis is on critical reflection and critical self-reflection, assessing what has been taken for granted to make a more dependable, tentative working judgment (Mezirow 2003: 60).

Mezirow notes how a "discourse ethics" thus emerges with a focus on "the particularity of differences in points of view" (2003: 62), a process that will be examined in the next chapter.

In this chapter, I elaborated on key components of communicative action that lend themselves toward "reading" Death Café talk. The major premise outlined in this chapter is that the lifeworld of death talk has been colonized by systems of the market, media, and medicine in ways that have caused the uncoupling of system and lifeworld. In this situation, the population thus relates to macro-level institutions in ways that satisfy a variety of legal regulations that contain few, if any norms, through a process Habermas terms juridification. Consequentially, communication to the populace is vertically linear, flowing from top to bottom of the social environment. Emancipatory practices in communication thus aim for mutual consensus by engaging participants to intersubjectively support or refute validity claims that surface in a variety of discursively generated discourses.

CHAPTER 4

Death Sentiments and Death Themes

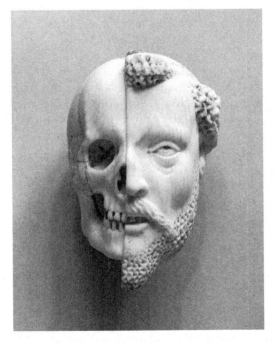

Monk and Death (sixteenth to seventeenth century). Walters Art Museum.

© The Author(s) 2017
J. Fong, *The Death Café Movement*,
DOI 10.1007/978-3-319-54256-0_4

87

We begin this chapter by examining the cues Death Café attendees most frequently conveyed to one another. Death Café events where data collection took place were on (1) January 18, 2014, (2) January 25, 2014, (3) February 18, 2014, (4) April 22, 2014, (5) May 22, 2014, (6) May 10, 2015, and (7) July 16, 2015. There was a total of 40 attendees across the seven Death Café events with 30 women attendees (75%) and 10 male attendees (25%). Three attendees (7.5%) are members of Generation X. As Death Cafés are meant to gather strangers, few disclosed their occupation or conveyed their class status.

Before we examine the themes communicated by our attendees, we must briefly discuss the key instrument employed in this study, Jonathan Feinberg's Wordle program. Wordle, a metadata generator, was employed to (1) create outputs, or canvases, that show each Café attendee's key words in ways that reflect the individual's most pressing thematic concerns about death and dying. We will also (2) discuss key words from Wordle canvases that capture each Death Café event in its entirety. Thus, two increasingly larger concentric dialog spheres that generate Death Café narratives and themes will be rendered by Wordle. We will also discuss the various validity claims that have been made throughout Death Café events as well as the discourses employed to support or contest the validity claims.

WORDLE CANVASES OF DEATH CAFÉ PARTICIPANTS AND EACH DEATH CAFÉ IN ITS ENTIRETY

Wordle is a tool for visualizing text by generating "tag clouds" ideal for communication analyses. Much of my elaboration on the utility of Wordle stems from my previous use of Wordle for research. Wordle takes inputted text and subsequently outputs word compilations where a larger word size indicates greater use of that particular word in the text (Viegas et al. 2009). The "cloud" reference stems from how the words are outputted in a manner that makes the compiled words appear as a rather chaotic lump of text, but only to a non-discerning eye. There is meaning within this compilation in that large-sized words imply the communicator's attribution of greater importance to the meaning of the word. Conversely, smaller sized words indicate infrequent mention and, by implication, less importance for the communicator. Each Death Café participant's dialog was transcribed and inputted into Wordle so as to generate an output of their thematic concerns about mortality. Similarly, a Wordle output was generated for each individual Death Café. From these canvases, words seen were then reread in their rightful passages as seen in the transcriptions.

The primary reason for employing Wordle stems from its utility for content analysis of text. Wordle has already established a presence in peer reviewed journals in media studies and their outputs have frequently surfaced in journals such as *New Media and Society*, as well as in information sciences journals such as *Communications in Computer and Information Science*. It must be emphasized, however, that Wordle outputs "make no scientific claims or inferences"; instead, "they offer their readers the possibility of unconstrained interpretations, based...on the assumption that word frequencies mean something" (Krippendorf and Bock 2009: 38). It should be emphasized, however, that my particular employment of Wordle will not be based on "unconstrained interpretations" but more rather, on cautious extrapolations. Wordle outputs are thus displayed in a manner that "helps the researcher to understand meaning and/or cause behind the patterns...as well as discover additional patterns" (Manovich 2010: 27). Fans of Wordle—in spite of it being a rather blunt instrument—agree that this program is filled with potential "Scientists wordle genetic functions, fans wordle music videos, teachers wordle literary texts, spouses wordle love letters, kids wordle their thoughts and journalists wordle political speeches" (Viegas et al. 2009: 1). However, to what degree the Wordle instrument is blunt is an important discussion to have for exploring different methodologies that could be employed for textual analysis, one not undertaken here given the focus of this study.

Before inputting transcriptions into Wordle, words such as "Death Café," "death," "died," "die," and "dying" were removed from all attendees' transcribed comments. The decision to remove these words was based on the need to eliminate the self-evident focus of the study, which is on death and dying and the Death Café. Removing key death words allow for an uncluttered archeological "dig" into what underlies attendees' views on mortality. Had the aforementioned words not been removed, they would have occupied large swathes of our Wordle outputs since our attendees extensively employed them. By removing the words tied to death and dying, additional space for Wordle outputs was secured for displaying important themes "orbiting" mortality concerns.

After the presentation of each Death Café's Wordle canvas, primary, secondary, tertiary, and quaternary words on the canvas will be analyzed.

Because these words are derived from countable words from within the dialog, the analysis will take place within the contexts, perspectives, and concerns of our Café participants. Krippendorff (2013) underscores the need for countable elements that can be used for extrapolations. This approach toward textual analysis has an early historical iteration through Berelson and Lazarsfeld's important work *The Analysis of Communication Content* (1948) where the authors emphasize the need to frame countable elements within political, cultural, or economic trends. Krippendorff (2013) shares similar views about how observed frequencies in content analysis would be "totally meaningless" were it not for the identification of context. Block quotes and parenthetical quotes from Café attendees will thus be employed to nest the words within its rightful context where the statement/s surfaced. When some quotes appear to be tied to particular speakers too frequently, such a scenario is due to particular speakers being more communicative than others (Kathy from DC6, for example, attended primarily as a listener and infrequently communicated). Indeed, not every attendee participated in death talk in equal amounts and there was communicative asymmetry at many Death Cafés.

The progression of our analyses will be based on attending to the largest primary and secondary words across each participant's Wordle canvas. Since these are the most frequently mentioned themes, they are given pride of place. Noteworthy, tertiary and quaternary words are then addressed as these usually begin to discern different attendees' sentiments from one another, as evinced in their individual Wordle canvases. The sequencing of discussion is chronological, from the first scheduled Café (DC1) and their attendees' Wordle canvases to our last Café, DC7, and the latter group's canvases. When possible, the flow of analysis will be through the words that seem to resonate equally across many attendees' canvases. Only then can we explore other themes that set the attendees apart. Additionally, when a theme on a Wordle canvas is discussed, the context of the different passages or block quotes that nested the word will be referenced with the thematic word within the passage italicized. When referencing the word that has appeared in Wordle during my analysis, the word will be set off in quotes. Finally, in situations where each theme appears in different iterations (as in when the word "like" functions beyond its verb status as a preposition, an adverb, or even an adjective), only the most death-relevant iterations will be discussed.

It is important to also note that as we examine our Café attendees Wordle outputs, the analyses of their thematic emphases can in no way be exhaustive or highly detailed since each individual attendee was never personally interviewed. Moreover, because Death Café attendees were strangers with one another upon the beginning of the Café event, a status that most desired to maintain until their departure, I respected this boundary so as to have complete leveling with other participants. Moreover, to query attendees about intentions and additional demographics robs the uniqueness of how Death Cafés are structured to induce death talk: that participants attend Death Cafés as strangers, *with many of who seek to remain strangers* with one another upon the conclusion of the evening. Yet, it is precisely this ensured anonymity that allows Café attendees' personal journeys in life while confronting death to be so candidly conveyed and so richly textured.[1]

Thus, key demographic data based on class, occupation, and specific age (with the exception that many identified themselves as Baby Boomers) were not forthcoming as these would require interviews or survey questionnaires to secure information, a procedure that would have influenced our attendees to violate the important status of being a stranger at a Death Café. Thus, words seen in Wordle have never been drawn from interviews, only through the participants communicative action seen in the transcriptions. Moreover, my desire to acquire demographic data would have been in vain: as my consent forms were handed out to Café participants during the opening sessions of death talk, any vocal query of each attendee about demographic information would have drastically slowed down the flow of the evening's discussion. Although interviews of attendees could have been structured to take place before the beginning of each Café session, the propensity for my queries to influence the content of death talk to follow made this approach untenable. The rhythm of rich conversation would have been severely compromised as well. Finally, given that environments like the Death Café, referred alternatively as public spheres by Habermas (1991) and third places by Oldenburg (1999), are deliberately oriented toward establishing leveling dynamics where social status is rendered inconsequential to interaction, the acquisition of detailed demographic data such as age, occupation, etc. was not pursued.

The concluding section of this chapter will explore the diverse validity claims and counterclaims via discourses if they exist. There were 159 instances where validity claims had been voiced and 39 discourses that responded to some of these validity claims. The final task of this chapter will consist of identifying thematic emphases and discourse responses of death talk that underpin emergent iterations of a death identity (see Tables 4.1, 4.2, and 4.3).

January 18, 2014: Wordle Canvases and Discussion
for Death Café 1 (DC1)

The January 18, 2014 Death Café took place at a locally popular yet quaint Afghani restaurant located approximately 35 miles east of downtown Los Angeles. The interior of the environment included awnings that broke apart the warm sunlight overhead, generating an evocative and relaxed atmosphere for conversation. Five attendees were present: Chloe, Cora, Pat, Stephanie, and Betsy.

Fig. 4.1   Betsy's comments (Betsy is event facilitator) January 18, 2014

Fig. 4.2   Chloe's comments (January 18, 2014)

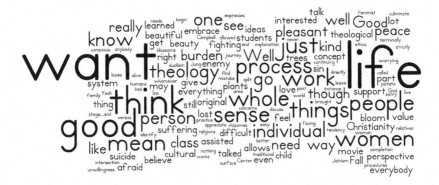

Fig. 4.3 Cora's comments (January 18, 2014)

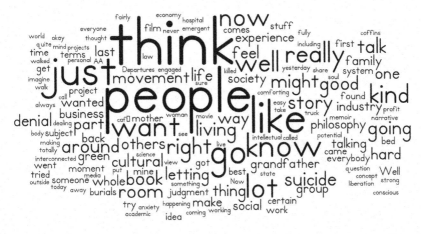

Fig. 4.4 Pat's comments (January 18, 2014)

Betsy's Wordle projection of the large word "hospice" (Fig. 4.1) reveals how formative her experience in hospice was in linking her with the "people," a word with the largest spatial dimensions in her Wordle canvas. Betsy indeed has familial links to the first hospice opened in the United States in Branford, Connecticut in 1974. Betsy's mention of "men," "cultures," and "African American" points to her celebration of Los Angeles' diversity as well as how

Fig. 4.5 Stephanie's comments (January 18, 2014)

Fig. 4.6 All attendees' comments (January 18, 2014)

the city's size makes it ideal for hosting many Death Cafés. Her love of Los Angeles manifests as an approximately quaternary "LA" in the Wordle canvas. Moreover, Betsy, more than others, saw the Death Café cartographically as conveyed during her discussion of Los Angeles Café sites, while recounting the history of her journeys across the county and beyond:

I mean I was like a therapist. No training whatsoever; just went in, driving around *LA* with my pager. There were no cell phones or internet at the time, no GPS. There was only my *Thomas Guide* (~), the pager, and the payphone. But it was the best way to do death because they taught me, the dying taught me. But I learned *LA* and this is why I want to go all over *LA* and do different Death Cafés, learn the cultures, take their coffee and their tea. But this is how I learned *LA*, the different neighborhoods, the different cultures, based on how they "do" death. It's like, "Oh, this is how you believe!" It was a great way to learn: not through books, not through studying, not through theory.

Betsy's continued emphasis on the people-oriented permutations of matters related to mortality at once captures its complexities as well as how these complexities unfurl in the context of community. Betsy's Wordle canvases from January 25, 2014 (Fig. 4.7), February 18, 2014 (Fig. 4.13), and April 22, 2014 (Fig. 4.18) thus reveal her appreciation and celebration of Los Angeles' diverse populations as ideal for Death Café meetings. Because Betsy's status as a Death Café facilitator meant she usually promulgates the evening's gathering with somewhat of a script, resulting in the consistency of her thematic emphases, the need for us to expound on Betsy's remaining Wordle outputs will be tempered so as to make analytical room for the voices of other Death Café attendees.

Like Betsy's, "people" occupies a large part of Chloe's Wordle canvas. Chloe conveys her experiences with people (Fig. 4.2) by framing their mortality experiences within the framework of "values," a gesture that is not surprising given her status as a doctoral theology student at a nearby college:

And I keep the conversation going so I know it's just not a matter of filling out forms and putting it in a drawer; it's about this dynamic process of reassessing my own *values* all the time—am a really big proponent of that— but at the same time they have limits. And one of the biggest limits is to believe that all we have to do is to fill out the forms. It's really much more about knowing what our *values* are and communicating with *people* we trust what those *values* are so that when *people* are put in that position to make healthcare decisions on our behalf they respect our wishes.

Pat's rendering of "people" (Fig. 4.4) is more expansive and critical. During discussion, she framed the human condition through the framework of capitalism, socialism, and feminism. She is a deep thinker of death and dying, yet she moves beyond ideology to remind her fellow participants that ultimately all people, along with our ecologies as well as our planet, are interconnected. "People" was often seen in conjunction with "think," a primary word that occupies the most space in her Wordle canvas. Indeed the most frequently employed word seen in Pat's Wordle canvas is "think."

> We *think* of ourselves as atomistic individuals but that sense that we're not a large part of some cultural whole is cultural, very American, very capitalist. I do *think* there is a role to be played in our educational system that is not explicitly preparing *people* for death, but you are making that pathway easier if you are narrating a metaphysical story that enables you to come to terms with death as part of life which is that we are all interconnected. We are interconnected on a planetary, ecological, system of a life support network.

Elsewhere Pat continues:

> When I *think* about my own death, like you said, I might feel differently on my death bed and because I do so much existential philosophy and I do believe in principal that we are our best selves, that we live up to our full potential, when we are keeping it real about the finite nature of our existence. I'm a 100% believer in that idea.
>
> So when I *think* about my own death I *think* about that kind of being, that state of acceptance where you hear the *people* in the room around you, and they're playing music and dealing with their anxiety and issues (~) but my hope, if you want to talk about a good death is that I would get to this place where I'm okay with letting go.

Like many attendees of DC1, thinking through concepts and ideas about mortality and how to confront it, as will be evinced by others in their respective Wordle canvases, provides greater clarity on mortality. It also allows for thoughtful validity claims that are articulated as social critique, as in Pat's statement: "The other thing about the denial: I *think* it's part of the cultural story because we as a society and culture are still in denial." Indeed, throughout the conversation, Pat was at the forefront of encouraging us to think about death and dying in all its iterations, and to know as a consequence what we "want" out of life, an approximately quaternary word, and what it is like to be living with such mindfulness. Not surprisingly, "living" also appears as a quaternary word in Pat's canvas and for good reason: As a philosophy professor, she again emphasizes how "death is the key to existentialists who seek an authentic existence. We're *living* more authentically, we're *living* more fully, if we're *living* in a conscious awareness of death." In her death talk, Pat references inspiring individuals and schools of thought, some from the grass roots while others icons in their respective disciplines.

Although "like" was also employed as an exemplar as well as a linguistic filler by many DC1 attendees, its most common usage occurred when participants indicated how they desired a particular encounter with death, a particular view, a particular idea, as when Stephanie describes why she likes driving by a cemetery (Fig. 4.5):

> So much of death is seen as morbid even though it's inseparable from life. I totally don't buy that. All the real mystics you read, whatever faith, they say it's actually energizing, literally energizing, to spend some time every day recognizing it, which is one of the things I love about my drive to and from work 'cause I live in Hollywood and I work in Pasadena. I get to drive by Forest Lawn every day. I really *like* that because it reminds me every day to remember the important stuff about life, because there is a shelf life.

Additionally, the word "like" was used by Stephanie to refer to other analogous elements, as in her account of loss when she "lost someone who was *like* a father and mentor and a dear friend."

Stephanie was most rhythmic during her interaction with other participants. At times, one to provide incisive humor, sarcasm, healthy doses of witty cynicism, and incisive critique, Stephanie also facilitated many moments of deep dialog. In this regard, she is unafraid of where her curiosities will take her. Stephanie is also well read, able to draw cues from Buddhism, Jung, and American spiritual teacher Ram Daas. She is a person of thought and spontaneity, driven by wants and the desire to know—indeed both "want" and "know" occupy the largest area of her Wordle canvas—but just barely. Like her compatriots, there was an emphasis on "people" which allowed her to engage in social critique of conventional assumptions and framing that distort our understanding of mortality. The same degree of emphases can be seen in the words "talk" and "think," both of which were employed by Stephanie to convey her experiences with people and their communicative orientation as well as with prominent thinkers that conveyed their views toward death and dying. In spite of her passion and emphasis for death talk, Stephanie was no proselytizer, especially to senior citizens, noting at one point that "there's no way I'd impose upon a fragile elder and make them *talk* about it, you know. I'm available but I'll play cards and live with my disappointment."

Wordle outputs for Cora and Stephanie (Figs. 4.3 and 4.5, respectively) show distinct emphases that differed them from each other as well as from our aforementioned trio. Cora's main emphasis was "life" as evidenced by the word's presence in her Wordle canvas. Her statement captures the importance of juxtaposing life and death so that the latter can hopefully inform the former: "One of the things I see as humans really embrace an embodied *life* is our unwillingness to embrace death as a natural process." With her theological orientation enriching her life trajectory, Cora is unafraid to hope or desire a better world where life and death are seen as a process. Her celebration of the former theme, however, had been conveyed through analogies of Jung as well as through some of her own during dialog, such as "individual trees and individual plants" are "one system," and that life is part of this entire system. Cora's mention of "want" is by no means self-serving. In her death talk, Cora noted how she wanted to "unpack more of the [death] stuff around" for people to find a more truthful relationship with living, further enhanced by her conviction—especially in the context of assisted dying—that she "would support the right to go when you *want* to go if you don't *want* to live anymore."

The Wordle outputs from all participants of the January 18, 2014 Death Café (Fig. 4.6) convey the importance of people in death talk, whether as activists, scholars, or simply members of the community. For example, Betsy, Chloe, and Pat's Wordle outputs (see Figs. 4.1, 4.2, and 4.4, respectively) reveal that "people" occupied a large swathe of the Wordle canvas area, reflecting their critique on the number of people in society that avoided the theme of death and dying. Additionally, large-sized words such as "want," "know," "life," "think," and "talk" are also visually explicit. They all reveal cues and themes of critical importance in death talk manifested by the DC1 group. Indeed, Pat felt that DC1 was "the most intellectual Death Café" she attended.

January 25, 2014: Wordle Canvases and Discussion for DC2

The January 25, 2014 Death Café took place at an airy and large Mediterranean-themed restaurant on a wonderfully mild day. No other patrons were present at the time of our death talk and Café participants had the entire venue to themselves, allowing for an atmospheric discussion in an evocatively empty restaurant. The context is a suburb approximately 15 miles northwest of downtown Los Angeles. Five attendees were present: Cheyenne, Steve, Trent, Troy, and Betsy.

Fig. 4.7 Betsy's comments (Betsy is event facilitator) (January 25, 2014)

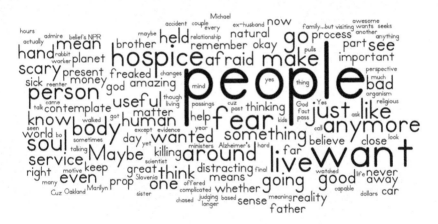

Fig. 4.8 Cheyenne's comments (January 25, 2014)

DC2 was dynamic event and "people" again emerged as the most popular theme, especially for Betsy, Cheyenne, and Trent (Figs. 4.7, 4.8, and 4.10, respectively). Cheyenne's people-centric orientation saw her frequent immersion with the theme of mortality in three distinct ways. The first approach was based on social critique, as in "We see evidence of *people* killing each other more and more, and they're killing the planet."

Fig. 4.9   Steve's comments (January 25, 2014)

Fig. 4.10   Trent's comments (January 25, 2014)

Fig. 4.11 Troy's comments (January 25, 2014)

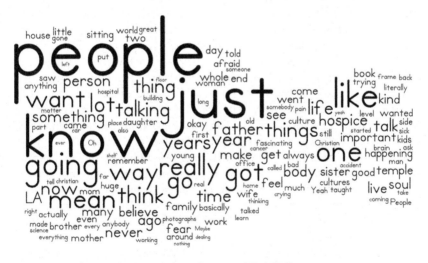

Fig. 4.12 All attendees' comments (January 25, 2014)

Cheyenne also noted tendencies she saw in people as they confronted mortality through statements such as, "Some *people* are afraid of it and some *people* aren't. Some are afraid to give birth and some *people* aren't." However, it would be Cheyenne's altruism and desire to make death operate as a catalyst for living and life that is dialectically noteworthy: "And so I want to help *people* live and live, to make their lives be as good as they can." At one point during death talk, Trent's query to Cheyenne about whether she felt there was a soul elicited a response that revealed her orientation to live in the urgency of the present: "What I see as useful for me is to go out and be as much service as I can to other *people*. Thinking about whether or not there's a god or a soul is not useful. It does not help one be a better person." When Trent again prodded her about whether she had any curiosities about the soul, Cheyenne continued to reinforce her view on life and death: "Not at all anymore. Not at all anymore. Doesn't matter to me anymore. What matters to me is that I'm part of this human organism, that for good or for bad, seeks to live as a human."

Betsy, Cheyenne, and Trent's Wordle canvases also include the word "mean." In the case of Betsy's usage, the term was employed idiomatically as in her view about how Buddhists approach mortality: "I *mean*, if you're Buddhist, they talk about it from day one." Cheyenne frequently used the term idiomatically as well in her view of a natural death: "I *mean*, it's a 100% natural process like going to the bathroom and having a baby. To me that's what it is." Regardless of which Café participant employed the term, when employed the term "mean" was able to effect simultaneously clarification and emphasis, as in when Trent conveys the value of the Burning Man festival that he annually visits: "It's powerful. I *mean*, that Temple of Remembrance. I *mean*, I've been all over the world and to many holy places, and this place is as moving as anything I've ever been to."

Cheyenne's experiences with bereavement of family members, hospice work, and her exposure to the fearmongering media as well as individuals' fear of dying have added a sense of urgency in how she views the existential condition of people, a point not lost on Trent, DC2's most communicatively dynamic attendee. Indeed, Trent presented similar social critiques against the media, specifically our use of social media, and its effects on "people." A notable account was his observation of our death voyeurism when he witnessed members of a community filming a death scene after a man was fatally struck by a car. From this episode, Trent implicates the group and their use of media devices to vulgarize death.

These *people* were filming the brain of this 21 year old kid on the street. And I'm thinking where do you come from as a culture where you're excited about filming a person's brain that's just landed on the street to put on YouTube as a sensationalistic kind of a thing, to put out there on your Facebook page or whatever you're doing. I mean, we're afraid of death, we have this whole industry that sanitizes it, yet at the same time we're worshipping it and reveling in it. It's weird!

However, Trent's employment of "people" in dialog was also ethnographic as evinced in his discussion of people's orientations toward sacrality during Nevada's Burning Man, particularly the "temple" in the guise of the Temple of Remembrance that honors those individuals who inspired. He recounts how people placed mementos of the deceased within the structure prior to its ritualized immolation. The crescendo of the event would see these structures burned, alluding to how fire—even ones that bring people together—can simultaneously exhibit connotations of death as finality, as farewell, and perhaps as renewal: "Well, I started to really pay attention to this particular structure at the festival and when my father passed away three years ago and I went to the *temple* and brought a photograph of him sitting in an airport somewhere—he traveled a lot—and I put it on the wall." He praises of how people can find community even in symbolic death:

So anyway, you're in an environment, a *temple* environment surrounded by *people* who are sobbing, crying, writing things for basically dead relatives—missing them, experiencing the pain of loss. My father's photo was up there. Then you know, two or three nights later, you stand with 10,000 *people* and you watch this structure burn to the ground in this huge pyre. They burned the entire building down.

Elsewhere, Trent notes:

In Burning Man I think it's cathartic. You will have literally thousands of *people* at night surrounding a building and there will be dead silence as these flames, these huge flames, burn the buildings to the ground! Then you hear someone shout out, "I miss you Aunt Mildred!" To me it's cathartic.

Notably, in Trent's Wordle canvas, we see the first visually explicit emergence of the use of "just" as adverb and occasionally as adjective. Although the word "just" could easily be dismissed as a ubiquitous word that has little existential value, its important function as a modifier of verbs, adjectives, other adverbs, and many types of phrases and clauses makes it an indispensable word for gauging the weight of emphasis in dialog. Indeed, Trent's use of "just" was often employed to emphasize one's proximity to the afterlife. An example can be found in Trent's astonishment when he learned of a medium's ability to know certain specific details about his life, "*just* things that there's no way this woman would know about" or after experiencing what he felt was a paranormal experience: "And I was like, okay, there's something *just* beyond the curtain trying to get attention." Ultimately, however, the greatest impact in the use of "just" was seen in Trent's existential query: "Without seeking it out, it's had me wondering, *just* as a curious person: You know, is this all there is? Is this it?"

Trent frequently emphasized the theme of knowing during death talk (Fig. 4.10). Trent's use of the word "know" is intimately connected to questions not directly related to death and dying per se, but on whether we could ever know about the afterlife, that realm or state—physical or transcendental—a dying person Trent believes we all transition to. Orbiting such topics were his sincere queries on whether there is one "way" or different ways to relate to mortality. For Trent, certainty about the metaphysical was a foregone conclusion. As such, Trent's Café orientation was to sloganeer certainties about mortality and an assumed beyond, but in a methodical way that often saw him requesting validations from fellow DC2 participants.

The Wordle canvas for Steve (Fig. 4.9) conveys how his orientations toward death were shaped by familial losses that deeply affected his "mother," a prominent word in his Wordle canvas. Steve's life experiences include his family system entering periodic crises, as when he lost his grandmother and sister, along with his mother's subsequent nervous breakdown and eventual passing. Indeed, the series of breakdowns experienced by Steve's mother internalized in him a foundational orientation toward death and dying that is shaped by fear. Moreover, Steve notes how his "father," in hopes of protecting his mom when she was not well, managed to "sanitize everything" related to mortality, an act which left in our participant unresolved issues about the fear of death and uncertainty about death and dying. The death of Steve's mother—a loss deemed by many thanatologists to be one of the most difficult loss an adult can experience save a loss of one's own child—was his first direct encounter with death, an episode that affected him deeply. For Steve, a former Christian Scientist:

My inner facing of death started when my grandmother died when I was seven. I had nothing to do with it. However my *mother*, who presumably was watching her *mother* die, had a complete nervous breakdown. And she was hospitalized. She was gone for a month. I don't remember any of that but I know it to be true.

My mom never came back from that in a way. She was never "there" again. So I grew up, you know, with a *mom* who was really not a functioning *mother* and she had another breakdown after her sister died about twenty five years ago. I was lot older for that and I was trying to nurture her back to health in a way. Between Christian Science which I view with a high level of disdain and what I think is reality and watching how death affected my *mother*, I basically had either been in denial of it or terrified of it my whole life. I have absolutely no interface with death at all until a year ago when my *mother* died. And I'm 57 years old going on 58 and that was the first death that I directly experienced.

Steve recounts his tensions and, ultimately, disagreements with his previous religious views, especially on matters of physical health and mortality. Still attending to some of the unresolved issues regarding his relationship to mortality, "going" figured prominently in Steve's Wordle canvas. For Steve, living had to become an ongoing project and process that he must be mindful of, lest in his words "I'm worried I'm *going* to be *one* of those guys who when he's dying is going to be flailing and screaming. I don't want to be." That the word "going" figures prominently in Steve's Wordle canvas and also in the aforementioned sentence suggests how Steve's view on mortality reveals his ongoing process at confronting it. Ironically, although rather self-deprecating during his moments of death talk, Steve's confrontation of end of life actually exhibited, and this was clearly not apparent to him at the time of our gathering, a great degree of courage that inspired much respect from his fellow participants. Steve exhaustively keeps at it, trying hard to harness from death talk a life project. Another example can be seen in the account:

But I don't feel like I have it in me. And I feel like the deck has been stacked against me because when you're seven years old and that happens it's sort of etched in you. And it's not for lack of time and discussing and going to therapy and really working hard on it but I have associations against it that are extremely uncomfortable. But I want to talk about it and bring it up, yeah.

Yet another example can be seen in Steve's sentiments about his former faith, sentiments that include another frequently employed word, "sick," to refer to the incompatibility of illness and religiosity in his former belief system:

> If you're a good Christian Scientist, then you'll get better. And if you're bad then you're going to be sick. Well guess what: I was bad a lot times when I was a kid because I got sick and I stayed sick, you know. You raise death to the nth level and you got what I got: you feel really, really defective, deeply defective, like what you just said [gesturing to Trent], like you're going to die.

Like Trent and many other Café participants in the study, Steve's Wordle canvas includes the word "know" to signify the importance of accessing meaning in death or accepting that such knowledge remains inaccessible, paths that allow our participants to skirt the horizons of nihilism. Perhaps, this is why for our other DC2 participant, Troy, there were many emphases during his discussion that employed the word "really," as can be seen in his Wordle canvas (Fig. 4.11). For Troy, "really" signifies the need for manifestations of experiences, of things as they actually are in their genuine individual and/or communal expression, a pattern also exhibited by Steve in the above block quote. Troy's approach toward mortality is based on the quest for some form of authenticity that can transcend conventional and stigmatized views on mortality. Such sentiments can be found when Troy addressed his sister's passing, "sister" being a word that drew in other important feelings: "I decided at that time that I was going to be there for her because I knew that all this avoidance was *really* hurting me and my whole family, so I spent the last couple weeks of her life being around with her" and "the whole thing was—her presence and comfort—compared to what I grew up with, a *really* stark contrast."

Troy's narrative also reminds us that death and dying is not only an individualized process for the person who is in life's terminal stage but one where community and family can be involved in the sacrality of death. That this was accomplished for Troy's sister is evocative, allowing the shared humanity of dying to resonate across time to those unknown and unnamed who primarily died—when there was no war or types of collectively experienced crises—within the home environment. Reassuringly for Troy, his family, and friends, was that his sister's passing did take place in the home, an environment often accepted by thanatologists as important for experiencing a good death. Unlike Steve, Troy made mention of other religious ideas like that from the "Baha'i" faith even though this was not his declared belief system. In the home hospice environment of his sister's passing, Troy recounted how the mourning ritual of washing the body, preparing it with oils, and wrapping it in a shroud before burial spiritually inspired him, transforming his "entire feeling about death because of the way she died: she basically at some point refused chemo after a while of battling cancer." For Troy, death was social and collective, orbiting around "family" as can be seen in his canvas. Troy's inspiration for participating in death talk also included emphatic critique with the word "really":

> And when she did pass, it was very graceful. They were all there, her *family* was there, her friends. The *Baha'i* people don't embalm. They use oils and wrap the body. The whole thing, you know, you talk about why hide it—it was *really* the first time I became aware of how American culture particularly hides death. And that was just revelatory... I still have a lot of fear about it, as you do [gesturing to Steve]; I don't want to have that fear.

By all accounts, among all of our participants, Troy had lost the most loved ones. As Café participant, Troy is also one of the few to have conveyed the warmth of the home hospice, noting how he was able to communicate with his sister in the weeks leading up to her death, even bringing his daughter to communicate with her. To what extent this promoted quality of life for his sister remains unknown. I am of the opinion that it likely did not detract from it.

The Wordle canvas of all participants' dialog in DC2 (Fig. 4.12) reveals, like DC1, that the processes, themes, symbolisms, and imminence of death are conceptualized within the context of being with people.

February 18, 2014: Wordle Canvases and Discussion for DC3

The setting for the February 18, 2014 Death Café was a restaurant with outdoor dining in a quiet suburb north of downtown Los Angeles. A small park lay across the street, filled with parents and their children. The small group met at a coffee shop late in the afternoon before relocating to the aforementioned diner. The context is a suburb about 20 miles northeast of

Fig. 4.13   Betsy's comments (Betsy is event facilitator) (February 18, 2014)

Fig. 4.14   Kaylee's comments (February 18, 2014)

Fig. 4.15 Renna's comments (February 18, 2014)

Fig. 4.16 Rosie's comments (February 18, 2014)

downtown Los Angeles. Four attendees were present: Kaylee, Renna, Rosie, and Betsy.

Like in many previous Wordle outputs of our Café participants, the word "just" found large and frequent textual exposition during DC3 as an adverb, idiomatic expression, and occasional adjective. Again "just" is an indispensible word for conveying precise emphases of conviction during death talk.

Fig. 4.17   All attendees' comments (February 18, 2014)

All participants at DC3, including facilitator Betsy, employed the word. The Wordle exposition of the word "just" found similarity in quaternary sizes across all DC3's participants. In Kaylee's case the word found its largest textual exposition (Fig. 4.14). Employed to articulate her view of the human condition at a time when she was experiencing the loss of her ex-husband, she poignantly notes:

> We know it's going to come. We know we're going to lose each other—we're all going to go. And you think you have an idea for how that will be but when it actually happens, it seems as if everything is so totally different and there's *just* no way that you can prepare. I mean I'm thinking that I have all this figured out on how I'm going to be when I die. I have to insist on it *just* to be present.

The capacity for "just" to allow beliefs to be emphatically felt and precisely described can be seen in Rosie's Wordle canvas. Figure 4.16 shows how "just" is employed in a manner that includes Rosie's account when she had her first graveyard encounter with the reality of death:

> Like I was telling Kaylee and Jack I've been interested in death since I was very young. And it kind of started at maybe six when I asked my mom to take me to a local graveyard because I was curious about it. While I was there I came across a grave of a boy who was about my age when he died so that was for me

really shocking and kind of traumatic. I can still remember *just* crying and being horrified realizing that I would die someday—and that someday could be at anytime. My mom didn't know what to say so she took me home and put me in front of a movie, the *Jungle Book*. I *just* remember no one ever knowing how to talk to me about it. So that kind of became something I became preoccupied with but also repressed because there was no one to talk to.

Both Kaylee and Rosie employ the adverb "really" frequently, a trend we shall see in many upcoming Wordle outputs of other Café participants. The rather consistent presence of "really" in many Wordle outputs highlights how Café participants are emphatic yet critical in their personal view of society—how it approaches mortality issues, and how it makes sense of their experiences. The use of "really" points again to our participants' search for authenticity—search for authenticity as they attempt—as they attempt to frame the death experience. For example, Rosie recalled how her parents shielded her from knowledge of her childhood friend's death. For Rosie, it was "*really* bizarre" in how "they made that decision on my behalf." A telling example can also be seen in Rosie's use of the word to emphasize her social critique while "just" is again employed to be emphatic in the sentence: "I've always noticed that for movies...like those slasher films where someone is killed, none of the friends care, *really*. They're *just* more afraid of their own death. So death becomes its own spectacle and we're supposed to get pleasure from this when you watch."

Other than the sometimes idiomatic use of "know," this frequently employed word suggests a desire to be informed about mortality. It can also point to the converse: how one can consciously be delinked from mortality. Regarding her 8-year-old son, Renna brings this point home in her discussion of wars, of which the word can be seen in her Wordle canvas (Fig. 4.15):

And the boys, they love shooting, fighting *wars*. I don't extrapolate that as them genuinely wanting to hurt anyone. They don't *know* the reality of that; it's a play thing for them at this point. But I mean people get bored and *war* is a relief from boredom. And I think people do get sucked into it, I think in America especially. We're so insulated from the rest of the world, so insulated from reality.

Renna cautions about people in a somewhat more somber light, however, noting how the truth about death and dying "can be manipulated in very dark and cynical ways by people who should *know* better in our society." Kaylee employed the term to remind fellow attendees that the notion of knowing includes its opposite, as in not being able to convey the vulnerable moments of a person in grief: "I think that's the dilemma—we don't *know* what we can do or say. And sometimes we say things that are inappropriate just to say something... It's because the silence is awkward. So to get comfortable with not being able to speak about the matter is the key."

Renna's Wordle canvas thus includes the word "war," italicized in the above block quote, as a rather large textual exposition as a quaternary term. Her concerns toward mortality accommodate how geopolitical conflicts, influenced by technology, shape our views on death and dying. Renna's orientation echoes the critiques of techno-medicine voiced by remaining Café attendees whose views we will later explore. Citing the dangers of recreationalizing war through videogames, she also implies that increasing technology for human use may mean "more deadly weapons," a justified concern given how the state often expropriates and frames collective death as sacrifice for the nation. This observation is not to be taken lightly. Indeed, from personal experience having hailed from Laos and Thailand, sites my parents relocated to after leaving South Vietnam due to the Vietnam conflict (mother) and the Japanese seaboard occupation of China, and later the Chinese Civil War (father), it is rather clear that the state desires to render epic mass deaths as but having one purpose: to die for country. Mass and epic deaths are genres of nationalist struggles and narratives, a point not addressed by many of our Café participants. Renna thus appropriately brings into the discussion a topic that should remind us how Death Cafés are actually privileged gatherings, gatherings that cannot possibly occur under systemic crisis or totalitarianism:

> Well technology makes it all possible. And videogames were developed by the military. In my background, I wrote on analyzing novels and theorizing on aesthetics, fascism and war in literature So I did some research on *war* history. The videogames are interesting. They were developed by the military. The shooter games come out of this. It's not a generally known thing but there is documentation. The trouble with *war* is that people get bored and there's a tendency for sociopaths to run things in our society especially where power and vast sums of money are at stake.

The emphasis of "people" is again apparent for the Wordle canvas that contains all DC3 participants' transcriptions (Fig. 4.17). Like previous Death Cafés, mortality is contextualized within community and between its interacting members. With the exception of Kaylee's Wordle canvas, "people" was emphasized by our other three participants, Betsy included. Although "people" found textual exposition in Kaylee's Wordle canvas, its smaller size reflects how Kaylee's orientation at the Death Café was one shaped by familial crises. For example, the textual exposition of "Mike" refers to Kaylee's ex-husband who passed away not long before her Death Café attendance. Experientials about family travails thus punctuated her dialog and, at the time, framed her attitude on mortality in ways that were comparatively more insular than Betsy, Renna, and Rosie's views. Death can thus be treated through paeans for a shared humanity or conceptualized as a nihilistic ambush that has claimed yet another life.

April 22, 2014: Wordle Canvases and Discussion for DC4

The April 22, 2014 Death Café took place inside a home that was made open to the public. Beginning at dusk during a warm Southern California spring, it welcomed a popular Los Angeles news anchor who expressed her interest in the Death Café. "Lia" and her film crew filmed the Death Café interaction that evening, with footage ultimately presented on the news a few weeks later. Nine attendees, including Betsy, participated in discussions. Lia's two-member film crew did not participate in the discussions. The context is a suburb approximately 15 miles northeast of downtown Los Angeles. Nine attendees were present: Carla, Chap, Kelly, Lia, Reese, Ricardo, Sarah, Tim, and Betsy.

Fig. 4.18   Betsy's comments (Betsy is event facilitator) (April 22, 2014)

Fig. 4.19   Carla's comments (April 22, 2014)

Fig. 4.20   Chap's comments (April 22, 2014)

DC4 was comparatively larger and more dynamic in attendance. With her two-person camera crew, Lia began the evening by first interviewing Betsy, querying her about her views on mortality and the Death Café project. Conceding that she probably belonged to that segment of the population that views death themes with discomfort, Lia asked, "Well it seems like if I were to see something on Facebook like the Death Café I

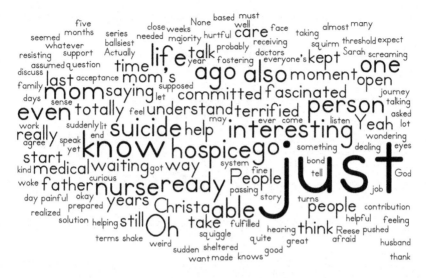

Fig. 4.21 Kelly's comments (April 22, 2014)

Fig. 4.22 Lia's comments (April 22, 2014)

Fig. 4.23   Reese's comments (April 22, 2014)

Fig. 4.24   Ricardo's comments (April 22, 2014)

Fig. 4.25 Sarah's comments (April 22, 2014)

Fig. 4.26 Tim's comments (April 22, 2014)

would never put your face [gesturing to Betsy] on it because you think about Goth, darkness. After all, we are talking about death. But is it because I am one of these US people that, you know, am afraid of it so it's dark to me? I mean is my view typical?" Later in the evening, Lia's question was answered by Ricardo, who noted how "beautiful" death talk can be for providing a deeper understanding of the sacrality of death, as evinced in his Wordle canvas (Fig. 4.24). His sentiments, "in our culture I don't think this discussion is had enough and it's really nice that this discussion is happening" and how it's "a really *beautiful* transition toward

Fig. 4.27   All attendees' comments (April 22, 2014)

talking about death and there's nothing to be afraid of" also embody such an orientation.

Sarah, a physician, added to the discussion by drawing inspiration from her hospice work: "That is what I saw as *beautiful* in a hospice experience, It's hard to describe to people the *beauty* of patients, you just see this glow about them. It's truly *beautiful*. And so that is the part that people who don't experience it will never know, and they will not know that there is incredible *beauty* within death" (also see Fig. 4.25). She poignantly conveyed the end-of-life experiences of her patients, noting that "it's as if the physical body is falling away and you can see their soul shining through." Perhaps more explicitly than any Café attendee, Sarah makes death functional for life and living because many of us will never "know" when our lives will end: "…from doing this hospice work, that's one of the lessons that came through to me about life and death in general. And still having the feeling of surrender and letting go because if I stay conscious the fact is at all times I don't *know* when I will die."

Although the words "really," "just," and "know" have been discussed previously, "know" will be revisited again in this section's discussion because many participants gave the word large textual expositions across our Wordle outputs, beyond its often idiomatic use.

In all its guises at DC4, the word "know" was epistemic in attempting to address the complex renderings of a potential soul and/or the possibility of an afterlife. For example, Chap expressed his interest in Tim's near-death experience (NDE): "Tim, what you said about the near death or death experience to me is really fascinating because from the concepts I believe in you *know* there's the separation of the soul and the body. So like in your case, what do you think is left? The soul or the body? And what came back?" (see Chap and Tim's Wordle canvases seen in Figs. 4.20 and 4.26, respectively). Tim replied:

> So my experience: the body did stop. I lost all my physical capacity. I couldn't move, I couldn't hear, I couldn't see. So, there was a separation from the body but there was still consciousness. I realized I couldn't do anything about what was happening and tried my best to resist the fact that I literally said to myself, "You're dying!" I finally had to let go because I was trying to hold on but I couldn't hold onto anything because I was all gone—couldn't see, couldn't hear, couldn't move so I had no capacity to hold on but there was still my interior going on saying, "Well you still can hold onto something, some DNA thing you can hold onto, some nerves or something" but I couldn't. And when I finally literally "died," then my consciousness and I went on the journey, and the shift of consciousness went from a "Tim" consciousness to a long journey into just consciousness. And what I would say from this is this was the journey of the soul and there was the unity of that with a sort of larger, whole consciousness, which was miraculous, spectacular.

Reese's epistemology on mortality also points to how some Café attendees are fully aware of their shared humanity on death and dying. Indeed, to "know" some feature of mortality was a popular theme for the evening. Although Reese appeared to be culturally aware that social differences are but referential, she drew rich cues from them to underscore how different peoples of the world "know" how to make operative their own death and dying themes. As one who studied with shamans in South America, Reese's experientials also blur the distinction between the metaphysical and physical, a process sometimes undertaken by Carla as well. In Reese's Wordle display, the presence of "spirit" becomes linked to epistemology: "You *know* with the shamans there is a common use of plant medicines, to take you to that *spirit* realm, to feel the soul leaving from the body. So there are ways and techniques on the planet that 'loosens' the soul from the body.

You can have an experience and because it's not your time, you come back" (Fig. 4.23). For many DC4 participants, experience is existence in the physical *and* metaphysical. The importance of "experience" thus found textual exposition in Reese's Wordle canvas. Carla, a psychic medium, follows up with further insight on the afterlife: "You *know* having those affirmations with the *spirit* world really does impact us and affect us. And we can heal what we have seen through stuff. I believe that many of us have had some type of *experience* with something from the other side and it doesn't end with death. I think this is a huge lesson" (Fig. 4.19). Kelly, however, was less certain when she responded to her dying mom's query about the soul and the afterlife: "I don't *know*. No one *knows*. None of us understands it" (Fig. 4.21).

Tim, a survivor of trauma that resulted in an NDE, was categorical in believing in something beyond death: "I'm not sure of the others here but I *know* from my experience that death is not the end of anything." Indeed, Tim's NDE was often referenced by participants of the event for its ability to be a highly formative yet transcendent episode of existence. "Experience" found textual exposition in both Tim and Reese's Wordle canvases. Reese's immersion in shamanistic practices allowed her existential awareness to transcend materiality, not unlike Tim's NDE if one were to believe in the simulacrum of alternative existences offered by psychotropics. Whereas many of DC4s Café participants attended to themes of mortality by observation and/or loss, Tim and Reese are firmly convinced that they had experienced something beyond on a first-person basis. The metaphysically transformative experience for both had their subtle differences, however. The Wordle canvas for both participants shows that Reese's connection to the metaphysical through the "spirit" world was comparable to Tim's ascription of an elevated level of "consciousness," inspired by the latter's NDE experience.

The use of the word "think" can almost always be seen interchangeably with "feel" in that both set up similar validity claims and opinions. For example, Ricardo observes how our culture is bereft of death talk and notes his appreciation for Death Café venues: "And in our culture I don't *think* this discussion is had enough and I *think* it's a discussion that shows talking about death is nothing to be afraid of." With both Reese and Ricardo approaching mortality and beyond from their shamanistic practices and worldviews, Carla adds to the narrative when she notes: " . . . I *think* that's what is so interesting to me is the people that I have brought through with their family, and they always talk about death as such a beautiful thing. And one of the things that most of them are grateful for is their family letting go."

Figure 4.27 reveals the Wordle output of all transcriptions from DC4 participants. Like previous totalized Wordle outputs of the entirety of each Café event "people" again was the most frequently emphasized theme in DC4. Interestingly, Lia, our news anchor, exhibited a Wordle canvas that paralleled the canvases of her fellow participants as it gave pride of place to "people" as well (Fig. 4.22). Although the word "people" existed in Kelly's Wordle canvas, it was much smaller in size since her accounts were primarily inspired and informed by her father's passing. The emphasis of "people," the need to "know," and the emphasis of exactness and precision via "just" (most emphatically employed by Kelly) points to how DC4 participants viewed mortality as a social, communal experience, but one where social critique about "people" who are not mindful were launched as well. Unlike other Death Cafés, DC4 participants include the voices of those who were certain they glimpsed the afterlife in some iteration, as in Tim's NDE, or in the case of Reese where her approach toward the liminality of consciousness was informed by the use of indigenously sacralized and non-recreational use of psychotropics.

May 22, 2014: Wordle Canvases and Discussion for DC5

The May 22, 2014 Death Café saw 10 attendees: Corrine, Helen, Irene, Lanay, Leonard, Lorraine, Naomi, Scott, and Warren, including facilitator Lisa S. Delong, participate in discussions. It was held at a small community center that was made open to the public. The event began in the early and warm evening. This venue is approximately 25 miles northeast of downtown Los Angeles.

Like DC4, DC5 was also an epistemic gathering. Hosted by Lisa S. Delong, the evening's discourse, more so than other Death Cafés, veered into engagements with the supernatural. The word "know" once again finds primary to quaternary exposition in every attendee's Wordle canvas. When in idiomatic use to pause and give emphasis to a statement—frequently employed to ground listeners into the intensity of the discourse—the word "know" frequently pointed to our participants' desire to accent their life struggles, grief, mourning, and/or loss. The pain compelled among them memories and contemplations that also articulated their desires for answers to life and death's mysteries. Although at DC5 the idiomatic use of "know" was persistent (and for grammar purists annoying), the topic of death and dying, when framed by recent loss, compels or behooves the search for some kind of certainty through worldviews, a dynamic exhibited at DC5's free-flowing communicative environment.

Fig. 4.28   Lisa's comments (Lisa is event facilitator) (May 22, 2014)

Fig. 4.29   Corrine's comments (May 22, 2014)

Fig. 4.30 Hera's comments (May 22, 2014)

Fig. 4.31 Irene's comments (May 22, 2014)

Fig. 4.32   Lanay's comments (May 22, 2014)

Fig. 4.33   Leonard's comments (May 22, 2014)

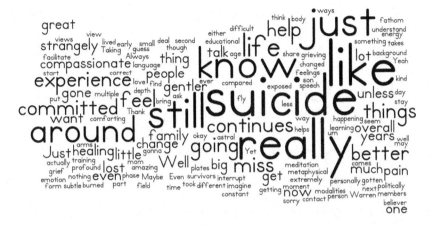

Fig. 4.34 Lorraine's comments (May 22, 2014)

Fig. 4.35 Naomi's comments (May 22, 2014)

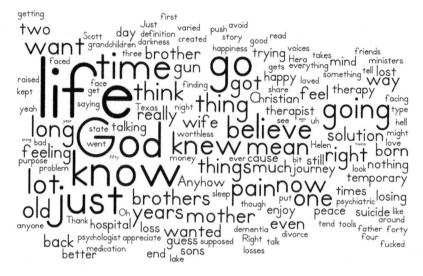

Fig. 4.36   Scott's comments (May 22, 2014)

Fig. 4.37   Warren's comments (May 22, 2014)

Fig. 4.38   All attendees' comments (May 22, 2014)

An emblematic use of "know" can be seen in Scott's (Fig. 4.36) raw assessment of "life," two themes that appear in Wordle expositions of many participants' canvases (see Figs. 4.28, 4.30, 4.32–4.34, and 4.36). However, only Scott's dialog displayed the theme of "life" larger (and thus, more frequently referenced) than "know." In one soliloquy, Scott established solidarity with fellow attendee Leonard (Fig. 4.33) because both had almost acted out their suicide attempts. After aborting his suicide attempt, Scott confronted the human condition and happiness' place within it, employing "know" in uncertain and certain terms that appear to, nonetheless, take Scott toward some important epiphanies:

And I was at your "lake" too (gesturing to Leonard who had driven to lake to attempt suicide). Not the same lake. But I was facing the end of a .38 caliber pistol one time back in 1988. I was going to end it all. Yeah. But what kept me from doing it was the thought of my mother who's about eighty years old that time, and my sons finding out their father blew his brains out because he was losing a few million dollars in investments. And I said, I can't do that to them. I love them too much. I'm not worth their suffering over. I am nothing. That's how I felt. I'm nobody. I fucked up my business, I fucked up my marriage, and I'm worthless, but they don't see me as that. I am their father and my mother would probably die from a heart attack if she knew I committed suicide because she raised me to be tougher than that. She was a tough woman. She went through a lot of hell. So I kept going, not because I wanted to, but because I feel I had to because I didn't want to cause pain to those I loved.

I got through it, but it was a slow process. I was on medication for a long time. Thank God for the medication. I was seeing a therapist every day for about three months; I'd see a psychiatrist. And I also signed myself into a mental institution after I attempted to end my *life*. I *knew*. I took my own cocked gun and put it down. I said something's wrong with me . . . at that time my wife was trying to get me to go to a therapist for a long time but I refused to. She saw the signs of my gradual withdrawal from *life* because I was losing all this money on this investment in Texas. And I was in a comatose state almost, a catatonic state, an even better description I guess. All I had to do was look out the window after getting a report from my manager in Texas about how much money we lost this past week and I just would obsess over how I'm going to kill myself. I didn't want anyone to find me, though. I just want to go up to the mountains somewhere to put a bullet in my mouth or push my accelerator down to go off the side. So, just weird stuff. But I *knew* when I finally faced the gun I couldn't go through with it.

But I don't *know*. I now do value *life* very much and one of the things I've noticed, growing since 1988, introspectively at first, is that I appreciate and am grateful for every day of my life. My heart's beating, I'm relatively healthy, I think. And, um, a little bit obsessive, I know that.

Unlike other Wordle canvases seen at all other Death Cafés, Scott's canvas exhibits a large-sized "God." However, he was not sloganeering paeans for a faith, but more rather, struggling to understand how a non-personified and non-anthropomorphized being might allude to a life purpose.

My own search for *God* is, uh, I do believe there may be a *God*, or some type of prime mover that created everything. But this does not mean I necessarily have any involvement with it personally in my life any longer. That's called deism, I guess: You believe that there's some power that created everything, but is not involved with the operation of it after all. I don't believe in a Christian *God*, I was raised that way though. I was a born-again Christian and me and my brothers were Christian and all this. I still have several uncles now that are ministers. I really fight with the *God* thing. So I do think there could be a *God* according to my definition. Not the *God* of the Bible, hell no. But the point is, whatever you believe in, if it gets you through this journey intact, believe in it! If it helps you, do it. It's not hurting anyone else. But, again, life is a struggle. Now, I loved reading Scott Peck's *The Road Less Traveled* back in '88 after I got out of the funny farm. And his first line of the book is, "Life is difficult." And once you can accept that fact. . . .

At this juncture, acknowledgment must be given to Leonard's discussion of religious themes. Indeed, it was Leonard's account of religion framing a series of familial tragedies and economic duress in his life, along with the articulation of an epistemic "know" that inspired Scott to share the aforementioned account. Leonard notes:

> So, it's tough enough to deal with the loss of a loved one but when your life basically falls apart around you, you don't even like the life you have anymore. And so I've been kind of working through that whole process. I talked about suicide for three days the last part of April. One night I decided I was going to try to kill myself and I wound up parked up at a cliff there by Lake Castaic thinking about just driving off.

To which Lorraine urgently interjected: "What stopped you? What happened?!"

> My wife and my kids. It would've never been fair to them. I mean I believe I still have faith in Christianity and *God*, but I tell you what, I've been screaming at *God* a lot lately. My wife's been screaming at *God* a lot lately. Organized religion doesn't really have a place in our lives anymore right now. So, I drove back from the cliff and went home that night.
>
> You've got to be pretty depressed to attempt suicide, which I was. Um, I'm happy to say I'm a lot farther along than I was eight weeks ago or however long ago that was. So, you *know*, there are the metaphysics. I mean I talked to a nurse in one of the units. You *know*, she kind of mixes Christianity up with metaphysics, which I thought was an interesting conversation that night. I've taught for our church school system for twenty-six years and that Church is like my life, including my job. And I've been the principal the last sixteen years. Last year I was wondering what's going on because something's not working like it use to.
>
> So, yeah, Church was my life. It was interesting. Part of our religion class was we always have the students go out and research other religions. So one day we went to the Hindu temple out there in Malibu Canyon. And we also went to a Buddhist temple. And I got to say if I was going to choose between the two of them, the Buddhist thing seems to be a lot easier way to go. (~) I'm not kidding, these guys got it down pretty simple! Life is pretty much this! (~) Hindu: it just depends on who you screwed up to. Whether it was adultery or whether you ate too much or whatever it was, that was the deity or the god that you had to go and talk to and give some food to and you *know*, to appease or whatever. It just seemed like a whole lot of work—too much work. The Buddhists seem to have a pretty simple down path.

Combining its idiomatic and action usage to point to epistemic awareness, Naomi employs "know" (Fig. 4.35) to convey her frustrations about people who lack a deeper understanding of mortality, noting that "I'm going through a big grieving process now. It is so lonely. People don't *know*. They think I will think 'Okay! It's been enough time, let's move on now!'" Recounting how she had to cope with the loss of her son, Naomi notes:

> Six months ago or so I saw a medium because I felt like I needed to touch base with my son, even though I was with him when he died at home. I still felt like I wasn't ready, as we had much unfinished business, you *know*. And all of a sudden he's dead. You go, "Oh my god, I didn't say this, I didn't say that." So I went to this woman who's amazing and my son came through. I mean, I *know* it was him and she did it through automatic writing. And there were things that he said that she was writing and she did not *know* me. She did not *know* anything about me except that my name was Naomi. She said, "Come on in," you *know*, and "How do you do?" and immediately she said, "I'm worried about Shannon." Well, Shannon's my granddaughter. Why would she *know* that? And my son proceeded to say, you *know*, "she's lost me and now she's losing you" because there are some issues between me and my daughter-in-law. So my son needed to talk to me.

When an idiomatic employment of "know" was amalgamated with its ability to ensure some semblance of certainty about mortality in all its iterations, the word was incisive, purposeful, and profound. Hera's Wordle canvas (Fig. 4.30) contains the largest sized "know" of DC5. However, we must allow her to first build her confrontation with death to understand her search about some certainty regarding mortality:

> My son had a medical patch and he just fell asleep and didn't wake up. And I found him three days afterwards. And I use to work with him so he didn't come to work and I decided to check up on his apartment and I saw three days worth of newspapers and I *knew* there was something wrong. But I never got to see him. I'm from the Jewish faith—let's just say originally, because I don't practice it now. But we bury our dead within twenty-four hours. It's our tradition. I never saw in my entire life a dead body until I saw my husband. And he died in a hospital. And I never got the chance to say goodbye. I'm hearing how wonderful it must have been to be with someone at that point in death. But what I'm trying to say is that we've always had a tradition in our family, ever since the kids were very little, that no matter what, no matter if we had a fight, that we always said "I love you." And my son's last words was, "I love you" on the phone and "See you at work" and so it's about

love. Why do we grieve so much? Because we love so much. And I guess some people say, "The more you love, the more you bleed," you *know*? But isn't that what it's basically all about? It's about the love.

Hera's crescendo to Café listeners follows:

But I don't think society is geared for that unless they really go through it. They don't *know* what to say or they'll say things they think are good for them. I'm sorry. I *know* probably there's some religious people here but people would say to me, "He's in a good place." And I want to say "Sorry, but no he's not," you *know*, and they were religious and I respect their religious beliefs, but, you can't say that to someone. I thought, why say that to me when you don't *know* me? You haven't lost a child. Why would you even say that? Even if I were religious, I couldn't even see myself saying that to somebody. So, I get that part where our society is not equipped. They don't *know* what to say.

Leonard echoes Hera's certainty and employs "know" definitively: "Whether we lose another loved one or whether we hit the lottery, *know* that happiness doesn't come from the outside. Happiness comes from right here [gesturing to his heart]."

The word "life" found frequent expression and exhibited many different nuances when conveyed by DC5 attendees, finding prominent places in Lisa, Hera, Lanay, Leonard, Lorraine, and Scott's Wordle canvases (Figs. 4.28, 4.30, 4.32–4.34, and 4.36, respectively). One of the evening's most intense accounts of confronting death and dying was found in Leonard, the aforementioned attendee that aborted his suicide attempt. After relaying to Café participants his account, Scott immediately conveyed his support to Leonard, noting how "there's a lot of your story—your autobiography—that really resonates with my *life*." Leonard's sentiments on life (indeed, much of the sentiments on life from the aforementioned DC5 participants) embodies the quintessential function of the Death Café itself: to confront death and dying for the sake of living well. In Scott's case, the theme of "life" is the largest word in his Wordle canvas.

I had three brothers one time and we all were in theological circles. I mean, two brothers were ministers and all four of us, still, had a thing about finding purpose and meaning in *life*. And I'm not going to spew forth my philosophy too much except there is no purpose in *life* other than what you make it out to be, is my belief. But, as long as you're here and you decide to stay on the pathway of this journey from womb to tomb, by God, you better enjoy it! Why stick around if you don't enjoy *life*?

For Scott, the process of life and living had to be informed by their contradictions: "I also signed myself into a mental institution after I attempted to end my *life*. I knew. I took my own cocked gun and put it down. I said something's wrong with me. My wife was trying to get me to go to a therapist for a long time but I refused to. She saw the signs of my gradual withdrawal from *life*. I knew when I finally faced the gun I couldn't go through with it." Scott's partner, Hera whose former husband died, discerned another nuance of life and living: "*Life* is difficult no matter where you live or how you live your *life*. There are things that will happen. None of us here have been immune to tragedy. I mean, some have it worse than others, but even that's a relative term." She continues by expounding her philosophy on living through dying:

Every day is a *life* that I walk away from the deaths of my husband and my son. They're not here to live but I am and I can live my *life* as much as I can. That's my journey. That's what I have gotten out of it, you know? I think that every time I think about it and people say to me, "How do you do it?" and "You've been through so much" and, you know what? We all go through tough times even without death. You know, maybe because there's this mystique about dying, that it's final and that's it! Maybe to a lot of people here, who think that's what it is and that's fine but, you know, I just live *life* a different way and carry them here [gesturing to her heart], not far away at all.

Lisa, the facilitator of DC5, employed the theme of life in a social critique of television and its tendency to distort death and dying. She lamented on how television warp one's capacity to understand the truth of mortality and makes the validity claim that "All we have is television, especially for nineteen year olds. You see a lot of reality TV and you have a lot of imagery that fictionalizes death over and over and over again... the most exemplary thing they have in *life* is what they see on television."

In contrast to other DC5 attendees, Lorraine—as a response to others hearing and commenting on Corrine's confrontation with death, a Café participant who lost her daughter to suicide—forwarded the need to sensitize the act of suicide by employing "gentler" language: "So, the politically correct way to talk about suicide is to say the person either 'died by suicide,' 'died of suicide,' or 'died from suicide,' or 'they took their own *life*.' Not that they 'committed' suicide. And it's amazing how that takes some of the energy off it when you don't say 'committed.'"

The theme of life was frequently referenced with the aid of "like" and "just" in their modifier and idiomatic use. As alluded to elsewhere in this work, a shared humanity view on mortality allows for such words to have tremendous personal significance. To be able to share the same contours of sensibilities about death and dying often activates the use of "like," as in Naomi's view on familial relations: "But when you're with your family, *like* my family, they don't know what to say. And sometimes, I don't want them to say anything." Similarly, Hera's frustration of certain communicative dynamics in society can be seen in the statement, "And I think that's indicative of what our society is *like*." The frequent search for and emphasis of certainty prompts the employment of "just." Warren's message is an example: "Really, you know, a grave, by nature, is any property that is only a place to remember. A memorial can be at a place like mine or a memorial can be in your bedroom, even a picture. It *just* serves as a place for you to remember a person."

Corrine's loss of her daughter to suicide represented the antipode to those who had chosen to live following their suicide attempts (as in Scott and Leonard's accounts). Still in the process of grieving, Corrine's use of the word "daughter" found prominent exposition in her Wordle canvas (Fig. 4.29). Indeed, during communicative action, Corrine's accounts on mortality were shaped by her reference to her daughter's life and death, one which was symbolically and viscerally felt by her mother. Corrine recounts how sometimes she too felt the need to join her daughter, noting that, "I always felt scared to die before my *daughter* passed away, but now I can't wait. Like, I just want to hurry up. I pray every day, like, 'God, please take me, not that sick person in the hospital. No, please, take me today.' But I don't know. He keeps me here." This sentiment was in contrast to Irene's view of mortality as shaped and enhanced by people. A breast cancer survivor and a Café attendee who spoke the least at DC5, Irene poignantly recounts a "beautiful" experience at a recent funeral of a friend and notes how "family members came from, you know, hours away" to view the body, and it was "*beautiful. Beautiful*, like they made a shroud. They had musicians come in. And it was a... very *beautiful* experience."

The people context of death and dying was given much attention by Warren (Fig. 4.37). Although DC5 was the only Death Café where "people" did not exhibit a large textual exposition on many participants' Wordle outputs, Warren's views on mortality were shaped greatly by his role as a mortician, an occupation that mandates an intimate connection with people, specifically grieving families. Indeed, his ethos of being an ethical funeral director revealed his intimate connections with and observations of people who experience bereavement. Many of his accounts orbited around people experiencing long-term grief and mourning.

> While one person may seem to cope or deal with a loss differently than someone else, we learn that, or at least I believe, that either way is okay. We have *people* that visit my location literally every single day to see a spouse that's in our care, every single day. And when we have conversations with some *people* it may seem like the occurrence just happened last week when it's already been like five or six years. Some *people* have books that take a little bit longer to get to that next chapter.

Warren continues, "some *people* don't want to shake my hand because I'm a mortician. But nevertheless, it's a chosen profession. I went to college to be a banker, an investor, maybe on Wall Street. But somehow I fell into this particular profession." He then critiques the medical profession and doctors "because a lot of them are very skilled in their craft and their art and being fantastic at saving lives, but they're just not social. Their bedside manners are not the greatest so they have to learn the technical. Same with any profession, you can study to get the licenses provided by the state of California but you can't be taught, like we're saying, the compassion."

DC5 included many attendees that have had acute encounters with death. From a cancer survivor to two who tried to die by suicide, to wives who lost their spouses, to mothers who lost their children to suicide or illness, the key theme of "know" reflected an urgency to find meaning and understanding in life (Fig. 4.38). Combined with its frequent idiomatic use, it is not surprising that "know" exhibits the largest textual exposition when all participants' comments were inputted into Wordle for analysis. DC5 participants' life histories, in this instance filled with greater degrees of tragedies experienced by attendees, resulted in a Death Café with greater bonding, clarity, and certainties about why and how to live in spite of ongoing pain experienced by many members. Mortality was transformed into a relational phenomenon in DC5, one based on stranger-to-stranger solidarity, support, and empathy toward the loss of loved ones, to those who tried to die. Although in this rare instance where a Death Café did not have "people" dominate the Wordle canvas, DC5 nonetheless revealed the intensity of epistemic and ontologic energies driving its communicative action.

May 10 and July 16, 2015 Death Cafés (DC6 and DC7)

Our last two Death Cafés have been combined for discussion due to their online orientation. The Death Cafés were conducted through Dr. Karen Wyatt's End of Life University (EOLU). Karen graciously offered me access to two events where she facilitated discussions, one of which was an online Death Café gathering on Mother's Day, May 10, 2015 (DC6) while the other, a July 16, 2015 (DC7) interview of Jon Underwood, focused on the rise of the Death Café movement in London and the United Kingdom.

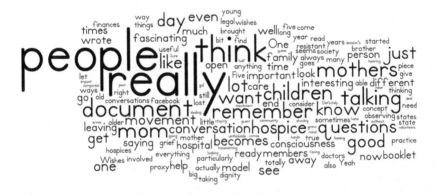

Fig. 4.39 Karen's DC6 comments (Karen is event facilitator) (May 10, 2015)

DC6 took place on May 10, 2015, Mother's Day. Karen creatively oriented the Death Café thematically, specifically for those who lost their mothers as well as those who are mothers but had lost their children. Attendees called in and the discussion was facilitated in a conference call format. Five attendees: Joan, Liz, Molly, and Karen participated in discussions while Kathy attended as a listener. In DC7, Karen Wyatt interviews Jon Underwood, again through her online Death Café portal.

Fig. 4.40   Joan's comments (May 10, 2015)

Fig. 4.41   Liz's comments (May 10, 2015)

Some noteworthy Wordle textual expositions have been derived from DC6. For example, although DC6 was held on Mother's Day, dedications to fathers also took place as in the case of Liz (Fig. 4.41). Liz's father's passing was a formative experience for her family. She recounted how her

Fig. 4.42 Molly's comments (May 10, 2015)

Fig. 4.43 All attendees' comments (May 10, 2015)

"mom," and herself as a "mom", and how her "kids" responded to the loss of "dad," words that found much textual exposition in Liz's Wordle canvas. That "years" found large textual exposition in Liz's Wordle canvas points to her account of experiences and encounters related to familial mortality, one which spanned over 30 years. Moreover, the word "counseling" in Liz's Wordle canvas suggests how people—in Liz's case her children—attend to

Fig. 4.44   Karen's DC7 comments (Karen is event facilitator) (July 16, 2015)

Fig. 4.45   Jon's comments (July 16, 2015)

mortality anxieties differently according to generation. Liz shares an anecdote about an interaction she had with her "daughter":

> One interesting thing that just came up recently was I had lost my *dad* when I was 10 and my brother at fourteen. And I thought my *mom* did a good job

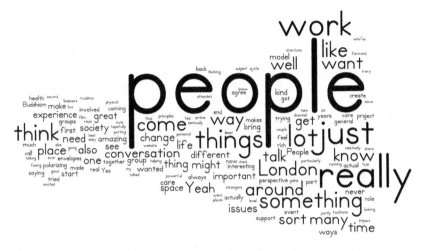

Fig. 4.46 All attendees' comments (July 16, 2015)

moving us on and you know, we've always kept *dad* in our memory and all that stuff. Well, anyway, moving on a few years: my husband passed away when my *kids* were 11 and 14, and so I kind of, you know, took the cues from my *mom* and whatever, and we moved on and kept *dad* in our memories. But this was 30 years ago. There weren't support groups, grief groups—all that good stuff—and I thought we did a pretty good job. But last weekend I was up with my *daughter*—who is now turning 40, and that's the age that my *dad* and her *dad* died. So she's approaching 40 now and she says to me, "*Mom*, how come you never sent us to *counseling*?" (~) I thought, "Wow!" Thirty years later and you're going to hit me with this? I don't think we had, like, grief counselors. "But there are counselors for everything!" and I said, "Yes, but for marriage, family, and maybe cancer deaths, but not sudden death!" you know. That was different. It wasn't something where you get a chance to say, "Bye *dad* I love you!" and all that good stuff. This was a sudden heart attack!

The incredulity surrounding some confrontations with death often blurs the distinctions between different nuances of dying. How one can prepare for an unprepared death is one of the least discussed trajectories in our life cycle, with Liz being the primary participant that makes visible such kinds of dying. She intimates whether one can ever be "ready" for an unannounced passing of the self or of loved ones. During the interaction, Joan relayed an account of a dying child in a hospital setting who innocently felt that it was her time, that she's "ready to go" and that her mother is "going to come get me and I'm ready to go" adds yet another context to dying, one framed by one's life chronology. As such, Wordle generated a large textual exposition of the word on Joan's canvas (Fig. 4.40).

For DC7, the unique exposition of the word "London" in Jon Underwood's Wordle canvas points to his Death Café activities in the city, one which will later have much implication for our discussion of Habermas' notion of the public sphere and Oldenburg's notion of the third place. One of the more compelling attributes of the existence of Death Cafés is that it is primarily an urban phenomenon replete with opportunities to confront death, as in settings like hospitals as earlier illuminated by Joan. At the very least, its emergence in Paris, London, across major cities in the United States and the world makes it very much part of a death system for urban angst. Urban life is indeed replete with hyper scheduling and intense stimuli and stressors. That Death Cafés are almost always urban phenomena might point to a new need for not just community but communities that are oriented toward existence. Urban life, one that almost always requires immersion and interaction with strangers as Lofland notes in her classic *A World of Strangers* (1973), may be catalyzing the proliferation of Death Cafés as secularizing members of community seek a greater depth within it. Jon's mention of London as a context, along with previous and frequent mention by Betsy regarding the merits of conducting Death Cafés in Los Angeles, suggests there is fatigue in the material-driven urban human condition that is inspiring residents to seek something beyond their concrete experiences.

The word "people" had large expositions in DC6 and DC7, again pointing to the importance of a people-oriented articulation of death and dying or as a subject of critique. Both Karen and Molly's canvases (see Figs. 4.39 and 4.42, respectively) have similar-sized textual expositions for the primary "people" and the secondary "really." The word "think" figured prominently in their discourses as well, with Karen's Wordle canvas projecting the word as an approximately tertiary word while Molly projected an approximately quaternary-sized word. The DC6 manifestation of the word "think" points to how attendees are continuing their reflections on mortality. For Karen and Molly, the word "people" was employed during their observations of those who exhibited a variety of patterned behavior, some of which they critiqued while others they compassionately responded to. Both Molly and Karen frequently synchronized with each other in terms of sentiments on mortality and steered much of the dialog for DC6. For Karen, dying was a people-oriented experience: "It's such a good point that we always have to consider the perspective of other *people* involved in these events. While death is a solitary event that happens to each one of us, it has an impact on so many *people* around us and we need to consider all those perspectives." In a social critique, however, Karen was incisive in her concern about people being led astray:

> I have a big concern about the anti-ageing movement. It feels to me like that movement is enmeshed with a denial of death and dying. And while I don't mind the concept of staying as youthful for as long as you can, I worry a little bit that it's a disguise for believing that we won't die, we don't have to die, we don't have to get older, and I am worried that the movement is leading some *people* astray and keeping them from really looking at the truth and reality that will be facing them.

Molly's incisive observations of young people included concerns about their lack of depth in comprehending mortality:

> So earlier we were talking about the young *people* being open-minded, and in a way, the Millennials are open-minded about politics, and gayness, and then therefore death. And also they're young *people* and they like to skydive and ride motorcycles and drink too much. It's easier for them to have be thoughtful about death because they really don't get it at all as compared to *people* who are 60 and really realize that the depressiveness that comes with ageing.

A welcome incorporation of people beyond atmospheric musings, critique, and philosophy, Molly also notes how:

> Some of things that *people* don't really think about—and certainly advanced directives don't ask about—is the temperature in a room. Some *people* spend their whole lives feeling chilly and when they're in the ICU they'd really like it to be a lot warmer than the average hospital is, or some *people* have had a giant family and they really like noise and chaos and radios and TV and laughter. Some *people* just want it to be quiet.

Although "people" only found an approximate tertiary textual exposition in Joan's Wordle canvas (Fig. 4.40), the value in Joan's observation about people was through her ability to see irony in their behavior:

> I think it's kind of ironic that we're talking about—I mean—publicly and nationally we're having this conversation about death all the time in the form of watching *people* being killed. We're always in this news cycle about killings and yet somehow it never gets to the realities of death and dying for most of us.

Such prescient and insightful observations are why, according to Jon Underwood in DC7, members of the community appreciate the Death Café, "because *people* don't have that opportunity so much" to talk about death and dying, they thus "come to Death Café on their own volition because they want to talk about this," and "what they say is really rich. It's a kind of thing that makes me feel privileged to hear." "Really" is again primarily employed as an intensifier about death in all its iterations throughout DC6 and DC7.

Jon's prescience is also grounded in a "people" context as evinced by the word having the largest textual exposition in his Wordle canvas (Fig. 4.45). Aware that Death Cafés are emergent in an important period that can be envisioned as a materially rich yet existentially impoverished metaphysical experience, Jon nonetheless was humble in his rendering of the timing of Death Café emergence:

> It's not because we're doing anything phenomenally clever. It's because there's a real need for this. *People* want this at this time. It's interesting because the Natural Death Center which has been going for 25 years—in the 1980s they tried to establish something fairly similar—and it didn't fly. So I think there's something—it's partly the internet and it's partly where we're at as a planet.

He continues, "It feels like . . . riding a wave. But there's a load of *people* also being propelled along by it as well, so in some ways Death Cafés are catalyzing change and in some ways it's sort of being carried along by it, but it's a fantastic and an exhilarating journey, at least from my perspective."

Karen's activistic orientation toward death talk is evident in DC7, with use of "people" and "really" taking place frequently. In support of

Jon's orientations about the need for more death talk, Karen notes how she "wanted to mention for our listeners too that it's relatively easy to start a Death Café compared to other ventures people might take on because you really just need to find a place to meet and a way to get the word out to people." She continues about how "every Death Café I've heard about or hosts I've talked to have said *people* just show up. *People* just come. Maybe it's just 5 or 6 *people* the first time but gradually the group gains momentum and more *people* are attracted." Affirming Karen's view, emphasis on the *people*-oriented nature of mortality is further expanded by an activistic Jon: "It's very powerful work because death connects with so many issues and things both on a macro-level where you can talk about inequality yet having it impact *people* also on a personal level."

Finally, the Wordle outputs for all attendees' comments combined can be seen in Fig. 4.43 for DC6 and Fig. 4.46 for DC7. "People" again appears as the most important theme in the context of a death discourse. "Know" appears as an important word alongside "people" in Fig. 4.43 for DC6. Adverbial components of idiomatic expressions such as "just" and "really" orbit many of the primary words of "people" and "know," serving to intensify the gravity of both discourses from DC6 and DC7. However, the unique attribute of DC6 is that conveyances about the loss of a mom or parent—perhaps processed by too many as a personal loss—still end up being another vector that fosters community and social relations in spite of death.

Our final Wordle output (Fig. 4.47) is derived from the entirety of all dialog from all Death Cafés (DC1–DC7). Again, the key emphases of "people" and the need to "know," along with adverbial compo- nents, as well as, crucially, the tertiary textual exposition of "life," reveal key death themes important to the grass roots. "Think" also figures prominently in the final Wordle canvas as does "know," allow- ing for the abundance of epistemic iterations to surface during death talk at all of our Death Cafés. Our panoply of Death Café participants, perhaps more justifiably framed at this juncture as existential activists, have essentially reminded us that we as a community must be mindful and contemplative of mortality for the sake of living. Knowing death is a function of community and its peoples, the latter of which can be seen as an exponentially crucial component for comprehending the death of others and of their own.

Fig. 4.47   All attendees' comments from all Death Cafés (January 2014 to July 2015)

DEATH THEMES, VALIDITY CLAIMS, AND DISCOURSE RESPONSES

Nine themes that orbited mortality in different permutations were frequently invoked at our seven Death Cafés. Validity claims are crucial for understanding themes that people prefer to forward for discussion and/or debate for the purposes of strengthening convictions and securing affirmations about how to approach mortality.

Table 4.1 displays the nine death themes and their associated number of validity claims derived from all Death Cafés. The themes, from those most able to generate validity claims to the least, are (1) death as a means to socially critique society, (2) death as experienced by culture, (3) the possibility of an afterlife, (4) normativity about death, (5) how confronting death can bring us closer to truth, (6) the emancipatory aspect of dying, (7) the legalities of dying, (8) the anxieties associated with dying, and (9) how to cope with death.

Table 4.2 displays the same nine death themes ordered by the most to least number of discourse responses per theme, along with the type of activated discourse and whether the discourse is affirming or contesting.

Table 4.3 displays six Habermasian discourse response types, from most frequently to least frequently used: (1) the theoretical discourse which was activated on 24 occasions, (2) the moral discourse which was activated on six occasions, (3) the practical discourse which was activated on four occasions, (4) the ethical discourse which was activated on three occasions, and (5) the explicative and (6) therapeutic discourses, both of which exhibited one activation per discourse. The aesthetic and pragmatic discourses were not activated during our examination of death talk. Table 4.3 also displays how discourse responses were sometimes affirmative, that is, vindicating the validity claims made by the speaker, and sometimes contesting, that is, challenging or requesting greater clarification about validity claims deemed problematic by listeners.

Because death talk themes have few institutional avenues for candid disclosure in a colonized lifeworld, Death Café participants' enthusiasms resulted in conveyances about death and dying that combined attributes of mortality in unique ways. Sometimes, death and dying is seen as physical state + fear + fact while in other instances, death is conveyed as loss + mourning + coping, and still in other instances, death is approached as religion + afterlife + spirits to name but a few formulations exhibited by our attendees. We shall have more to say on this matter toward the conclusion of this chapter.

Table 4.1   Death themes and frequency of VCs from all Death Cafés (lowest to highest)

Nine death themes ranked by number of VCs per theme	No. of VC statements (lowest to highest)
1. Death as social critique	38
2. Death as cultural experience	33
3. Beyond death	17
4. Normativity of death	14
5. Death as authenticity/truth	14
6. Liberation in life and/or death	14
7. Legalities of death and dying	11
8. Anxiety and fear of death	10
9. Coping with death	8
Total VCs	159

VC: Validity claims

Mention must also be made about the validity claims that did not inspire a discourse response. Some speakers' validity claims were nested in relatively lengthy monologues. When such long monologues were

Table 4.2   Discourses per death theme from all Death Café events (highest to lowest)

Nine death themes ranked by discourses challenging VCs	Discourse response types and their frequencies per theme		No. of discourse response/s per death theme (high to low)
Beyond death	Moral affirming	$n = 1$	11
	Moral contesting	$n = 1$	
	Theoretical affirming	$n = 2$	
	Theoretical contesting	$n = 7$	
Death as cultural experience	Ethical contesting	$n = 1$	9
	Moral contesting	$n = 1$	
	Practical contesting	$n = 1$	
	Theoretical affirming	$n = 1$	
	Therapeutic contesting	$n = 1$	
	Practical affirming	$n = 2$	
	Theoretical contesting	$n = 2$	
Anxiety and fear of death	Theoretical contesting	$n = 5$	5
Liberation in life and/ or death	Explicative contesting	$n = 1$	5
	Moral affirming	$n = 2$	
	Theoretical contesting	$n = 2$	
Normativity of death	Ethical affirming	$n = 1$	3
	Practical affirming	$n = 1$	
	Theoretical affirming	$n = 1$	
Death as social critique	Moral affirming	$n = 1$	2
	Theoretical contesting	$n = 1$	
Death as authenticity/ truth	Theoretical contesting	$n = 2$	2
Legalities of death and dying	Ethical affirming	$n = 1$	1
Coping with death	Theoretical affirming	$n = 1$	1
	Total		39

VC: Validity claims

completed, participants usually affirmed and reflected on the profundity of the speaker's message with no need for clarification or contestation toward the validity claim. Moreover, because some listeners have themselves experienced acute crises indirectly or directly related to death and dying, a sense of calm resignation toward other speakers' crises was displayed as a gesture of empathy, respect, and deference.

Table 4.3   Affirming and contesting discourse responses by discourse type

Discourse type	Total	Affirmative	Contesting
Theoretical	24	6	18
Moral	6	4	2
Practical	4	3	1
Ethical	3	2	1
Explicative	1	0	1
Therapeutic	1	0	1
Total	39	15	24

Even when participants did not experience personal loss or encountered death in some manner, their philosophical support of death talk obliged them toward the same affirmation as well as resignation. Others were simply taken by personal matters when the profundity of a message took root. Because most listeners experienced deep reflections, sometimes awe, after hearing a particular message conveyed, the intermittent long silences that followed did not necessarily compel rebuttals toward the speaker making the validity claim.

Perhaps most surprising about the findings of this study are that most forwarded validity claims garnered no contestations, but quiet affirmations and contemplations. In most instances, even when a problematic validity claim is attended to by different listeners, each of them fielded no more than one or two topics in their discourse responses to the validity claim-maker. When such a round of discussion concludes, other listeners took it upon themselves to begin discussion on another theme of mortality. When such speakers are not yet forthcoming due to the profundity of the moment, the Death Café facilitator will thank the speaker and encourage other speakers to communicate. Invariably, new validity claims from new speakers emerged in the prior speaker's wake, and these then become core themes articulated by a new speaker engaging in death talk. Frequently tucked within these exchanges are humor and wit, often drawing out the community's solidarity and lightening the "load" of death. Because everyone at a Death Café is a speaker and/or listener, the vast majority of participants paced themselves rather effectively in how they spoke and granted the floor to others.

The examples in the following sections were selected for exhibiting what are arguably the more incisive validity claims as well as validity claims with discourse responses as they relate to the nine mortality themes presented in Table 4.1. The communicative action themes are sequenced in order from those with the highest frequency of discourse responses to themes with the least discourse responses (see Table 4.2 for sequencing of themes). It is within each thematic section that only the most notable validity claims are presented. To present the discussion as systematically as possible, validity claims that have discourse responses are placed toward the end of each thematic section. These discourse responses are set off by a further indent that classifies them. Like the presentation of validity claims, only notable discourse responses are presented. Some of the following passages have already been quoted during our Wordle discussions. However, their importance as validity claims warrants their presence in the following discussions as well.

Beyond Death

Table 4.2 reveals that the theme "Beyond death" inspired 11 discourse responses. A question for some, a problematic for others, an impossibility for yet others, speakers and listeners during the dialog were most animated and curious. Personal narratives and accounts, along with validity claims about the supernatural, paranormal, and/or afterlife, were conveyed. NDEs were invoked, often inspiring discussion to orient itself toward topics about the soul. Deference to spirits and the way other cultures welcomed them was also discussed as was speculation about their benevolence. Desires to know about the truth of the afterlife as conveyed by Café speakers (theoretical discourse) and whether such a search consumes precious time that could be better used to reflect on our current reality (moral discourse) generated the dynamics of the dialog. However, the depth of discussions about a corporeal death resulted in a lack of staying power in the discourse responses, with listeners primarily responding with but a few contestations, if at all, to validity claims. Some examples of validity claims made and those that inspired discourse responses can be seen in the following statements.

> **Carla from DC4**: As a psychic medium I think that's what is so interesting to me is the people that I have brought through with their family, and they always talk about death as such a beautiful thing. And one of the things that most of them are grateful for is their family letting go. And we talked about how important it is for us to let go when it is our time and it is also

important to know that when your family leaves you they, they don't really leave you. They are still there with you, helping you, protecting you. But... just the process of going, of leaving the physical body, whether it is temporary, that process is so beautiful. The death itself. And Tim asked a question about pain, and in every single case that I brought through, every spirit communicated with, that death is always a beautiful thing, so indescribable, there are no words for it.

Tim from DC4 (commenting on his NDE): And when I finally literally "died," then my consciousness and I went on the journey, and the shift of consciousness went from a "Tim" consciousness to a long journey into just consciousness. And what I would say from this is this was the journey of the soul and there was the unity of that with a sort of larger, whole consciousness, which was miraculous, spectacular.

Reese from DC4 (commenting on the metaphysical experience from psychotropics): So there are ways and things and techniques on the planet that "loosens" the soul from the body. You can have an experience and because it's not your time, you come back. And then, there's an ally that's being made and then there's this whole concept of spirit allies, which is really interesting.

Trent from DC2 (commenting on cryogenics): This gets back to the notion of the soul. If there's a soul and it leaves the body, then the body is just a piece of meat. You know, not to be disrespectful, but it's literally just a body and the soul is gone—all this energy freezing for hundreds of years and science will revive and we can transplant the head and revitalize the body, if there's a soul and that's literally a life-force, this is just a desperate pathetic attempt by people dealing with the material world, you know... we're spiritual beings in a material world, not material beings in a spiritual world, you know.

Theoretical discourse challenge from Cheyenne: Maybe they're in this reality where they believe they can save their soul in the body? Maybe I'm thinking that when I'm revitalized, whoever revitalizes me, my soul will reenter. And then I'll be all right.

Theoretical discourse challenge from Trent: It's just a body. It's just skin and bones.

Theoretical discourse challenge from Cheyenne: But the person who selected that are people—I'm assuming there are people that would like to never die.

Moral discourse affirmation from Betsy: Google is going to try to prolong life. Did you see that recent *Time* magazine? Apparently Google has now teamed up with a group and they're trying to make people live longer by doing away with disease. So, it was on the cover of *Time* magazine and it caused this huge uproar. They want to try to do away with disease.

Troy from DC2: In a sense quantum physics does sometimes sound like spirituality, very much, you know. The idea is that what's real is the life force and the materiality is the illusion. So, the body is an aspect of that, so you know it's a very interesting thing.

Theoretical discourse affirmation from Trent: That's what Einstein said. He said basically that one day we'll have instruments that will be able to pull the curtain up and we'll be able to discover a whole universe on the other side that's been right here with us the whole time but have been unable to measure.

Death as Cultural Experience

The second most popular theme is "Death as cultural experience" (see Table 4.2), one that inspired nine discourse responses. The most diversity in discourse responses can be seen in this theme because many participants considered, often with much alacrity, how other cultural and religious practices framed death and dying. Communicative action within this theme thus had the intended or unintended effect of relativizing cultural certainties and practices about death and dying. It thus entertained unfamiliar cultural renderings of mortality through theological views, gender, demographics, and religiosity, all of which serve as epistemological and ontological sites for the reworking of personalized death trajectories. The trajectory of one attempting to draw cues from different sites of social life can be seen in how participants are assembling, *in situ*, ideal cues and discarding those that stem, for example, from the market. In terms of the latter, there was much critique about culture, one that has been given its own section titled "Death as Social Critique."

The process of accommodating diverse cultural practices and views under one's authoring of a personalized mortality suggests that death talk provides for participants a forum for resolving or finishing their personal life and death narratives. Discourse responses include messages that centered on whether one's cultural approach can benefit only groups (ethical discourse) or all of humanity (moral discourse), whether certain views espoused by the speaker with validity claims are correct or accurate (practical discourse) as well as whether the claims about cultural orientations and practices regarding death and dying contain elements of truth (theoretical discourse). Even the therapeutic discourse was activated in one instance, after journalist Lia from DC4 shared her qualifications to attendees, prompting Tim to politely ask whether her report will distort Death Cafés like the media distorts everything else.

Cora from DC1: Sometimes people in ministry will talk about how theology works when you're facing a mother who has just lost a child. And I'd say I don't think that's the point of all theology because there's nothing to say to that person who has just lost a child other than "I'm sorry and I'm here." There is no explanation for that. But there doesn't need to be a theology that explains that. I think there needs to be a theology that allows us to embrace life and allows us to appreciate—as Joseph Campbell says—to experience the rapture while alive.

Leonard from DC5: So, yeah, Church was my life. It was interesting. Part of our religion class was we always have the students go out and research other religions. So one day we went to the Hindu temple out there in Malibu Canyon. And we also went to a Buddhist temple. And I got to say if I was going to choose between the two of them, the Buddhist thing seems to be a lot easier way to go. (~) I'm not kidding, these guys got it down pretty simple! Life is pretty much this! (~) Hindu: it just depends on who you screwed up to. Whether it was adultery or whether you ate too much or whatever it was, that was the deity or the god that you had to go and talk to and give some food to and you *know*, to appease or whatever. It just seemed like a whole lot of work—too much work. The Buddhists seem to have a pretty simple down path.

Jon from DC7: Ok, so I have to go back a bit really. I first came to contact with this subject matter about 15–16 years ago. And it was through my connection with Buddhism and because Buddhism places an emphasis on focusing on death and dying in general, I think. My tradition is the Tibetan tradition but I think Buddhist traditions in general do that. So I was really struck by this.

Betsy from DC1: In my many years of doing this, it's the men that do not want to be the burden. You can't believe the conversations I've had with men. I've talked to hundreds of men and it's like "is it cheaper for me to be dead?"

Ethical discourse affirmation from Cora: Well for women there's this whole sense that I don't want to leave my husband having to care for me—he might find it too difficult, or I don't want my children to be sad, or I don't want people worrying and so on, to have other people run the household.

Moral discourse affirmation from Chloe: In all of these jurisdictions there are conditions that have to be met before anyone can actually go through with it. So there are psychological evaluations by more than one doctor. There needs to be more than one medical doctor that confirms that this person truly has the state of mind, that they want to end their life and that they feel there truly is no other solution. But statistics show that very few people, that is, those people who have fulfilled these conditions, very few actually use it. And where it's been legalized, the percentage of people with terminal illness who go through this option is so miniscule.

Molly from DC6: But culturally too I think the baby boomers are much more used to taking control of their bodies, of exercising, of eating healthy or you know, having that message that you are sort of responsible for how your health goes, and the message that you're in control of things and that we don't bow down to the experts like doctors, we want to research it ourselves. So I think there's really just a whole lot that has to do with the way we culturally and generationally approach all questions that have a big impact on the question of how our dying experience will be like also.

Practical discourse affirmation from Joan: That's a great point. I just wonder how significantly more difficult it would be for people that have focused their whole lives by being healthy and doing all the right things and exercising. It could be interesting to see how that transition is made, or to get to an acceptance of something that's happening.

Anxiety and Fear of Death

The issue of fear of dying (see Table 4.2) is likely as old as the human condition itself. Along with millennia of cultural reproduction of dying as a process of unphotogenic corporeal decay where there is, at the very least, discomfort and at worst excruciating pain, it is no wonder that even a cursory thought on why death is "scary" can be attributed to the fear of a painful and prolonged exit. At our Death Cafés, most participants did not communicatively confront this aspect of mortality. Reflecting on Stephanie's anecdote (DC1) derived from her volunteer service with senior citizens who were averse to exploring mortality, the fact is some people will never desire to confront the facticity and finality of their mortality, at least in a public community setting. Perhaps we are intuitively aware at this stage in our technological development that medicine can eliminate the physical pain of death. Or perhaps this is their defiance and resistance, their right to not confront what should be confronted. The fear that was most pronounced—often through implication—was the fear of dying alone. Experiencing death as a solitary, final act of existence means for some an absolute extinction of all that is the self. Those from different sensibilities found the inevitable process euphoric in its crescendo, whereby the self is potentially liberated into another state or cyclicity of existence.

Betsy from DC2: When people die many are afraid of being forgotten. That's a huge thing—even 20 or something years ago when I started this. When people are dying they want to be remembered. It's a common theme with everybody, of like "I'm here, I was on the planet, and made a mark. But is anyone going to remember me?"

Cheyenne from DC2: The fact that you're here is just awesome. To think that there should be judging. There shouldn't be. It's not bad to have a scary death. For me it's okay—even if I'm freaked out.

Chap from DC4: Well I encountered a person who was fascinating to me. His biggest fear was that he was going to die alone. Now think about that. He wasn't concerned about pain although I know he was in great pain. But his fear was to be left alone to die.

Stephanie from DC1: Where I worked there's a senior group—and you know, I'm 61 and I want to look at this reality about what I really feel—I spent a month in Benares, in India, both times I went to meditate there daily and watch the cremations and the comings and the goings. But I have to say there's not a single person in the senior's group that was into this. I even brought in Jung's Seven Tasks of Ageing—and they were going "this is kind of heavy."

Theoretical discourse challenge from Chloe: Not everyone's like that. I've seen a lot of people at the end of life that did contemplate their mortality because anyone in the hospital has the potential of dying, obviously.

Theoretical discourse challenge from Pat: Not everybody is self-reflective, you know. There's only a certain percentage.

Ricardo from DC4: The common theme that I have heard amongst people, people I often speak to about death, is that it must be terrifying alone. It's a huge thing among people. And, the time I came close to actually having an accident where I was swept out to sea and almost drowned, I can see the people on the shore having their dinner, lights were coming on, it was getting dark. There was a rip tide and I couldn't make it back in. Suddenly the thing that came to me the most, the strongest feeling of that moment, is that I'm going to die here and I am alone. And now that was the most frightening part of that moment. You know, I'm glad I made it back but I think there is that theme of not wanting to leave, alone.

Theoretical discourse challenge from Reese: We come into this world through our mother. We're not alone. We are not alone when we are here and there is this sense of a major transition through death and we want that, that mother, we want something that is invaluable to make it okay because death is that huge unknown. Kinda' scary even for grown-ups but still you are going somewhere.

Theoretical discourse challenge from Tim: I had the same exact same experience that you are describing. I was alone. But the alones have no more meaning. The experience itself was so profound, serene, ecstatic and awesome. Being alone isn't an issue even though the way it happens leaves you alone. So I guess it's like if you're going through an experience of reliving our lives, like if we were to go through a time machine, yet that's still just one moment.

Theoretical discourse affirmation from Sarah: I was just going to say that I think it's the ego that has the fear of being alone. And I see many patients who voice that, "just don't let me be alone!" At least in hospice they make sure someone is always with the person so they don't have to be alone. But then you mentioned you were chased out of the room and I've seen that as well and I've seen patients not die when we thought they would until everyone in the family, for some reason, left the room, and the person dies in 5 minutes. I think some people cling too much to life and can't make that transition because they are clinging to their loved ones around them. So being alone is helpful for them to let go.

Liberation in Life and/or Death

A theme that most of us will likely never hear elaborated by health professionals in medical environments, many Café participants emphasized the importance and the need to understand this final attribute of the human condition (see Table 4.2). Indeed, what the Death Café represents is but an exceptionally early way of preparing—through personalization and self-authoring—one's own path toward mortality. The process is intuitive in its ethos as exemplified by Betsy in one of her sentiments about beginning preparations communicatively, emotionally, and logistically while we still can. Other participants saw death and dying as integral to what can only be described as a death consciousness: a regular and mindful employment of our mortality for enhancing life in the present. Thus, death can lead to freedom in life. Yet, even in this trajectory exists wonderful nuances that are framed by religiosity, ecology, spirituality, all of which inform one another to promote a death identity.

Betsy from DC4: So I really believe in your own path with dying. For me, I've seen so many people die so it's an experience and it gets to be a blessing.

Sarah from DC4: And still having the feeling of surrender and letting go because if I stay conscious the fact is at all times I don't know when I will die. My life is limited so I have to enjoy this moment right now.

Karen from DC6: And it seems like we've been doing that for a long time: observing death from a distance. But it's so good to see this higher consciousness. Now we're bringing death into our own consciousness, where we're able to think about it for ourselves and relate to it within our own lives.

Cora from DC1: One of the things I see as humans really embrace an embodied life is our unwillingness to embrace death as a natural process. And I want to unpack more of the stuff around—the ideas that begin with the whole thing of the "fall" and how this makes death the enemy.

Theoretical discourse challenge from Stephanie: But wait, wait, are you sure that Christianity sees death as an enemy? I mean you're going to go to heaven if you do good.

Theoretical discourse challenge from Cora: Traditional Christians believe that original sin brought death into the world, God is only for life. I work part time at XX Health Center and I work with people who work directly with students across disciplines. And they'll give them cases and various things to discuss. If there's an instance where a patient supposedly is dying and expresses wishes not to have certain procedures done, so many of the students say "Oh, I'll just do it anyway." There's a whole culture of egocentricity that says "I can't fail and let that person die."

Trent from DC2: I saw an interview with Frank Zappa, the great musician. He's a pretty smart dude in his own way—I mean if you've ever sat and watched him you'd realize he was no dummy. He was a real thinker. And on his deathbed, I think he died of cancer, there was an interview with him on his hospital bed, and I'm still trying to deconstruct this and to understand it. But he said, "It's not important for me to be remembered. And then he said "That's for guys like Bush"—he kind of made it a political thing—he goes it's really important to them to have monuments so people remember them. He goes "it's not important to me, it's not important that I'm remembered."

Explicative discourse challenge from Betsy: I'm wondering if he was just referring to things music-wise. I mean I'm just talking about people who are like "Did anybody love me?", "Did anybody care for me?", or like "Will somebody talk about me when I'm gone?" I'm wondering if he's just talking about this at the musical level.

Tim from DC4: Now, death itself, having experienced it through a near death, that is not the issue. It isn't. It is a gift for all. Many people have had equal and similar experiences and so I'm not alone in this. The commonality of the experience is absolute ecstasy, bliss, total communication, union, and the most peaceful and aware sense of self consciousness that I ever had, and other people share that. Now I have seen others who have died easily and I have seen some people resist in terror. I'm not even sure how one even chooses that. I was wondering about the issue of pain and of the fear of the unknown.

Practical discourse affirmation from Sarah: Your point about resistance: Because of what I have experienced is that people are more resistant and more afraid because they haven't even thought about dying until the last moments of life. They seem to have more difficulty, they seem to have more discomfort and suffering and so that's why I am excited for Death Café: For people to become more educated and more aware and more comfortable in general with the idea of death and dying. This will make that transition time easier in general for most people.

Normativity in Death

Norms drive the orientation of many Café participants (see Table 4.2). Many participants by virtue of being an attendee will attest on different occasions the important need to have venues like the Death Café. Attending the Death Café is a means of righting a sort of cultural wrong. In the process, attendees are fully aware that they're participating in the process of shattering what they believe is the taboo and stigma surrounding death talk. Others saw the utility of Death Cafés in how it provides what can only be described as life steps for our participants. Death Cafés had taught them something of value about living—but only, as can be seen in our examples of Scott and Leonard (DC5)—when one is pushed to that brink so as to reemerge with a greater purpose in life. The vast majority of participants saw the simple goodness of living. They saw this goodness in the compassion meted out between members at Death Cafés, as well as in the charitability of Death Cafés themselves. Playing an important role in civil society, Death Cafés are praised for being able to encourage a more nuanced, rather than absolutist approach toward life and living, death and dying.

Chloe from DC1: I'm very much shaped by relational theology, by very progressive Christian views and Buddhism as well. Thus my framework is a liberatory one and I truly believe that's what we're here to do. But my only personal values are that people will live to very end, to the very fullest, that no one should ever have to go through this. I too have lost people to suicide and because of my work I truly see how miserable some people are and I don't think we can impose our own values and I don't think everyone's freedoms look the same and I very strongly believe that people should have some choice.

Betsy from DC2: It's important you get people talking now so that you're not in the hospital crying, screaming, feeling guilty for taking them off life support.

Leonard from DC5: So, yeah, I don't really know. I know I came real close to dying. By my own hands. But, uh, I won't go there again. That's just wrong.

Scott from DC5: My wife wanted a divorce and I knew I was a horrible husband and I don't blame her for divorcing me. I faced a lot of therapy. And I really got serious about God, then, or looking for God. And I did have a few experiences around that time because I put the gun down. Didn't mean I didn't think of doing it again later on. I had some really bad times. Some bad nights. When the sun sets, those were my worst times.

Lorraine from DC5: You seem like you are really compassionate and I guess you have to be so compassionate to be in your work.

Theoretical discourse affirmation from Warren: I feel a lot of compassion, well, and that's the thing about our profession. I'm not sure if there's any formal training that a person can get, um, but I know people when I interview them for positions and staff. I can teach them, you know, how to write a contract or what's the best practices in speaking to someone about these services we're going to provide. But you can't teach compassion. You can't teach people when to say something or just to say nothing. And I believe I am fortunate because I grew up with a really compassionate family. And that's what made me who I am today.

Leonard from DC5: I think suicide is selfish. That's why I don't believe in it, personally.

Practical discourse challenge from Corrine (who lost her daughter to suicide): My daughter, she's not selfish. She was the go to girl. Her friends would always say she always listened. And she was just a kind, sweet, happy soul. And, like, my help that I'm getting is, uhm, you don't think about anything but getting the pain away.

Death as Social Critique

Most Death Café events visited in this study communicatively articulated social critiques more frequently than other themes (see Table 4.2). Yet interestingly, the validity claims that were highly critical of how society frames death and dying garnered the least contesting discourse responses. This outcome suggests that listeners agree with the validity claim-maker, further evinced by the many nods exhibited by listeners to the speaker. The three main areas of criticism include the media, medicine, and the market. No substantial discourse responses followed many validity claims made against this "trinity." What surfaced was deferential listening, a means of affirmation that need not find validation through verbal or communicative action but simply by an "it's all understood" type of implicit acknowledgment. Sentiments from speakers that made validity claims about society's inability to foster a more respectful view of death and dying include resignation, frustration, concern, and disappointment. Café participants frequently implicated the media, medical establishment, and market for its tendencies to vulgarize death and dying, either through its techno-management of mortality or its use as a form of entertainment. Frequently, Café listeners shared the same sensibilities as the speaker when critique of the trinity took place. At my data collection sites, no attendees took issue with validity claims made against the trinity.

Criticism of the Media

Exacerbating the issue of Americans uncomfortable about death and dying matters is how online communities function as personal, sometimes hermetically sealed worlds that promote the delusion of immortality. One can see this in how individuals relate to interest sites on the internet. With alacrity, aesthetic representations of the self are uploaded with the most charitable intentions, all for the sake of attaining cyber-immortality. Indeed, through social media, such immortality is ensured through uploaded videos and photographs, through comments posted by gadflies, professional malcontents, and genuinely helpful people.

For noted sociologists, such as Kellner (2000), Ritzer (2003), and Virilio (2000), technology and online worlds primarily rely on recreation and narcissistic identities that are etched into cyberspace, detracting from the rich dynamics of interpersonal interaction. In this postmodern dilemma, the simulated and the real are almost indistinguishable, and death as phantasmagoria and death as reality blur. Exacerbating the issue is how televised programing vulgarizes the dying process, promoting extremist views of mortality. News channels frequently function as repositories for sensationalized excess. In the United States, death and dying are thus envisioned almost exclusively as outcomes of violence, of drive-by shootings, murders, explosions, beheadings, school massacres, gang violence, and so forth. This is not an unfamiliar observation for the populace and many Café attendees in our sample have shared such critiques.

Renna from DC3: To me the biggest misrepresentation of death in popular culture, like when you watch soap operas and movies, is that grief ends. It's like when someone dies, everyone is sad, then they go on, and the other subplots unfold. But the reality is grief never ends. But you're just different. It never ends. My father died 26 years ago last week and I miss him every day. It kind of deepens. I mean it changes but maybe for shallow people it ends.

Rosie from DC3: I've always noticed that for movies, in particular, like those slasher films where someone is killed: none of the friends care, really. They're just more afraid of their own death. So death becomes its own spectacle and we're supposed to get pleasure from this when you watch.

Hera from DC5: And to tell you the truth, I have not watched a newscast on television in over 20 years, the reason being that I cannot—I don't want to be—witness to the sensationalism that is thrown in my face or blasted on the radio. Tragedy is around the corner but they go on, and on, and on, and it instills fear. But I don't understand personally why society doesn't make things more positive in manner. It's so depressing.

Lisa from DC5: All we have is television, especially for nineteen year olds. You see a lot of reality TV and you have a lot of imagery that fictionalizes death over and over and over again. And that's the deepest conversation or the most exemplary thing that they have in their life is what they see on television. And, you know, and then so often they mimic that.

To appreciate how Death Cafés are still nascent in the age of hypermedia, Anastaplo discusses how television "not only . . . fails to inform but also that it deceives people into believing they are informed" (1986:21). Anastaplo sees a negative correlation between political discourse and the increase in television program offerings. That is, with the onset of television, citizens' capacity—specifically grassroots citizens' capacity—to participate in political discourse has declined. Indeed, Café attendees are fully aware of these tendencies exhibited by the media, as can be seen by the preceding passages. By breaking away from how the media constructs social roles, expectations, and approaches toward mortality, Café attendees are engaged in the process of decolonizing the lifeworld from what Habermas would describe as "mediated" roles. For Eley, these roles are shaped by "newspapers and magazines, radio and TV" all of which are "the media" of a colonized public sphere (1994:289). Garnham elaborates on this concept with greater clarity:

> Our everyday social relations, our very individual social identities, are constructed in a complex process of mediations. We see ourselves as husbands, wives, lovers, fathers, mothers, friends, neighbors, workers, and consumers increasingly in terms of...identities that are constructed in and through mediated communication: soap operas, novels, films, songs, etc. And we often act out those roles using objects of consumption provided and in large part determined by the system of economic production and exchange." (Garnham 1994:365–366)

Criticism of Medicine

Participants who are critical of the medical establishment did so on principle. The issue of contention is how medicine conceptualizes and micromanages death. For Café attendees, this manifests as orientations and practices that aim to restrict sovereignty over the individual at the time leading up to death. Much could be made of this contention by examining the debate surrounding the topic of assisted dying. This theme did surface at our Death Café gatherings and was used to counter medicine's technocratic management of the body as machine, even though it also challenged some of the fundamental religious beliefs of some participants. Moreover, the need to critique medicine can also be seen in the accounts of participants profiled by a variety of journalists whose coverage of the Death Café was noted in Chapter 1.

Stephanie from DC1: We do have this culture of "take a pill now!" Everything is supposed to be easy. But death is tough. Like birth, it's tough. I just wanted to throw this in.

Kelly from DC4: Yeah, the medical system is terrified of death itself. So that is fostering a lot of the problems because the majority of the people who die are receiving medical care, probably from a doctor.

Tim from DC4: The medical profession's job is to keep them alive. It's not their job to help people transition. We can keep people alive now longer than we ever could at any time in history. But are we doing a disservice? It's a question I have no answer to but it is a question I feel.

Chap from DC4: It's sad because in this country death is controlled by the medical profession and by lawyers who are the legislators of this country. And we have to take it away from them, and the only way to take it away is to be like some countries in Europe or given some states in the United States where the person can choose, you know, the time one wants to go. And here, we feel that we are very advanced but really we are way behind.

Very few attendees targeted health-care costs during their examination of mortality. Although the costs of health care in the United States are high, this surprising omission requires us to appreciate how Café attendees, as individuals, have already begun their delinking from the materiality of the lifeworld in which the notion of costs can be quantifiably linked to mortality. Ever so slight a renunciation, it is a renunciation nonetheless. Additionally, at many Death Cafés, the medical establishment was often referred to with a sense of reification. Attendees are fully aware of its power, its impressive vernacular, and its current domination in framing our path toward end of life. Tied into these concerns are references to changes in public policy that, at the time of this writing, resulted in California's passage of the End of Life Option Act. To what extent juridification will be imposed remains to be seen.

Some compelling discontents about the medical establishment can be seen in Katy Butler's important work, *Knocking on Heaven's Door* (2013) as well through Atul Gawande's *Being Mortal* (2014). Additionally, Ann Neumann's work *The Good Death* (2016) forwards the same concerns: that death and dying today is complicated by legalistic, bureaucratic, and procedural details, exacerbated by a lack of bond between many doctors and patients. This distance allows medical practitioners to keep the terminally ill alive longer than is necessary. Butler employs this important criticism that my work acknowledges, that is, how the health "care" system remains flawed and ill-prepared to attend to people's existential needs, offering them instead costs and reimbursement issues.

Criticism of the Market
The deathcare industries are acutely aware of the criticisms meted out against the medical industry and have intensified their marketing for funeral preplanning. Mullins reported on this prescience by the deathcare industries as far back as 1998 in a report published in the *Milwaukee Business Journal*. In the article, Mullins (1998) documented how activities such as funeral preparation, a will, and end-of-life medical care are pitched in ways that aim to capture the patronage of this demographic. John Klemmer of the Heritage Funeral Homes Inc. forthrightly acknowledged that "the main reason we are doing this is

to retain market share." This is a rather urgent strategy when more and more Americans are opting to be cremated. Indeed, by 2011, Slocum and Carlson note that 36% of Americans have opted for cremation, with some states "approaching 70 percent" in its utilization of this practice (2011:43).

> **Pat from DC1**: The funeral industry is really operated in a very monopolistic fashion and so I like it that there's this new entrepreneurial spirit that's stealing that corner from manipulative people. I don't have a problem with Costco selling coffins.
>
> **Ricardo from DC4**: There are a lot of people that work very hard throughout their own lives to provide for their families, buy a home and save money for their retirement and they might not have any chance to go quite often to the medical establishment. But there's no legacy there. You know, you work your whole life and then you give all of them away—not to your family—but to the medical industry. That doesn't seem right.
>
> **Karen from DC6**: ...we've had a real rise in for-profit hospices that are really taking money out of the system, which is really sad to see the hospice movement going in that direction but I guess that's just the nature of things here: In our capitalistic society everything ultimately becomes a business and becomes corporatized.
>
> **Molly from DC6**: Yeah, and economics in a way brought a lot to the forefront, you know, just how much it costs us to do all this medical care, how much it costs our families to keep us alive in ICUs somewhere, and people's retirement plans being decimated by the last three weeks of their lives. There's a lot of reason, practical reasons, to get over our squeamishness.

Mortality in a free market system like ours is not unlike the dynamics of living itself: Both involve business transactions based on profit motives, and these transactions take place at a time when the dying and grieving are most vulnerable and impressionable. Moreover, the deathcare industry in the funeral services sector is now ensconcing themselves in American superstores such as some Costcos where coffins are now sold in nicely decorated dioramas. Classic works like Jessica Mitford's *The American Way of Death* (1963) continue to be reprinted because of its prescience in illuminating the less than desirable practices that still remain in some areas of the industry.

Death as Authenticity and Truth

Confronting this final corporeal inevitability is done dialectically by Café attendees who remind themselves and others that living life fully can be had from such a view (see Table 4.2). Here, one sees the optimism, alacrity, and passion expressed by many participants to live well and to enjoy life and living. As we shall see, Molly from DC6 reminded her fellow attendees about the importance of how our living in the moment provides cues for how we will die, a realization that places the onus—perhaps a cathartically emancipatory one—on the participant to take action, to take responsibility for personalizing and conceptualizing their own path toward death and dying. Yet, in advanced industrialized societies with populations living in comparative prosperity, we see militancy toward life through the employment of technological contraptions to destroy one another, a paradox addressed by Adorno and Horkheimer as well as Erich Fromm, fellow Frankfurt School thinkers that informed much of Habermas' thinking and critique. Moreover, Jon and Karen's dialog from DC7 illuminates a possible trajectory for the Death Café movement to take in such a context.

Stephanie from DC1: So much of death is seen as morbid even though it's inseparable from life. I totally don't buy that. All the real mystics you read, whatever faith, say it's actually energizing, literally energizing, to spend some time every day recognizing it, which is one of the things I love about my drive to and from work 'cause...I get to drive by Forest Lawn every day. I really like that because it reminds me every day to remember the important stuff about life, because there is a shelf life.
Cheyenne from DC2: So it's been very important to me to keep death and the reality of what it means to me and my perspective on the world: death is as individual as each person. It's something we all do and it's something we all do alone. So everything that happens around death for me, well, I don't build anything in my head that's more powerful than death. I mean it's a completely natural process, a 100% natural process like going to the bathroom and having a baby. To me that's what it is.
Molly from DC6: I find that almost everybody approaches their dying in pretty much exactly the same way they approach their lives—whatever that way is: how they deal with crisis and how they deal with fear, and how they deal with God, so getting familiar with that really gives you a perspective that isn't so overwhelmed by "Oh my gosh I'm dying and I'm thinking about these issues!"

Jon from DC7: One's thought around death has a massive role to play in what we collectively define as important: The way we structure our whole society is in some ways strongly connected to our thoughts around death. So from my perspective, all this work around death is a way of trying to change society for the better.

Moral discourse affirmation from Karen: Absolutely, for me as a physician, I see how much these conversations can change our entire healthcare industry in ways that desperately need to change. It's so important to healthcare but then I agree with you: I see the impact our denial of death has on how we structure society. In a way our materialism and consumerism, I see that in part as trying to convince ourselves that we're immortal and avoiding the true issue that life is fleeting and that we need to enjoy the parts of life that have the deepest meaning instead of losing ourselves in the superficiality of materialism.

Legalities of Death and Dying

Echoing Betsy's often cited sentiment about how procedural details and the logistics of death and dying make dying "hard," participants at the Café also exhibited nuances on how to address the procedural details that frame end-of-life priorities (see Table 4.2). These ranged from matters of principle to matters of state. In between these concerns, even the merits of an ecological death were voiced. In this thematic context, one sees the core elements of how the Death Café functions as a transformative movement, one where creative conflations of mortality and ecology, political empowerment, constructive self-criticism, and existential self-actualizations inform us about practices of Death Café participants. However, Café participants seemed to limit the duration and depth of critique against such regulatory topics, and the topics' staying power remained weak during communicative action. This is not surprising for legalities are but mundane matters when seen against the backdrop of exploring one's mortality. Death Café attendees appear to relish in just enough information about one or two key forms, books, and other issues to be mindful of, and once the merits of these items are illuminated, they segue toward other genres of mortality. Such a process, however, illuminates Café attendees' awareness about Habermas warning that systems speak to the population through regulations and laws, and in ways that are frequently bereft of norms.

The expected responses and reality checks can be seen by some of the following examples.

Karen from DC6: Some people have said when patients get into a hospital and there is a lot of contention about whether they should have a certain type of treatment or not, sometimes the *Five Wishes* document doesn't cover enough situations to be useful in the hospital.

Pat from DC1: It always struck me as so, speaking of arrogance, so arrogant to make suicide against the law because if you succeed, the law has no recourse.

Theoretical discourse challenge from Stephanie: But God help you if you fail.

Pat from DC1: Coffins take up a lot of space and then it's hard to imagine what the super-green solution is because you had mentioned cremation, but what about the carbon emissions? So there are quite a few things to consider. This month's issue of [...] has a thing on green burials—or the green way to go out.

Ethical discourse affirmation from Stephanie: There are some green burials where your body is wrapped in a really simple shroud and put into the ground. For the longest time I just thought I'd be cremated but that makes a lot of sense too. The idea of me being in a natural setting is nice. I kind of like the simplicity of that.

Liz from DC6: Here in California we're having the death with dignity legislation coming up in and it's already getting heated as far as the conversations on both sides go, you know. Hospices are kind of fighting it with: "Hey if we can provide you with pain relief and your wishes and keep you comfortable and provide that dignity in dying, then why do we need the legislation to opt out early?"

Theoretical discourse affirmation from Molly: Oh, don't get me started. Actually I'm going to the appropriations committee meeting tomorrow, they're holding legislation on the costs of it for California and so now the debate is going on. A lot of people have their fingers in the pie but at least it's happening.

Coping with Death

Coping with death was a complex theme (see Table 4.2). It included communicative action articulated by the bereaved in various stages of grief. However, it also included the protagonists' confrontation—be it direct or indirect—with dying. In the case the former, our speakers and listeners in their capacity as sons, mothers, fathers, sisters and brothers, widows and widowers continued their lamentations, often making accommodations to themes from beyond life.

Leonard from DC5: Whatever it takes, you got to find it. Death Café seemed like a really great way, another avenue. I don't think there's only one avenue, I don't think, for, you know, dealing with your grief. There's no one avenue. You've got to try different things, so for me, it's cooking, it's starting my photography, it's not that easy to do it.

Lisa from DC5: But there are lots of things we can do to help our minds, I think, ease into adjusting to life without them and the sooner we put something into practice the better, whether its journaling or planting a garden or tree—something that gives that grief some place to go every day.

Karen from DC6: One thing I love about the Death Café is that it gives us a place to explore talking about death and dying with other people who are open to the conversation. And we get to practice having these conversations and talking with one another. And I think that alone can help us feel more confident to go to our loved ones who might be less comfortable and be more resistant to it and this can help us get ready for that.

Joan from DC5: I've heard that when you get to the age that's the same age as the time when one of your parents just passed, it's very hard for you. So I'm just noticing the significance that she's [referring to a fellow attendee's daughter] turning 40, the age when people have passed. That could be part of what is propelling her into these thoughts.

Theoretical discourse affirmation from Molly: I also think there's really quite a lot of cultural and generational difference about how we approach things and also the style of whatever age we are. So earlier we were talking about young people being open-minded, and in a way, the Millennials are open-minded about politics, and gayness, and then therefore death. It's easier for them to have a thoughtfulness about death because they really don't get it at all as compared to people who are 60 and really realize that the depressiveness that comes with ageing.

One of the most important revelations from our transcriptions regarding Death Café communicative action is that the vast majority of Café attendees are not polemical during death talk. Although many validity claims were conveyed, they remained infrequently challenged by different Habermasian discourses. Participants are intuitively aware that too many contestations via discourse responses will only serve to rob the momentum and violate the shared humanity derived from the meaningful activity of death talk. This feature of Death Café group dynamics points to, at the very least, the intersubjectivity, and at best, mutual consensus that is sought during death talks for the sake of promoting a deeper comprehension of our mortality.

Although a dearth of challenging discourses that characterized all of our Death Cafés may appear to initially detract from Habermas' theory, it should be noted that such an outcome is to be expected because of the content of the Death Café itself: to empower and inspire people to live by confronting death and dying, a process that generates profundities that cannot but be approached reflexively. Yet, because of the fearsome process of examining one's mortality, all participants are fully empathetic and mindful of not impinging on someone else's worldview or narrative. Charitable accommodations toward speakers making validity claims are especially true of speakers whose claims were directed against the trinity of the media, medicine, and market. The few instances where counterpoints surfaced thus expressed alternative visions on mortality rather than defensive dogmatism. Where discourse responses to certain validity claims were launched, even these did not inspire a domino effect of responses to a speaker's validity claims. Instead, deferential listening took place between speakers and listeners of validity claims. In the vast majority of instances where discourse responses were forthcoming, these rarely extended beyond three different listeners attempting to vindicate or contest the speaker making the validity claim. Most discourse responses thus had little staying power beyond listeners' immediate affirmations and reflections. A town hall-like environment where exchanges become heated and vitriolic did not surface at any Death Café events. Moreover, because discussion times were carefully managed by the facilitator, listeners, and sometimes the speakers, the propensity for discourse responses to drag on did not occur frequently.

In spite of the promise for death talk to build community, communication dynamics at Death Cafés do reveal some limitations to Habermas' theory of communicative action. Chief among these is that the contours of time expended for discourse exchanges were never fully articulated by Habermas. That is, to what extent do participants engage in their dialogic exchanges until intersubjectivity and mutual consensus surface? Habermas' theory of communicative action contains another oversight in that no discernment is made on how different types of topics engaged by communicative action may foster community solidarity in rather quick and decisive ways. That is, if there is a great degree of thematic interest for a topic, then intersubjectivity and mutual consensus can be established in rather short order. However, such an outcome requires a foundational facticity that all can agree upon at the outset. Given the mortality theme of Death Cafés, it is thus pointless to contest the facticity of our death. This was understood by all Death Café participants in that not one I have witnessed debated to "win" during death talk. At the Death Café, the empowerment felt and exhibited by its participants is primarily existential and transcendental, and very infrequently political, the latter dynamic of which Habermas derives his communicative action analyses.

What surfaced at Death Cafés was how death talk inspires personal and collective empowerment at the existential level. The personal catharsis and self-authoring of one's own trajectory toward mortality becomes a process that finds it unnecessary and irrelevant to disempower any other group. Whereas a politicized communicative action might sway a contingent of listeners in ways that may alter their vote for a candidate or inspire them to devise new strategies for changing public policy, death talk communicative action ensures only the verifiable fact that the corporeal end of one's body is certain. In this regard, the topic of death and its associated death talk is an important community *and* communicative leveler, an attribute we will revisit in Chapter 6, for death and dying are equal opportunity employers of us all. From all walks of life, Café attendees are reminded that they have a shared humanity that can be seen in the inevitability of death as transition for some or as the absolute extinction of self for others. Because empowerment over death is a corporeal impossibility, empowerment for living until death thus becomes the chief aim of the Death Café.

The Death Café contains a myriad of cues that constitutes it as a bona fide social movement, albeit in its very prototypical phase, a phase where simply "talking" about what is perceived as forbidden is itself an expression of activism. I would thus like to emphasize that in spite of the aforementioned critique of some of communicative action theory's limitations, what did categorically emerge at Death Cafés was a decolonizing of the lifeworld through the confrontation of death, a process that allowed our participants to engage in, among other things, social critique of the trinity of media, medicine, and the market. Here, Habermas's contributions toward understanding lifeworld colonization, and in this work, its converse of lifeworld decolonization, remain vital for understanding how the community and the self assemble a good life and good death.

At this juncture, I hope to have demonstrated that regular community gatherings that address death and dying, along with all its concomitant ideas and practices, constitute a social movement. Kemmis and McTaggart's contention that those engaged in communicative action activism do not "aim to overthrow established authority . . . but rather to get them to transform their ways of working so that problems and crises can be overcome" accurately describes the dynamics of Death Café gatherings (2007: 301). By confronting mortality issues proactively through death talk, often with a great degree of incisiveness, humor, and a visceral sense of solidarity among attendees, and with a sprinkling of discussion on onerous legal matters and other procedures that one must engage with when working with bureaucracies attending to end of life, Death Café participants are essentially breaking the forbidden status of discussing death, revealing the underlying social themes that frame their notions of mortality. In the next two chapters, we examine ideas of additional thinkers that further enhance our understanding of Death Café angst, emancipation, and even its spatiality.

NOTE

1. With the exception of two of the greater Los Angeles area's Death Café hosts, Betsy Trapasso and Lisa S. Delong, and Karen Wyatt, MD through her online Death Café, all other attendees whose messages were selected for this work have received pseudonyms so as to ensure their confidentiality. Since Betsy and Lisa are iconic activists and public figures in Southern California's Death Café community, this work does not refer to them pseudonymously. Similarly, Jon Underwood, a much loved public figure, was not assigned a pseudonym. The same orientation was also adopted for Colorado-based Karen Wyatt, MD, a public figure who founded the online EOLU and hosts virtual Death Cafés monthly. Karen has graciously allowed me to transcribe her callers' discussions from two of her online events (one of which interviewed Jon Underwood).

CHAPTER 5

Enhancing Habermas with Erich Fromm and Kurt Wolff

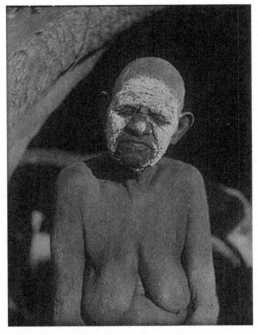

Herbert Basedow's *Old Woman Mourning* depicting mourning practices in aboriginal Australia (1919). National Museum of Australia.

© The Author(s) 2017
J. Fong, *The Death Café Movement*,
DOI 10.1007/978-3-319-54256-0_5

In this chapter, considerations as to why some people retreat from death talk while others engage it with alacrity are examined through the lens of sociologists Erich Fromm and Kurt Wolff, respectively. In our continuation of examining the Death Café and its participants engaged in personalizing their death trajectories, consideration of metaphysician Robin LePoidevin's views on time are worth noting so as to funnel our discussion toward Fromm and Wolff. In the Peter Oxley-produced BBC documentary *Cosmic Time*, LePoidevin notes how time is "highly paradoxical" because it forces us to consider "notions of infinity, of beginnings, and endings" (LePoidevin cited in Oxley 2006: 11:40 minutes). In spite of its heavy empiricism (the documentary series is hosted by physicist Michio Kaku), its presentation of other views, especially of science fiction writer China Melville, was arguably most insightful for framing mortality. Melville forwards the view that every human being has at one point marveled at his/her experiences with time since "questions of time are...incredibly important to us in our everyday lives." For Melville, "mortality is the horizon of time for each of us individually" and "anything that allows us to have a sense of escaping that kind of inevitable end of our own time is quite appealing" (Melville, cited in Oxley 2006: 30:00 minutes).

Melville's observation provides another contour toward understanding death: as end of time, a continuum that we *attempt to master with material stimuli as hyper-time technology, but only during independent and mobile periods* of our lives. And in the latter phase of life when less time is left for our corporeal existence, when dependence on systems, kinship groups, and social networks for quality of life matters, the existential angst and urgency to maintain personal sovereignty is exacerbated by the bureaucratic imperatives that consume precious time. These details, meted out primarily from powerful macro-level institutions, add clutter to one's trajectory toward end of life. Thus, for the dying protagonist, the symbolic immortality afforded by, for example, online professional and lifestyle profiles—so important and crucial for our personal accomplishments and quality of life—now offer less comforts than dying arrangements that must be engaged with at a time when the protagonist is most vulnerable. It is not surprising that many people from cultures shaped by industrialization, worlds that iterate a robotic life of constant acquisition of goods from industry, escape from the freedoms they have to personalize, author, and confront their mortality. The refinement in their decision-making to discern material culture for consumption is tempered by their inability to make decisions on what may ultimately mean the extinction of self, time, and everything they had acquired, a point emphasized by Frankfurt School's Erich Fromm.

The richness of the Death Café movement can thus be further enhanced by harnessing the ideas of Fromm's *Escape from Freedom* (1969) and *To Have or To Be* (1976) and other relevant thinkers. Describing the human condition as a dichotomy between those who desire to acquire and those who seek to "become," Fromm privileges the position of the latter. Fromm notes how the process of the human "being" is "epistemic." More importantly, Fromm suggests that the profundities that allow people to become reflexive are in principle "indescribable" (Fromm 1976: 76). Additionally, to add to our reading of Death Café dynamics, I weave in the ideas of Kurt Wolff. I will be discussing how Wolff's surrender and catch method, one that serves as an important catalyst for forming a death identity, is useful for explaining how surrendering to mortality can be harnessed by participants to live well and to personalize their trajectories toward having a good death. Death can be an identity that informs an ethos for readying oneself to confront mortality. It expresses a set of values emphasizing the capacity we have to author our own life and death.

Understanding Death Café Communicative Action with the Ideas of Erich Fromm

The surprising findings of the dynamics of the Death Café movement are that Café participants are fully aware that sages, philosophers, prophets, and loved ones have already responded to the meaning and mystery of death in numerous iterations across millennia. Indeed, attendees draw inspiration from their particular icons' wisdoms to compose their personal narratives, regardless of which period in history the wisdoms had been conveyed. Yet in spite of the wise proclamations on life and death by prophets, sages, and philosophers, their answers still do not compel many outside Café culture to articulate a nuanced and personalized rendering of mortality, even though their learned ones provide a surfeit of different metaphysical frameworks to work from. Why is this case?

In *Escape from Freedom*—a timeless work that continues to have much explanatory power for the twenty-first century—Fromm outlines the human condition of freedom historically, drawing cues from the medieval period onward. Fromm contends that freedom required a process of individuation that began during the Reformation, a process that continues into the era of his writing. A compelling and prescient work, Fromm notes that although modernity had inspired people to celebrate their subsequent freedoms afforded by this individuality, it came at a heavy price: the ultimate loss of the authentic self, one that can transcend ubiquitous systemic control by social institutions. With such a loss, the individual—although more free than their medieval predecessors since the latter group had to identify with caste, ethnicity, and religion at a time when individuality was not yet "born"—is trapped in a context of despair, desperation, and isolation.

> Man was deprived of the security he had enjoyed, of the unquestionable feeling of belonging, and he was torn loose from the world which had satisfied his quest for security both economically and spiritually. He felt alone and anxious. But he was also free to act and to think independently, to become his own master and do with his life as he could—not as he was told to do (Fromm 1969: 99).

Fromm also presciently notes how Protestantism freed people "spiritually" while capitalism "continued to do so mentally, socially, and politically" (Fromm 1969: 106). However, freedom—and the need to repeatedly make important decisions because of it—exists in such multitude within our lifeworlds that freedom becomes a "burden" (Fromm 1969: 74). The individual thus tries to escape from this freedom, handing over authority to macro-level institutions or those with fascistic agendas. People thus live in a Durkheimian profane world, relegating the sacrality of life and death to cultural peripheries.

Fromm examines Hitler and the Nazi party's rise to power in the precarious political and socioeconomic conditions of post-World War I Germany to substantiate his assertions. Fromm notes how pre-Third Reich Germans escaped their freedoms offered by the fledgling Weimar Republic, a representative democracy that existed between 1919 and 1933, to embrace fascism. The population ceded power to the Nazis so that the weight of Germany's cultural, economic, and political travails could be attended to by a paternal and oligarchal despotism. Germany under Hitler was the quintessential example of how freedom can have unanticipated consequences. In the case of pre-Third Reich Germany, the individual needed to be "saved from making decisions, saved from the final responsibility for the fate of his self, and thereby saved from the doubt of what decisions to make" (Fromm 1969: 155). Fromm's observations highlight the plight of the individual given a surfeit of freedoms, so much so that they escape from freedom toward profane systems that can make decisions on their behalf, ignoring the fact that such systems have always robotically spoken to their constituencies through juridification. In the case of Nazi ideology, this regulatory narrative served the interests of jingoism and the military industrialists that supported Hitler's rise to power during the pre-World War II period.

For Fromm, capitalism and its symbiosis with the scientific industrial complex has created a human condition like that which has consequently befallen those that have escaped freedoms in the past. Thus, the "modern individual has lost to a great extent the inner capacity to have faith in anything ... not provable by the methods of the natural sciences," a system that opened up humanity to greater freedoms by providing material culture that, while removing social and natural limiting conditions, out-putted copious amounts of life problematics that had to be solved by decision-making. (Fromm 1969: 105). Thus, although the individual today is "free from all ties binding him to spiritual authorities ... this very freedom leaves him alone and anxious" and "overwhelms him with a feeling of his own individual insignificance and powerlessness" (Fromm 1969: 80). Consequently, the "isolated individual is crushed by the experience" (Fromm 1969: 80). For Fromm, people no longer hail from a world where universal frameworks are uncontested in ways that pro-moted some form of teleological certainty, where all knew their place in the larger scheme of things. The modern individual in a democratic system is swimming in a surfeit of freedoms yet it overwhelms the person as it imposes its incessant demands for all forms of heavy decision-making. Freedom thus paradoxically generates, among all things, insecurity, angst, and fear in modern humans where this "new freedom" generated a "deep feeling of ... powerlessness, doubt, aloneness, and anxiety" (Fromm 1969: 63). Lost in the protagonist's own world of relativism and subjective motivations, Fromm contends that people are forced to seek their answers for meaning of life from different sites of social life, rendering them vulnerable to control by key institutions in society.

Fromm thus argues that people who escape freedom end up becoming automatons living in a world of negative freedom, where they show a "marked dependence on powers outside themselves, on other people, or institutions" (Fromm 1969: 141). Moreover, Fromm notes that such citizens are highly susceptible to submitting to the "factual or alleged orders of these outside forces" (Fromm 1969: 141). Alas, the contradiction of the human condition in search of freedom is presented: give the person too much freedom (which always is accompanied by the baggage of requirements for decision-making) and that person will run from it, escape from it. In this regard, Fromm makes visible an important attribute of capitalism: the escape from freedom is precipitated by those free individuals who no longer wish to, or lack the wherewithal, to take on heavy responsibilities needed to assemble their lives in an uncertain, liminal, world.

For Fromm, even though people surrender their freedom to sociopolitical institutions and begin to function as cogs, "sometimes small, sometimes larger, of a machinery which forces its tempo upon him, which he cannot control" (Fromm 1969: 125), they nonetheless believe they are still free to make their own decisions to remove their personally socially limiting conditions on their own terms. How is this possible? That is, how do people stay deluded when a slow reification of macro-level institutions takes place in ways that, in turn, mete out social control upon the populace? Habermas's response will likely be that these actors' lifeworlds have already been colonized over a long chronology: community has weakened, and members of the weakened community are thus indoctrinated into the need to compete against one another. Indeed, Fromm paralleled Tönnies's notion of *gesellschaft* as well as Habermas's sentiments, noting how "the concrete relationship of one individual to another has lost its direct and human character and has assumed a spirit of manipulation and instrumentality" (Fromm 1969: 119). Freedom is thus myopically employed: to outdo one another.

Another factor Fromm identifies as a social mechanism that influences people to give up their freedom is what he terms anonymous authority, one that distributes and sometimes dilutes for the population solutions, value systems, and ideologies. They accomplish this in ways that are highly suggestive as top-down narratives, with the most conventional orientation to mortality based on the vulgarization, desacralization, and commoditization of death and dying. Anonymous authority then, is an effective means for macro-level institutions to establish their hegemony and social control in civil society. To the extent this affects our orientation to death and dying, distortion about mortality is the outcome. In an almost resigned manner Fromm continues:

It is disguised as common sense, science, psychic health, normality, public opinion. It does not demand anything except the self-evident. It seems to use no pressure but only mild persuasion... Anonymous authority is more effective than overt authority, since one never suspects that there is any order which one is expected to follow. In external authority it is clear that there is an order and who gives it; one can fight against the authority, and in this fight personal independence and moral courage can develop... in anonymous authority both command and commander have become invisible. It is like being fired at by an invisible enemy. There is nobody and nothing to fight back against (Fromm 1969: 166).

An alternative employment of anonymous authority can be seen in the pluralized notion of anonymous *authorities*: the trinity of media, medicine, and the market that metes out juridification trajectories— that is, top-down regulations if not orders—as it colonizes the life-world. The vast majority of those in leadership positions at these institutions are primarily faceless, save the few charismatic executives that receive publicity. In this regard, this work conceptualizes their attempts at hegemony as authoritarian in nature, one that limits interaction between population and system, and one where juridification has the effect of constraining the ability of the grassroots to formulate counterresponses that can challenge formally sanctioned regulations of social control.

I am fully aware that constructing certain macro-level institutions as having the same means of social control as the state may be a contentious one. However, it behooves us to remind ourselves that in fact, juridification of social life is the most common form of "rule" inside democratic states between election cycles. Indeed, in between election cycles bureaucratic entities constrain dialog through juridification and political correctness, while entrenching their power through the economy and the culture industry, an outcome noted by key Frankfurt School thinkers such as Theodor Adorno and Max Horkheimer (Horkheimer and Adorno 1972) as well as Herbert Marcuse (1964). Indeed, for Fromm, juridification trajectories are designed to "befog the issues" as if "problems are too complicated for the average individual to grasp," requiring "specialists" to decipher the cryptic regulatory language that emanates from macro-level institutions (Fromm 1969: 249). This contention is also supported by sociologist of postmodernity Zygmunt Bauman in the classic work *Liquid Modernity* (Bauman 2000) where he argues that people increasingly defer to experts to configure their lives. Bauman also suggests why people defer to experts in his other important work *Wasted Lives*:

> What we all seem to fear...is abandonment, exclusion, being rejected, blackballed, disowned, dropped, stripped of what we are... We fear being left alone, helpless and hapless...We fear to be dumped...What we miss most badly is the certainty that all that won't happen—not to us (Bauman 2004: 128).

Fromm repeatedly reminds readers that these conditions coexist alongside the freed individual. He is more critical, however, noting how the "insignificance of the individual in our era" is further exacerbated by people adopting roles of being only a "businessman, employee, or manual laborer, but also...a customer" (Fromm 1969: 126).

With the advent of the internet, people have begun to build communities through preferred brands that reveal their preferences for certain aspects and objects of material culture. Although Fromm notes how capitalism freed the individual to "stand on his own feet and to try his luck" so as to become the "master of his fate," money "became the great equalizer of man and proved to be more powerful than birth and caste," such that it manipulated people to employ their freedom to seek primarily what is quantifiable in corporeal existence (Fromm 1969: 61–62). Fromm laments how members of society believe this is a bona fide freedom, unaware that such an orientation is a result of steering by anonymous authorities. He notes how "we can have thoughts, feelings, wishes, and even sensual sensations which we subjectively feel to be ours, and yet...these thoughts and feelings...have been put into us from the outside, are basically alien, and are not what we think, feel and so on" (Fromm 1969: 187). Because this is primarily the mode people in modern capitalist democracies experience freedom, they lack the acumen to employ freedoms for other important decision-making episodes such as addressing mortality. Elsewhere Fromm notes:

> Most people are convinced that as long as they are not overtly forced to do something by an outside power, their decisions are theirs, and that if they want something, it is they who want it. But this is one of the great illusions we have about ourselves. A great number of our decisions are not really our own but are suggested to us from the outside; we have succeeded in persuading

ourselves that it is we who have made the decision, whereas we have actually conformed with expectations of others, driven by the fear of isolation and by more direct threats to our life, freedom, and comfort (Fromm 1969: 197).

Fromm's sentiments suggest that societies in late capitalism do not institutionally pitch secularized views toward epistemic, ontological, or self-actualizing freedoms for their constituents. Yet, it allows the pageantry and the rituals, the scripts, aesthetics, and forms of culture and religion to express themselves in commodified form. However, as an institutional protagonist that affects one's tangible quality of life, the market in the last instance dictates social behavior of those less informed.

Fromm's most critical statement against a market-oriented culture is that its manifestations through pageantry and rituals reveals how humanity's "biological weakness" establishes "the condition of human culture" (Fromm 1969: 32), allowing anonymous authority to flow through its contexts and practices, shaping people's narratives on death and dying in ways that delink it from informing life and living. It is not surprising then, to observe why there can be informal sanctions on death talk, even in the most intimate of settings, to address end of life issues. No matter the pageantry, rituals, and scripts to honor those who die, the endgame is the same: unless one is cremated, the corporeal manifestation of death, given time, is garishly unphotogenic, requiring some type of cultural "packaging" to deny its gnarled forms that embody this final material consequence of living.

Did Fromm simply abandon his readers to a dystopian view of the human condition? Fortunately, Fromm offers a means for the actor to experience emancipation and positive freedom through what he terms as spontaneous activity, or activity that passionately harnesses the "total integrated personality" (Fromm 1969: 257). He further elaborates that only "those qualities that result from our spontaneous activity give strength to the self and thereby form the basis of its integrity... This implies that what matters is the activity as such, the process and not the result" (Fromm 1969: 260–261). Thus, the spontaneous dynamics of death talk engaged by Death Café participants become a form of resistance toward systemic, cultural, and institutional controls that frame the narrative of death and dying. Indeed, the decolonization of the lifeworld from its distorted representation of the deathworld is underway at Death Cafés. The process is to intra- and intergenerationally dismantle—through communicative action as spontaneous activity—the building blocks of an immortality complex, one which was addressed and critiqued by many Café participants. Only then can the individual and the community's journey toward a more sincere and non-pretentious understanding of life and death remain uncluttered. For Fromm, spontaneous activity thus unites the self "anew with the world" (Fromm 1969: 259). The spontaneous dynamics of death talk communicative action also unites fellow human beings with one another, and with the nature of death as a whole. The key catalyst propelling spontaneous activity is love, "not love as the dissolution of the self in another person, not love as the possession of another person, but love as spontaneous affirmation of others" (Fromm 1969: 259).

The institutions cited by Café attendees, along with their operations and orientations, are contested because of their tenacity to condition people and their lives into a state of impoverished understanding of mortality. This situation cannot be dismissed as a factor, for Fromm notes the individual is but the "most helpless of all animals at birth," requiring social systems to adapt the individual to the "process of learning, not on instinctual determination" (Fromm 1969: 31). Fromm's prescient elaboration evokes the critiques Café participants had made against the marketing of immortality, through, say, antiaging creams or the use of cryogenics:

A vast sector of modern advertising.... does not appeal to reason but to emotion; like any other kind of hypnoid suggestion, it tries to impress its objects emotionally and then make them submit intellectually. This type of advertising impresses the customer by all sorts of means: by repetition of the same formula again and again; by the influence of an authoritative image.... All these methods are essentially irrational; they have nothing to do with the qualities of the merchandise, and they smother and kill the critical capacity of the customer like an opiate or outright hypnosis.... As a matter of fact, these methods of dulling the capacity for critical thinking are more dangerous to our democracy than many of the open attacks against it, and more immoral—in terms of human integrity... (Fromm 1969: 127–128).

Large systems of the market thus mete out misinformation for the populace to learn in ways that disrupt knowledge transmission from, say family. This misinforming process, norm-free and regulatory, advocates incessant consumption with little distinction between healthy and unhealthy consumption. For Fromm, the outcome of this form of lifeworld colonization is that:

...the individual ceases to be himself; he adopts entirely the kind of personality offered to him by cultural patterns...The person who gives up his individual self and becomes and automaton, identical with millions of other automatons around him, need not feel alone and anxious anymore. But the price he pays, however, is high; it is the loss of his self (Fromm 1969: 184).

And herein lies the segue mechanism—in the form of a question—that will take us into Fromm's next important work, *To Have or To Be* (Fromm 1976): who are those that can distance themselves from the immortality complex, that system that lures us away from confronting our mortality in our lifeworlds? For Fromm, it is those who live *to become*, while those who live *to have* end up the automatons that so riled Fromm and Marcuse. For Fromm, those who choose to have consequently envision an arithmetic rendering of time. In such instances, time is envisioned as something one presumably has control over, as in the number of years one has to live. This orientation generates fears about death, allowing it to develop and proliferate in our psychical makeup not unlike what Melville noted at the outset of this chapter. However, Fromm notes how if one were to conceptualize our lifetimes while "in the being mode, time is dethroned; it is no longer the idol that rules our life" (Fromm 1976: 110).

Since Café participants are in the process of being and becoming, they appear more mindful than most in acknowledging that, even in the most ideal conditions of being surrounded by loved ones at home upon death—indeed, the process is sociological—the crescendo of life, that final instance of vital functions, will force the actor to invariably engage with death alone, a facticity that will allow Café participants to prepare logistically as well as metaphysically. This view illuminates a death identity that no longer gives emphasis to physiological renderings of death as a cessation of a variety of bodily functions. A death identity is meant to remind us of our available agencies in *being* as we journey toward end of life. Such an iteration of death and its implications for living well with our mortality can be contrasted with simply viewing life as a biological imperative, the latter of which Fromm deems problematic.

The need to have has still another foundation, the *biologically given desire to live*. Whether we are happy or unhappy, our body impels us to strive for immortality. But since we know by experience that we shall die, we seek solutions that make us believe that, in spite of the empirical evidence, we are immortal. This wish has taken many forms: the belief of the Pharaohs that their bodies enshrined in the pyramids would be immortal...fame, celebrity, even notoriety—anything that seems to guarantee a footnote in the record of history—constitutes a bit of immortality. The craving for fame is not just secular vanity. It has a religious quality for those who do not believe in the traditional hereafter anymore...Publicity paves the way to immortality and the public relations agents become the new priests (Fromm 1976: 70).

A death identity is an identity that will ultimately proclaim that actual death, along with its symbolisms and sentiments, should be symbiotically internalized everyday for the purpose of celebrating a life for which actors may still lack full control and understanding. Such a transformation is sought so that we can brace ourselves for that period when we sequentially lose corporal others and ultimately, the corporeal self. Café attendees are displaying this ethos—though its cues are just on the verge of being understood unanimously—of loving without control for the object that is the human body. Loving a person in a way that one can have as an object—including loving the self as an object—"transforms everybody and everything into something dead and subject to another's power" without the actor able to critically interrogate the futility of acquiring such power (Fromm 1976: 65).

Café attendees are constructing a death identity that is about learning to value their lives and the lives of their loved ones in the present or the spirits of those in the timeless infinite, in ways where nothing is sought in return. For Fromm, there is a distinction between existential having which will at the very outset provide a theme or essence for the actor to grasp—a process Fromm lauds—to the idea of materialistically having, which he views critically:

Existential having is rooted in human existence. It is rationally directed impulse in the pursuit of staying alive—in contrast to the characterological having...which is a passionate drive to retain and keep that is not innate, but that has developed as the result of the impact of social conditions on the human species...Existential having is not in conflict with being: characterological having necessarily is (Fromm 1976: 73).

Fromm's views thus remind us about the importance of completing the self-authoring of our existence along with its intimate ties to transcendence, for which the Death Café potentially functions as a conduit.

Finishing the unfinished narrative of dying well on one's own terms, if possible, constitutes the core drive of a death identity. It is a process that Fromm envisions as existential having, one that results in major changes to one's character. How one finds an ethos toward mortality in light of such changes requires faith in a shared humanity that is derived from being, where a "process of self-renewing and self-increasing" can be derived from confronting a hollow materialistic death with one that is liberating and emancipatory (Fromm 1976: 39).

The changes to self and community assumed to follow when members of society transition toward being is the first salvo against conventional materialism, the latter of which forwards the goal of having until fellow members of society are described as having *more or less of something*. Fromm is critical of such a position, warning how this notion of gesellschaft is reproduced intergenerationally to espouse the view that "if one *has* nothing, one *is* nothing" (Fromm 1976: 13). For Fromm, having and being are two existential antipodes, both of which shape the characters of people as well as generate different types of characters, of which the "marketing character" is most suspect. The notion of the marketing character, albeit a rather overarching generalization, is nonetheless rich as a strategically essentialized category. Fromm's notion of the marketing character adequately frames much of the angst and discontents that Death Café participants have against materialistic society. Indeed, such individuals reproduce the notion of having directly upon the body in ways that make it prone to being lost in death. Thus, for Fromm, the marketing character is

> based on experiencing oneself as a commodity, and one's value not as "use value" but as "exchange value." The living being becomes a commodity on the "personality market." The principle of evaluation is the same on both the personality and the commodity markets: on the one, personalities are offered for sale; on the other, commodities (Fromm 1976: 127).

True to the orientations of critical theory, Fromm offers no quarter even for those market characters that self-actualize in their respective careers: "A stock broker, a salesperson, a secretary, a railroad executive, a college professor, or a hotel manager must each offer a different kind of personality that, regardless of their differences, must fulfill one condition: to be in demand" (Fromm 1976: 127).

A motivating force for Death Café participation is that it allows for its actors the process of assembling their life trajectories in unique ways, freed from being a marketing character trapped in institutionalized scripts and larger macro-influences, yet retaining all of its existential hopes. Café attendees, through an evolving death identity, are thus aiming to unfetter themselves from the fear of "losing what I have . . . my body, my ego, my possessions, and my identity; the fear of facing the abyss of nonidentity, of 'being lost'" (Fromm 1976: 108). Thus, generating a death identity is a resolution to Fromm and anthropologist Ernest Becker's rendering that people intuitively fear mortality. Café participants' death identity, derived from cues offered by their personal compilation of sages, their personal experiences with life and death struggles, and their memories set in the context of infinity and timelessness, are sacralizing the process of returning to a healing or healed self for the coming moment of death. For some, this manifests as new horizons of being and becoming while for others the absolute extinction of all that is the self. Death Café attendees are informing us about the importance of acknowledging our own narrative toward mortality as legitimately sacred by seeking meaning across time and across cultures, a process facilitated by communicative action.

The examination of death talk dynamics suggests that Habermas's communicative action can do well with a death discourse, one that can provide purpose for the corporeal, and for some, beyond the corporeal. Ironically, the death discourse—in spite of the weight of its profundities— may be the least antagonistic of the discourses for challenging validity claims because there is little to challenge the facticity that is the end of life. It serves as a basis for our shared human condition *and* shared humanity. Café attendees are keenly aware they are in the process of being and becoming and there is no need for vitriolic or long-drawn out contestations against validity claims, that is, the doctor talking about death is allowed to be a doctor, the shaman talking about death is allowed to be shaman, the medium talking about death is allowed to be a medium, and the near-death experience survivor is allowed to be a near-death experience survivor, all of whose validity claims are intersubjectivity accepted *in situ* and on good faith. Yet, Fromm was incisive enough to discern two types of faith.

Faith, in the having mode, is the possession of an answer for which one has no rational proof. It consists of formulations created by others, which one accepts because one submits to those others—usually a bureaucracy. In the being mode, faith is an entirely different phenomenon. Can we live without faith? Must not the nursling have faith in its mother's breast? Must we all not have faith in other beings, in those whom we love, and in ourselves? Can we live without faith in... our life? Indeed, without faith we become sterile, hopeless, afraid to the very core of our being. Faith, in the being mode, is not, in the first place, a belief in certain ideas... but an inner orientation (Fromm 1976: 36–37).

Death Café gatherings, in spite of its critical orientations toward social systems, remain apolitical town hall events that allow participants to accept, even romanticize, the many horizons of mortality. Although this may be perceived as a haphazard means of forming community, the converse provides some insights: no attendee at our Death Cafés has ever joined a gathering with incontrovertible facticity about the whys and hows of death and dying, and the possibilities or lack thereof regarding an afterlife. Claims to such power do not therefore exist. By default this thematic leveling removes the pretentiousness of titles and labels and renders irrelevant earthly matters shaped by concealed motivations, all of which clutter our capacity to live. This reason alone explains why Fromm celebrates the state of being, for "optimum knowledge in the being mode is to *know more deeply*. In the having mode it is *to have more knowledge*" (Fromm 1976: 36). The atmosphere of each gathering exhibits too much depth for heated contestations. In the safe spaces where strangers realize that they can actually bond with one another, solidarity and empathy, along with Habermasian intersubjectivity, mutual understanding and consensus, as well as the process of opening up of communicative space, permeate the setting. A death discourse, in spite of its morbid moniker, actually creates an environment that is alive.

Habermas' communicative action can well do with a death discourse, one that concerns itself with how to live life through our address of mortality, one which might provide a resolution to his view of an unfinished project of modernity. A death discourse situates speaker and listener in a most unique context of Sartrean freedom, where one can choose to author a quality of life that is nourished by the mindful awareness of our inevitable end. A death discourse finishes the modernity project because it starkly reveals that the bearers of modernity, which have rapaciously colonized nature in many ways, cannot in the final instance, steer the body and whatever practices we bestow upon it toward corporeal immortality. It reminds modernity, if we can make it a protagonist, that it cannot be a charlatan. Ignoring such venues where a mindful appreciation for mortality through a death discourse can be articulated for community may well open our lives to profit-based institutions and organs of the state to dictate how we live and die. In the latter case as can be seen in too many historical epochs, we may be rendered susceptible to how the state force feeds its rendering of death and dying for jingoistic purposes, as in to die for the "motherland" or "fatherland."

The Role of the State

The issue of how the state has historically appropriated death and dying by determining people's mortality through political means was visited in my discussion of how political prisoners confronted their mortality (Fong 2014), with key themes reparaphrased in this work. Indeed, the state is a significant actor in framing death and dying for nation, one that can draw its citizens to willingly give their lives for a sloganeered cause. To what degree state cooptation of death and dying for a national cause affects our imagery of death as a product of war remains to be seen. However, its role in thematically appropriating death and dying as well as meting it out against those deemed as enemies bears mention.

The state has not been included as part of the trinity that has juridified death, namely, for two reasons, the first of which is that Café participants rarely addressed the issue and there are no thick communicative action data on this sentiment. A secondary reason is that the state can only appropriate mass death and engage in death talk during times of conflict, and even then its narrative must coexist with media renderings of the conflict. That said, state-related death processes do project a sense of helplessness, a sense that we must give our lives to protect those who will protect our geographical womb. To what degree Death Café dynamics can be framed as an antipode to such agendas, that is, to serve as a public sphere for a new antiwar or nonviolent consciousness remains to be seen as the movement continues to grows globally.

Insofar as humanity's reliance on the state for its life cues is concerned, Nietzsche cautions that "the state is a clever institution for protecting individuals from one another" but "if one goes too far in ennobling it, the individual is ultimately weakened by it, even dissolved" (Nietzsche 2006a: 183). Nietzsche's view on war was damning, that "war is the sleep or wintertime of culture" (Nietzsche 2006a: 271). The state, in its

capacity to wage war, can thus be seen as an agent of lifeworld colonization, one where nationalist narratives conflate the system *with* the lifeworld. As such, many in nationalist conflagrations are compelled to die not
as their own authors of mortality, but to die for the state and whatever
cues it employs for the survival of the nation.

Nietzsche's criticism can also be directed toward those revolutionaries
whose notion of death grants little sovereignty to one's mortality. In such
contexts, the mortal self disappears into an indignant collective, one ready
to identify heroes for cultural consumption as they overthrow old societies
for the establishment of new ones. Yet, Nietzsche notes how "an overthrow can well be a source of energy in an exhausted human race, but it
can never be an organizer, architect, artist, perfecter of the human character" (Nietzsche 2006a: 281). However, Nietzsche, unlike most Café
attendees, spared the institution of science criticism since it had "as its goal
the least pain and the longest life possible—that is, a kind of eternal
happiness...a very modest kind in comparison with the promises of
religions" (Nietzsche 2006a: 105).

Arthur Koestler (1905–1983), author and novelist, was forced to confront death established by the state. While covering the Spanish Civil War
in Spain as a journalist, he was captured by Francisco Franco's troops in
early 1937, suspected of being a left-wing sympathizer. Sentenced to be
executed by firing squad, Koestler spent months in prison until June of the
same year. Koestler was indeed a member of the Communist Party of
Germany, and that his assigned interview of Franco as a journalist was
done on behalf of the *Comintern*,[1] using the London-based newspaper
News Chronicle "as a cover" (Koestler 1966: 5). Koestler's accounts were
detailed in his prison diary and through recollections after his release. The
experiences of this period was published in the classic *Dialogue with Death*
(Koestler 1966), where Koestler retold accounts of the many nights where
he would hear prisoners being led away to face Franco's firing squad,
hearing them being shot, and uncertain if he would be next. One account
told of the pending execution of a neighboring cell mate in March of
1937:

They went on to the next cell. When my neighbour was called, he said
nothing. Most probably he was already awake, and, like me, prepared. But
when the priest had ended his prayer, he asked, as if of himself: "Why must I
die?" The priest answered in five words, uttered in a solemn voice but rather

hurriedly: "Faith man. Death means release." They marched him off (Koestler 1966: 165).

Koestler survived the ordeal because he was ultimately freed through a prisoner exchange. *Dialogue* contains, along with psychological themes, insight into the acutely simplistic and artificial demand of war: death for country or death by the enemy. War functions as a cultural mechanism to instruct those in society to survive or die with the state. Festooned by parades, flags, medals, and the proverbial hero, this romance can quickly be fatigued: trapped in raw despair, Koestler noted that "the only consolation you could give to a condemned man on his way to the electric chair would be to tell him a comet was on the way which would destroy the world the very next day" (Koestler 1966: 92). Mortality meted out by the state apparatus is, if anything, grossly vulgar in spite of heroification practices that are situated inside the epic of mass death and slaughter.

Koestler tried to find morsels of strength during his perceived date with death by downplaying the suffering meted out to him by society: "This is why situations lived through are never so bad in reality as in imagination. Nature sees to it that trees do not grow beyond a certain height, not even the trees of suffering" (Koestler 1966: 117). Koestler also harnessed the acquisition of prison resources as an analogy for social struggle, noting that "here inside the prison walls the struggle is waged for a cigarette, for permission to exercise in the courtyard, for the possession of a pencil. It is a struggle for minimal and unworthy objects, but a struggle for existence like any other" (Koestler 1966: 197). After acquiring his freedom, Koestler concluded rather sociologically: "Those who... deny the influence of environment on the development of the human being should spend a year in prison and observe themselves daily in the mirror" (Koestler 1966: 197). We can see in Koestler's sentiments how transformations in character occurs when the state is involved in authoring our mortality.

Milada Horáková (1901–1950) encountered a more dire outcome. A Czech lawyer, freedom fighter, and politician, she was the most prominent pan-European feminist executed by Stalinists during Cold War Czechoslovakia. Horáková's life, clearly shaped by a powerful calling, was dynamic in its feminism as recounted by Markéta Doležalová on the Czech Republic's *Institute for the Study of Totalitarian Regimes* website.

During her youth in the 1920s, Horáková's activities with the Women's National Council and later the International Women's Council were supplemented by her travels across Europe to promote women's issues. At home, she attended to important issues affecting unmarried women and children born out of wedlock, as well as drafting bills that would improve the status of women in family law and in blue-collar professions. During this period, she was inspired by Senator Františka Plamínková, founder of the Czech women's movement. Plamínková would later be captured and executed by the Nazis in 1942. Not surprisingly Horáková became active in resisting the Nazi Occupation of Czechoslovakia. She was ultimately captured by the Nazis, sent to prison, and spent the remainder of World War II at the Theresienstadt concentration camp located in the country. After World War II concluded, she served in the country's parliament until the 1948 Communist takeover of the country. A year later Horáková was arrested again under fabricated charges, accused of trying to overthrow the regime, and forced to stand trial in a kangaroo court, this time by the communists she worked hard to put in power.

Subjected to torture and forced to stand in the sham trials orchestrated by the Stalinists, she was sentenced to death on June 8, 1950. Her observations of societal dynamics during her solitary confinement, fully aware that her imminent death by the state, deserves mention. On the night before her execution, jailers allowed Horáková to write three letters. The evocative letters were written to her husband, Bohuslav, teenage daughter, Jana, and Horáková's mother-in-law, who would be Jana's caretaker upon her mother's demise. However, it would be Horáková's letter for Jana that included an important section that instructed Jana about the ways of society, and, how one dies with integrity. Authoring her mortality through final tasks and writings, she noted to Jana:

> Don't be frightened and sad because I am not coming back any more. Learn, my child, to look at life early as a serious matter. Life is hard, it does not pamper anybody, and for every time it strokes you it gives you ten blows. Become accustomed to that soon, but don't let it defeat you. Decide to fight (Kelly 2012).

Elsewhere in the letter, and in a spirit that many Death Café attendees would acknowledge, Horáková wrote of life:

> Of course, you will only be able to solve it correctly and truthfully by knowing very, very much. Not only from books, but from people; learn from everybody, no matter how unimportant! Go through the world with

open eyes, and listen not only to your own pains and interests, but also to the pains, interests and longings of others.

You know that to organize one's scale of values well means to know not only oneself well, to be firm in the analysis of one's character, but mainly to know the others, to know as much of the world as possible, its past, present, and future development.

I have changed my mind many times, rearranged many values, but, what was left as an essential value, without which I cannot imagine my life, is the freedom of my conscience. I would like you, my little girl, to think about whether I was right (Mills 2012).

In her last paragraph to Jana, Horokava instructs "Just one more thing: Choose your friends carefully. Among other things one is also very much determined by the people with whom one associates. Therefore choose very carefully" (Mills 2012). As Horáková's notes attest, the period before death still affords the social actor a modicum of freedom to author one's anthem for death.

At 2:30 A.M. on June 27, 1950, Horáková was hanged with a coterie of similarly condemned in spite of appeals by Winston Churchill, Albert Einstein, Eleanor Roosevelt, Bertrand Russell, and many others. As an anti-Nazi and anti-Communist crusader, Horáková's political stance was simultaneously an apolitical one that brought her back to womanhood, society, and humanity as a whole, a process which granted her emancipation from the dysfunctions of authoritarian state narratives on how one's death is most noble only when offered to nation.

Enhancing Communicative Action with the Ideas of Kurt Heinrich Wolff

Although it may seem that a discussion of state appropriated practices to frame death and dying is but a digression away from the trinity that inspired Death Café communicative action, it is worth mentioning that the human condition under state articulation of death and dying can never fully stifle the sovereignty actors have about living and dying on their own terms. We have seen incisive conclusions about love, family, and society through the examples of Koestler and Horáková. It can just as well be expected that members of the civilian population who skirt the horizons of mortality, whether directly or indirectly, can similarly be resurrected into life, informed by the new profundities and realizations acquired from their experiences.

Kurt Heinrich Wolff, a sociologist that enhances our understanding of mortality, examined how key moments of lucid awareness about experiences in the social world can inspire transcendence. A younger contemporary of Fromm, Wolff hailed from a distinguished cadre of German immigrant sociologists that migrated to the United States by the late 1930s (see Fong 2014). However, Wolff's important conceptual contribution to our Death Café research, his notion of surrender and catch, is not well-known in the discourse of American sociology which was highly positivistic at the time of his writings. In spite of this, the concept of surrender and catch serves an important function in helping us appreciate the Death Café movement's capacity for accommodating the epiphanies of existence in ways that systems cannot.

For Wolff, surrender and catch, *a moment and methodology*, are able to seize that totalizing experience and existential realization of one's predicament in the web of life. Wolff observed that in certain periods of the human experience, we discover epiphanic profundities, sometimes divine, regarding our human experience. Wolff's ideas suggest how the profound realizations that do take us closer to a deeper understanding of death and dying can also stem from surrender and catch experiences that are joyful (1976). Surrender and catch are thus important processes that have great implications for understanding the motivations of speakers at Death Cafés as they illuminate life and death accounts through communicative action. Invariably both states provide for actors the fluidity to link themselves to empowering wisdoms drawn from across the present and across time. When listeners at the Death Café also empathetically immerse themselves in the conveyed experiences of those who have experienced surrender and catches, they are exposed to cues that help personalize their trajectory toward end of life.

The aims of this section examine surrender and catch in ways that can assist us in postulating its antecedent. This is an important task because Wolff himself did not specify nor elaborate upon kinds of human episodes that are catalytic in generating surrender and catch experiences. I am of the view, however, that Wolff may not disagree that indirect experiences, but more importantly direct experiences with death and dying (for example, being next to a loved one about to die, having experienced a near-death experience, failed suicide, or having survived severe illness) are catalytic in inspiring people to participate in death talk. Surrender and catch episodes conveyed by Café participants during death talk are able to generate a sense of community because such experiences appear to render encounters with death as rebirth. Listeners can join the speaker in transformation because all have confronted death and dying in some iteration and now see people, society, and the world differently. My contribution to Wolff's view is that having experienced a direct or indirect death is a catalyst that brings people toward some kind of surrender and catch episode, compelling them to share their experiences at venues such as the Death Café. Indeed, through the ideas of Wolff, we can appreciate how the rich Café narratives generated by those confronting death through death talk are but products of many participants' surrender and catch experiences.

Wolff describes surrender as one of "total involvement" in the moment where the subject, the act, and the object disappear, followed by the subject realizing certainties that invariably are. In surrender, there is also a "suspension of received notions" in that other socially imposed frameworks, concepts, and even the plausibility of theory are suspended (1962: 41).[2] That is, such moments cannot be made to occur superficially by acquisition or formula. Perhaps a stage of transcendence, fact, theory, hypothesis, metaphor, image, and poetry become one. Moreover, Wolff notes how there surfaces a "pertinence of everything" where time, place, feelings, and events are reassembled for the subject. This process of uncluttered knowing can be a jovial or fearsome experience because it renders the subject completely vulnerable to new realizations. The state of surrender is one that is explicitly an experience that "cannot be commanded," thus yielding a profound level of authenticity for understanding the self in relation to society (Wolff 1962: 46). For Wolff, the entire process contains the dialectic of dying and becoming (1962: 47). Wolff's biographers note:

> The experience of surrender can be explicated through its components: total involvement, the suspension of received notions, and pertinence of everything...Total involvement or absorption means that the surrenderer's whole being is involved in the experience such that the subjects-object distinction disappears (Backhaus and Psathas 2007: xxv).

The state of surrender, where the social actor has a "totalizing state" of knowledge and "expansion of consciousness" (Wolff 1976: 63) begets the epistemological and ontological knowledge that is the content of the catch, a process that reorients one's life and purpose. Wolff's renders the catch as when the experiencer is able to see the

"structure that emerges from it" (1974: 549) for it is a "yield, harvest-
...necessarily emerging structure" (1974: 318). In this regard, we see
how surrender and catch assists participants to comprehend one
another at their Death Cafés. Wolff notes in his seminal work
Surrender and Catch: Experience and Inquiry Today (1976) that "as a
method it is characterized by openness toward its origin...it is self-
correcting and therefore, in the spirit of the essence of knowledge,"
one that is inherently existential (1976: 79). Wolff pushes the para-
meter of epistemology even further by noting how scientific findings
are but theoretical and relative, while existential truth is "absolute—
also philosophical, artistic, poetic, if you will" (1976: 79). Here, Wolff
provides his philosophy with a crescendo, one that unites the existential
self with society in that human beings "are thrown back on what we
really are, which is what we share with mankind" (1976: 54). This
profundity frequently generates Death Café communicative action,
interpersonal relations, group dynamics, and community solidarity. In
these times of totalizing inspiration "words burst forth in...meaning
from the immediacy of experience...[and] we have a sense of what we
are talking about" (Backhaus and Psathas 2007: xxv).

Surrender and catch is thus a process that amplifies social awareness
beyond a Maslowian self-actualization. The lucidity experienced by the
actor allows for a departure from socially constructed boundaries. The
concept also points to how crises can be catalytic in generating surrender
and catches among social actors, seen, for example, in our discussion of
Koestler and Horáková. For Wolff, in such realizations, the actor experiences a "certainty of full communication with his fellow men: as long as his
experience lasts, he can convey anything, and he who listens cannot help
but understand" (Wolff 1962: 40). Indeed, the experiencer is thrown back
on what is shared with humanity, perhaps internalizing the view of how
the self invariably belongs to the human race. Wolff's ideas mesh nicely
with Habermas' view of communicative action, both of which aim at some
sort of deeper comprehension: surrender and catch utterances become the
validity claims that draw inspiration, or at the very least, minimize the
degree of discourse contestations while maximizing discourse affirmations.
A plausible outcome of this symbiosis is intersubjectivity and mutual
consensus between communicators.

To understand how Wolff came upon such an approach requires us to
understand the dislocations and crises that affected his life. During the
pre-World War II period, Wolff's life was that of a transnational European,

but due to circumstances seemingly beyond his control. Born in Darmstadt, Germany, he ultimately had to flee Germany in 1933 because of its nascent fascism. Settling in Italy, he was again forced to relocate in 1939 with his wife, Carla Bruck, as a result of Benito Mussolini's anti-Jewish stance and growing partnership with Hitler. After a brief stay in England, they migrated to the United States while the Holocaust unfolded in Europe. Wolff thus found no comfort in the human condition of postwar modernity: with the conclusion of World War II, the onset of the Cold War and its numerous associated proxy wars, and the threat of nuclear annihilation, mass social catastrophe suddenly became very real. Here Wolff' sentiments would later be framed by Giddens's (1990, 1991, 1999), Giddens and Pierson's (1998), and Beck's (1992) notions that the modern era manufactures much of its own risks. Although Wolff and his biographers point to Wolff's field research in New Mexico as constitutive of his surrender and catch formulation, the horrors of the Holocaust and his concerns at the time that there may indeed be a nuclear conflagration, became tropes for his view of humanity's existential crisis. Indeed, these themes "far more than any other, shaped his thinking" (Kalberg 2007: 79).

Wolff's concerns echo the same themes as the Frankfurt School comprised of German sociologists that emigrated to the United States during the first half of the twentieth century, and of which Habermas and Fromm hail from. Although certainly not the first to envision a crisis of humanity, Wolff's views should be discerned from other great thinkers who approached the subject, such as Friedrich Nietzsche, who viewed the crisis of humanity in the timeless *Thus Spoke Zarathustra* (Nietzsche 2006b) as borne from the death of God. Yet perhaps the distinction is superficial. Both Nietzsche and Wolf, in spite of attributing causal factors to emergent nihilism and deeply profound moments, respectively, may simply be illuminating the fluctuations in the human condition in one long chronology, one that experienced two big existential disappointments. For Nietzsche God was supposed to assist humanity but "died." For Wolff, science was supposed to reflect our advancement and civilization but instead employed some of the most brilliant people in society to serve madness (that is, war), a point echoed by spiritual philosopher Eckhart Tolle in *A New Earth* (2008). For Nietzsche, the death of God ushered in an age where one had to be an *übermensch*, an "overman," to survive and transcend. For Wolff, to be this *übermensch* required nourishing doses of surrender and catch. The social actor in a Wolffian human condition must now rely on these moments of truth and the super-human labor to maintain it so as to navigate through life. Both saw in the wake of their respective disappointments the need for profound realizations to proceed and to survive, and both illuminate through their own philosophies humanity's long search for sanity, purpose, and direction in life and death.

Wolff insists that social theory must be adequate to confront the consequences of evil. For Wolff, the social sciences as "science" did not—perhaps dared not—address this important theme of social existence (Gordon 2007: 67). Wolff's scions note in affirmation:

The age of modern science brought with it the project of predicting, controlling, and manipulating the natural world. Its project was to discover the principles of linear causality, or natural laws, by which all phenomena are to be reduced . . . Wolff rejects this modern form of reason that denies the unique transcendent(al) capacities of humankind (Backhaus and Psathas 2007: 77).

Surrender and catch was thus a necessary method that allowed Wolff and his proponents to confront the "tragic contradictions of history" (Godway 2007: 83). Wolff felt that by failing to account for the such possibilities of humankind, science also failed to account for the human capacity to "create new meaning [and] existential truth on the basis of transcending socio-historically conditioned everyday life" (Backhaus and Psathas 2007: 77).

Through surrender and catch Wolff is able to conduct a historical diagnosis of the human condition—its meanings and material consequences—all through the conduit of the individual whose discernment from society is blurred (Stehr 2007: 55). Surrender and catch's distinguishing feature is its methodological acceptance of profundities that forcefully displace traditional ideas about what constitutes knowledge (Backhaus and Psathas 2007). One such profundity was found in Wolff's concerns about the Holocaust, and his surrender and catch aimed therefore at mining for cues about the human condition that, for Kalberg (2007: 79), could be harnessed to demolish the "invidious dualisms at the foundation of the Holocaust." For Kalberg, such dualisms, as in "German and Jews, Germans and Gypsies, Germans and Communists— called forth the greatest evil. 'Surrender' reacts with unequivocal clarity, forcefulness, and horror against dualisms" (2007: 79).

Wolff's subjectivized epistemology thus emancipated qualitative sociological methods from its status as arguably the softest sociological method in an already "softened" science. He accomplished this by situating humankind in systemic crises, "hard" events that forced characters, thinkers, and social actors to confront their respective mortalities as their communities collapsed around them. Such an approach was predictably beyond the purview of positivist approaches that rendered subjects into objects, and more inimically, separated facts from values, a divorce that resulted in, again, those dualisms whose political appropriation resulted in the insanity of war and genocide. For Wolff and his sociology of knowledge, such a divorce is untenable because facts and values are indelibly intertwined into, if surrender and catch runs its course, truths that are articulated about the human condition; that is, Wolff's methodological approach accommodates how we are guided by values that operate in the selection of what is significant to research in the first place (Imber 2007: 71). In this manner, method and values become inseparable to the social thinker. Such a perspective Wolff did not see in American sociology even after his many transplants across a variety of universities. For Kalberg:

> Wolff's sociology...has to this day been received only in fragments in the United States...American sociology remains to this day predominantly Durkheimian, Parsonian, positivist, uncritical of...modernity in any fundamental sense, and uninfluenced by the Holocaust (Kalberg 2007: 80).

It is thus not surprising that Wolff's chroniclers have described his sociology as taking an existential turn. Given Wolff's surrender and catch stems from his lamentations of the Holocaust as a key symbol for his crisis of humanity, of death appropriated by not the family but by an anomalous state, we can begin to appreciate the frequency of surrender and catch moments that must have been experienced by all of humanity, from the subaltern to its greatest thinkers and sages, when members of their respective societies encountered their greatest existential crisis: death.

Thus, death talk requires a social context of peace for our surrender and catch self-actualizations to become salient. Dying well is a privilege that only some of us on this planet have, as can be seen in the case when pop icon David Bowie passed away peacefully, glorified and deified. His penultimate task—the release of the *Blackstar* album in 2016—could only have transpired by his access to top physicians working through stable social networks and systems. And author his mortality he did, with fantastic imagery seen in the eponymous music video as well as in "Lazarus," both of which harness motifs to serve as paeans for what he envisions as the essence of mortality. The converse suggests that people's deaths in many parts of the world reflect the state and a variety of other institutions' cooptation of their destinies. Many people may encounter deaths while their social systems are in less than ideal conditions due to poverty, political crises, or when encountering the wrath of nature.

Death talk, like death, is a new frontier, a new communicative horizon that aims to free the individual by reinforcing values for a very mortal existence. Informed by Wolff's surrender and catches, death talk becomes a mechanism for decolonizing a Habermasian lifeworld.

> Our own era simply denies death and with it one fundamental aspect of life. Instead of allowing the awareness of death and suffering to become one of the strongest incentives for life, the basis for human solidarity, and an experience without which joy and enthusiasm lack intensity and depth, the individual is forced to repress it. But, as always the case with repression, by being removed from sight the repressed elements do not cease to exist. Thus the fear of death lives an illegitimate existence among us. It remains alive in spite of the attempt to deny it, but being repressed it remains sterile (Fromm 1969: 245).

Thus, the new rationales, queries, and efforts of Death Cafe activists point to a potential shift toward a consciousness about a shared humanity that can be found not only locally but in our global village. By examining those who confront their mortality through communicative action, we can create points of entry into understanding that there can be sort of unanimity in how the human experience communicatively responds to death and dying, and thus, life and living. This is a rather urgent task in an age where celebrating diversity has frequently taken on an aesthetic trajectory, one which overlooks how diversity is sometimes borne from voluntarily segregating groups not yet fully reconciled with other groups due to the painful historical and material consequences for simply being who they are. Thus, the love of the ethnie is accompanied by the fear and need to compete against and challenge historical "others."

More than biological decay framed by the supernatural, death is also very much an identity, one that encourages practices of reflexivity when the continuity of life is ruptured within the antipodes of living and dying. This existential pivot ultimately binds all humanity together when it turns its page toward the mortal phases of our life cycle, breaking apart one's immortality complex. Yet, regardless of whether we are taken to our horizon of mortality through systemic crisis or through the privilege of being able to fully author our own good death, Fromm's wisdoms are again pertinent: "The instruction on how to die is indeed the same as the instruction on how to live. The more we rid ourselves of the craving for possession in all its forms, particularly our ego-boundness, the less strong is the fear of dying, since there is nothing to lose" (Fromm 1976).

Because the weight of institutional and bureaucratic dynamics on the self can generate reification directed toward systems of mortality, Death Café activists are engaged in fostering social change that will have important implications for generating a paradigm shift toward embracing mortality on one's own terms. Ideally this will occur in ways that check on reification and juridification meted out by social systems. The author of death is aware that dying requires planning and preparation. It requires work and exponentially intense emotional labor by the person dying and by the community that claims the dying person as one of their own. Aside from the existential work needed to frame oneself toward end of life, the process also entails much decision-making, is logistical, requires accounting, and the need to deal with local, state, and for some, even national bureaucracies whose purviews will author the death and dying process for those unwilling to do so. If the freewill most of us have to author or personalize our own trajectory toward our end is ignored because death and dying dynamics are deemed too much of a "burden" as Fromm notes, we will give up our freedom—and escape from the freedom—of determining our emotional, psychical, social contexts, and physical well-being as we near end of life.

But for many in the materialist generation, we have done exactly this. By avoiding the logistical, emotional, and metaphysical preparation for death early on, we escape from freedoms we have to be authentic in living. It is much too convenient to not deal with death and dying, which for much of the human condition, exclaims, proclaims, and even defames the horrific and nerve-wracking fears we have of a corporeal end. Into this denial, the trinity inserts itself with its fantasies and dreamscapes, juridified talk, and techno-gadgetry that robotize humanity. We let lotions and creams, botox, and dreams keep us ensconced in the immortality complex, we let experts dictate how to live so as to live forever, and we let bureaucracies and systems do the same with juridified communication that promote health. Consequently, we do not know how to live, so we do not know how to die. Many of us remain automatons, willingly waking up during the wee hours of the morning to stand in the frigid cold for an updated mobile phone release, yet never waking at the same time to contemplate death in a state of relaxation, as so poignantly noted by Soygal Rinpoche in the *Tibetan Book of Living and Dying* (2012).

Fromm and Wolff allow us to appreciate how Death Café attendees are not escaping from this freedom. Indeed, they are employing Death Café venues as their site for spontaneous activity, most passionately engaged with by attendees who experienced totalizing and epiphanic surrender and catches that emerged during their confrontations with death and dying. With norm-free systems—primarily the trinity, along with the intermittent demands by the state for its citizens to die for it— unwilling to take existential sentiments and concerns to weave into a social narrative about mortality, Café attendees are thus using their freedom *to* rather than their freedom *from* to enhance their understanding of life and living, death and dying. Perhaps Edward Tiryakian's timeless observation, hauntingly prescient in its profundity, is worth invoking: "As societies grow larger in area and denser in population, and as individual differences multiply the time will come when the only thing members of a society will have in common is that they are human" (Tiryakian 1962: 56).

In the next chapter, we again attempt to make operative theoretical assertions that can be amalgamated with our analyses of Death Cafés. We explore the notion of Habermas' public spheres and how this concept can be greatly enhanced by Ray Oldenburg's seminal work on third places. In our examination of the public environment of discourse that are Death Cafés, Habermas' discussion, historical and theoretical, is integrated with Oldenburg's notion of the third place, a public setting that is jovial and elegiac. The formulation I am hoping to reach is how communicative action is a function of third places, and ultimately, that Death Cafés are community and collective environments that can only materialize through them.

NOTES

1. The *Comintern*, or Communist International, was an international Communist organization. Initially founded by Vladimir Lenin in 1919. Its main agenda was to create an internationalized movement to overthrow the world's bourgeois (capitalist) class. Although dissolved in 1943, the onset of the Cold War allowed its resurrection by many Third World nationalists who embraced socialism to fight and end colonial rule in their respective countries.

2. Wolff (1962) concedes that "surrender" implies "passivity" and of "giving up," but reminds readers that this is an issue of semantics. Indeed, Wolff critiques other terms that allude to surrender, terms such as "abandonment" (which is not ideal because "it suggests a dissoluteness quite alien to surrender"), "exposure" ("... but this has a gratuitous ring of voyeurism"), and "devotion" or "dedication" ("... these limit the meaning of surrender to an attitude and inappropriately introduce a moral note") (Wolff 1962: 21–22).

CHAPTER 6

Enhancing Habermas with Ray Oldenburg

Gustav Klimt's *Death and Life* (1911).

© The Author(s) 2017
J. Fong, *The Death Café Movement*,
DOI 10.1007/978-3-319-54256-0_6

In this chapter, the utility of combining Habermas's views on the public sphere with that of Ray Oldenburg's notion of the third place is examined. The chapter aims to illuminate the spatiality of death talk conducive for communicative action and the decolonization of the lifeworld. An amalgamation of Habermas and Oldenburg's ideas will allow Habermas's notion of the public sphere elaborated in *The Structural Transformation of the Public Sphere* (Habermas 1991), to historically "arrive" at the ideas of Oldenburg, explicated in *The Great Good Place* (Oldenburg 1999). As noted at the outset of my work, I hope to only employ theoretical concepts in ways where they can be made operative and/or validated by tangible, visceral, or corporeal manifestations. However, such an amalgamation is vital for other important reasons that inform this chapter.

One important reason is that the public sphere and third place, in spite of their sometimes deviating trajectories insofar as how they are envisioned to function, are quite interchangeable concepts. In short, Habermas documents their emergence historically as environments where mutual exchange can be seen first for the court, then for the bourgeois class that emerged as capitalism took root in Western Europe. Oldenburg's notion of the third place illuminates the same architecture, but adopts an enthusiastic yet elegiac view of their importance as an *informal public* sphere, one to be discerned from the second place of work where we are enmeshed in a formal public sphere, and the first place of home and family, where we experience an informal private sphere.

A second reason is that Oldenburg's ideas help frame how Habermas's communicative action unfolds and disentangles itself from the frequently chaotic, community-robbing dynamics of contemporary urban experiences. It should be noted, that although Habermas went through great pains to demonstrate the historical evolution of the public sphere through the elaboration of its dynamics and functions, he does not explicitly formulate the public sphere as contingent upon urban configuration and dynamics. In contrast, Oldenburg saw third places spatially, and because of their intimate configurations, as the *sine qua non* for enriching whatever community life exists within the urban context. Although this appears to be an intellectual gulf, the bridging of the two concepts is not without merit. If urbanity is conceptualized as an outcome of modernity borne through industrialization, then the proliferation of Death Cafés in primarily urban areas reflects how the venues are contesting the discontents of modernity at its source: within cities. Within cities we have what Habermas describes as the exhaustion of utopian energies (Habermas 1986) stemming from the city apparatus colonizing the lifeworld, juridification, cold technocratic bureaucracies, lack of systemic ethics, hollow materialism, alienation of the subject, and alienation of the subject from mortality. It is not hard to envision such a scenario if we realize that cities are essentially large supermarkets where their highways and roads—analogous to the different shopping aisles within a supermarket—take citizens to their destinations of consumption. Death Cafés can thus be construed as an urban movement as well, responding to urbanity's undesirable effects upon lifeworld autonomy.

Finally, amalgamating the public sphere with the third place allows one to envision how communicative action at Death Cafés unfold in ways that can be enjoyable and cathartic—attributes that Oldenburg so frequently celebrate in his historical and cultural examination of third places. As alluded throughout this monograph, Death Cafés are not depressive environments; whatever themes death talk addresses have been conveyed through community support, humor, and collective displays of empathy, all of which allow each event to conclude on a positive, life affirming mode.

THE PUBLIC SPHERE

Although the English translation of Habermas's work first found textual exposition by 1989, the original German work under the title *Strukturwandel der Öffentlicheit* was published in 1962, 27 years earlier, predating the German edition of the first volume of *Communicative Action* by almost 20 years. *Structural Transformation of the Public Sphere* (Habermas 1991) introduces spatial, demographic, and historical references to how public fora evolved. Moreover, patterns of its infiltration by macro-level systems established by the new bourgeois class hints at the colonization of the lifeworld thesis to come as Habermas profiled such transformations in the public spheres of Britain, France, and Germany. However it would be the *Theory of Communicative Action* that illuminated the communication dynamics *within* public spheres in post-Enlightenment modernity. That said, Habermas was apparently unhappy with the work. For Calhoun, he was "at least conscious of the large amount of empirical research done on themes relevant to it during the 1960s" and thus cited "one of the reasons for the delayed translation was that he had intended for years to rework this text. He never did, but readers may be surprised how many of Habermas's later themes are pre-figured in this work" (Calhoun 1994: 5).

For Habermas, the public sphere is "public" in that they are "open to all" in ways where freedom can take root beyond institutions and the "obscurity of the private sphere" (Habermas 1991: 2–4). Ideally, the public sphere had to allow for the disregard of status, relying instead on "justifiable trust," the promotion of rational argument as the "sole arbiter of any issue," along with the address of issues "that until then had not been questioned"; finally, the public sphere had to remain inclusive (Calhoun 1994: 12).

> First, they preserved a kind of social intercourse that, far from presupposing the equality of status, disregarded status altogether.... Secondly, discussion within such a public presupposed the problematization of areas that until then had not been questioned.... Thirdly... the public... could never close itself off entirely and become consolidated as a clique; for it always under-stood and found itself immersed within a more inclusive public of all private people, persons who-insofar as they were propertied and educated-as read-ers, listeners, and spectators could avail themselves via the market of the objects that were subject to discussion. (Habermas 1991: 36-37)

Not unlike Oldenburg, Habermas views the public sphere as one that "stood or fell with the principle of universal access." He also notes how, "a public sphere from which specific groups would be ... excluded was less than merely incomplete; it was not a public sphere at all" (1991: 85). However, Habermas was stringent with his notion of the public sphere because of its vital function as a politicized environment, an orientation that sets him apart from Oldenburg, who saw third places as where primarily recreational community dialog takes place. Invoking Kant to warn us about its constriction, one that was "the effective cause of all secret societies" (1991: 107), Habermas saw in public spheres a realm of "freedom and permanence" that exhibited democratic energies beyond elections (1991: 4). For Habermas, it thus became imperative to reclaim the public sphere "regulated from above against the public authorities themselves" so that citizens can "engage them in a debate over the general rules governing relations in the basically privatized but publicly relevant sphere of commodity exchange and social labor" (1991: 27), if only for the "natural vocation of man to communicate with his fellows, especially in matters of affecting mankind as a whole" (1991: 107). For Habermas, such an environment was unique and without historical precedent because of the "people's public use of reason" (1991: 27). Other scholars have contributed their renderings of the public sphere as well, with Eley defining the concept as that "realm of social life in which something approaching public opinion can be formed" and where "access is guaranteed to all citizens" (1994: 289). In a manner that frames the dynamics of Death Cafés, Eley emphasizes how a "portion of the public sphere comes into being in every conversation in which private individuals assemble to form a public body" (1994: 289).

Historically, public spheres did not always exhibit such a degree of egalitarianism, having gone through different atavisms where its publicity was initially tied to monarchical dynamics following the Middle Ages; that is, the queen and king "largely monopolized public authority" (1991: 68) and determined with the court what was worthy of being in public discourse. This older iteration of top-down juridification is problematic for Habermas. During this period, the growing propertied class still unfettered from its deference to monarchy, employed public spheres as environments to display material culture acquired by those with social and cultural capital. This dynamic meant that the early bourgeois voluntarily segregated their ilk into a closed communicative community. In the case of eighteenth-century Germany, the nobility's sense of self-worth was completely dependent on the validation of the court and thus "failed to develop strong enough lines of communication with bourgeois intellectuals to participate in creating a strong civil society separate from the state" (Calhoun 1994: 15). Aesthetic discernments were also involved as fashion came to signal occupation and class standing in ways that Lofland (1973) terms as *appearational ordering*, the process by which members of preindustrial society decipher and decode strangers in their midst by observing attire. Habermas echoes Lofland's views:

The staging of the publicity involved in representation was wedded to personal attributes such as insignia (badges and arms), dress (clothing and coiffure), demeanor (form of greeting and poise) and rhetoric (form of address and formal discourse in general)—in a word, to a strict code of "noble" conduct. The latter crystallized during the High Middle Ages into the system of courtly virtues, a Christianized form of the chivalrous and courteous. Characteristically, in none of these virtues did the physical aspect entirely lose its significance, for virtue must be embodied, it had to be capable of public representation. (Habermas 1991: 8)

This public representation signaled the actor's links (or lack thereof) to the court. In this regard, public spheres were spheres to show one's proximity to the ruling class and to the monarch. Strangers were not *that* strange after all, as visual cues identifying social class predominated the lifeworld. That Death Cafés no longer rely on these visual cues while still celebrating a community of strangers points to how public spheres would ultimately transform into settings where class distinctions are less explicit and less reliant on aesthetic presentations, if at all, a point that Oldenburg frequently celebrates about third places.

By the time the bourgeoisie found form in the frenetic pace of economic development leading up to the Industrial Revolution and beyond, guilds functioned as a segue mechanism toward the public spheres we are familiar with today. Aristocracies were no longer hegemonic in all matters of life and would ultimately lose their function and purpose. Guilds, however, are but atavisms of previous forms of the public spheres that, in spite of their attempts to break free from whatever aristocratic systems had constrained their power, now had to contend with a controlling secular and industrialized society. This arrangement was not catastrophic economically since production of exchange values had yet to take on the intensity of mass production for the local and, later through imperialism and colonization, global markets. The delinking of this group from court dynamics was a drawn-out process in that the "towns...had local markets from the beginning" yet remained "in the hands of the guilds and the corporations," and that "these remained strictly regulated, serving more as instruments for the domination of the surrounding areas than for free commodity exchange between town and country" (Habermas 1991: 15). Yet the trajectory of the bourgeois public sphere continued to evolve:

> While the early institutions of the bourgeois public sphere originally were closely bound up with aristocratic society as it became dissociated from the court, the "great" public that formed in the theaters, museums, and concerts was bourgeois in its social origin. Around 1750 its influence began to predominate. (Habermas 1991: 43).

The country that at the time shaped the Industrial Revolution more so than any other, the United Kingdom saw its political public spheres emerge at the turn of the eighteenth century (Habermas 1991).

Given the historical contexts that shape the character of public spheres, the position taken in this work is that Death Cafés could not have arisen in earlier epochs where the church, aristocracy, the bourgeois, were tugged and influenced by institutions that would need to be bureaucratically engorged so as to foster the birth of the nation-state. Thus, the aforementioned institutions were lifeworld colonizers of their respective time periods. Even the early atavism of a bourgeois public sphere orbited around the state in spite of having severed its ties to the court. They did so because of their dependency on the state for legitimation, but also because these early members of the public sphere were members of the bourgeois class; that is, they were elites emanating from a "narrow" segment of Europe's population, "mainly educated, propertied men, and they conducted a discourse not only exclusive of others but prejudicial to the interests of those excluded" (Calhoun 1994: 3).

It should be noted that Habermas's observation of bourgeois dominance as one that still had to defer to the state is a distinctly different reading from Marx, who condemned the intimate links between the state and its capitalist class, one where the former does the bidding of the latter. Habermas saw the public during Western European industrialization as still "state-related" and state-dependent in that the public functioned as an "apparatus with regulated spheres of jurisdiction" (1991: 18). From the bourgeois public sphere, journals and literature emerged to address issues related to the state, as did intellectuals aligned with merchants, bankers, entrepreneurs, and manufacturers. Yet social changes were underway: the press now had a purpose as the public sphere would transition toward being a "reading public," one that brought civil society into existence to further depersonalize state authority. Aided by the press, which Habermas notes had "developed a unique explosive power," the public sphere was slowly acquiring more sovereignty (1991: 20). However, the state was not yet ready to be relegated to the periphery and opened up its own access to the press, and "very soon the press was systematically made to serve the interests of the state administration" (Habermas 1991: 22).

The first journals in the strict sense, ironically called "political journals," appeared weekly at first, and daily as early as the middle of the seventeenth century. In those days private correspondence contained detailed and current news about Imperial Diets, wars, harvests, taxes, transports of precious metals, and, of course, reports on foreign trade. (Habermas 1991: 20).

Elsewhere Habermas notes:

> Besides the carriers of commercial and finance capitalism, a growing group
> of entrepreneurs, manufacturers, and factory owners became dependent
> upon measures taken by the state administration whose intent certainly
> was not merely that of controlling commercial-entrepreneurial activity but
> also of encouraging initiative through regulation. (1991: 23–24).

However, with a depersonalizing state that began to concede territory to
civil society, the bourgeois class then became the "real carrier of the
public" (Habermas 1991: 23), one that, in a nod to Hobbes, expressed
public opinion, consciousness, and conscience (Habermas 1991: 89–90).

> This stratum of "bourgeois" was the real carrier of the public, which from
> the outset was a reading public. Unlike the great urban merchants and
> officials who, in former days, could be assimilated by the cultivated nobility
> of the Italian Renaissance courts, they could no longer be integrated . . . into
> the noble culture at the close of the Baroque period. Their commanding
> status in the new sphere of civil society led instead to a tension between
> "town" and "court." (Habermas 1991: 23).

Just as importantly, private concerns within a confined spatial environment, what Oldenburg terms the first place, the environment of family
dynamics, now emerged into public discourse that expressed and attended
to issues related to household economics. The free market would soon
devour these concerns, outputting services and commodities that inserted
themselves into a burgeoning middle class and their households. Not
surprisingly, death and dying patterns experienced major shifts in social
and cultural configuration. The personal matters of death now became
subject to appropriation by macro-level institutions such as the healthcare,
deathcare, and media industries, systems that Habermas assigned colonizing and juridifying tendencies to. Systems, then, appear to exhibit a very
consistent historical tendency to consume public sphere discourse: concerned communication by the public are appropriated by industry, the
contents of which are rendered catalytic in generating new products, and
returned to the public through juridification where warranties and warn-
ings related to its use are surfeit.

In the United States, one can see very explicitly the mediated manner in
which healthcare appropriates concerns about human health. For example,

the numerous pharmaceutical medications that can be seen on television advertisements, presented in familial or lifeworld backdrops where friends and kin are in highly sociable settings, seem, on the surface, a lovely *mise-en-scène*. A less critical observer may not realize that such scenarios already serve as tropes for a colonized lifeworld. Indeed, the drug maker is "there" with the folks at the barbecue suffering from acid reflux, there swimming in a lake with fellow Baby Boomers, there with a group of characters who suffer from incontinence, and there always in empathy. Then appears the fine print on the side effects of the drug, the need to see your doctor or physician to see if you qualify for the drug, the prohibitions of taking the drug with another drug, etc., its textual exposition presented in diminutive and narrow font typesetting so as much legal stipulation as possible can be crammed into the video imagery.

Habermas's critique of the mass media is not unlike the many sentiments expressed by Café attendees, namely, that at this juncture in our social development, "the mass media recommend themselves as addressees of personal needs and difficulties, as authorities for advice on the problems of life" (1991: 172). Habermas reminds us to return democratic dynamics into the public sphere because regardless of its atavisms, the public sphere is an ideal type.

> Publicity was, according to its very idea, a principle of democracy not because anyone could in principle announce with equal opportunity, his personal inclinations, wishes, and convictions...it could only be realized in the measure that these personal opinions could evolve through the rational-critical debate of a public into public opinion. (Habermas 1991: 29).

Garnham argues that Habermas clearly distinguishes the public sphere from that of the state and market and, as a result, positions the observer to view "threats to democracy and the public discourses upon which it depends" (1994: 361). The aforementioned conditions are why Habermas believes that democracy remains an unfinished project: the systems above actors are not democratic beyond institutional mechanisms that allow for voting, which in itself can only occur intermittently through political cycles. Beyond this election cyclicity, other systems are at work, engaging in the process of colonizing the lifeworld, stifling democratic deliberation. A quick transplantation of implications from our observations of past public spheres toward the present suggests that the process of colonizing the lifeworld of mortality is still ongoing, with systems stigmatizing, if not technically controlling death talk in ways where a more determinately free public sphere such as Death Cafés can counter.

Death Café participation by its attendees are thus taking place in a Habermasian manner where "the public concern regarding the private sphere of civil society was no longer confined to the authorities but was considered by the subjects as one that was properly theirs" (Habermas 1991: 23). Social movement theorist such as Goldstone carves out just enough analytical space to accommodate Habermas ideas when he notes how democratic institutions provide "laws and practices in which citizens and groups are given rights to assemble, speak, write and associate freely" (2004: 333). Yet Goldstone forwards an erroneous position typically seen in much of the social movement literature: that success of democracy is still dependent on political action through "elections of officials or voting on ballot issues" (2004: 333). In other words, the determinants of social movement success must come from how it contests the state, and whether the state acquiesces to or adopts the views of the social movement. However, this condition is not sought after at Death Café meetings given its frequent orientation toward transcendence (we will have more to say about this orientation as it pertains to social movements in the final chapter of my work).

The bourgeois-driven public sphere, in spite of its ability to insert itself into society, ultimately declined in influence. By the mid-1800s, new social conditions adjusted to the inadequacies of laissez-faire capitalism. This prompted state transformation toward that of a welfare state where provisions were provided for citizens by decree, a process that nonetheless did not prevent the private and public from becoming amalgamated further by consumerism and commercialism. In this manner, the "state and society, once distinct, became interlocked" (Calhoun 1994: 21). Habermas laments on how such developments allowed infiltration into the lifeworld by a capitalist welfare state that is intimately tied to market dynamics, thus obstructing venues for "conflicting private wills of rational people" to "be brought into harmony" (Calhoun 1994: 18).

A key shortcoming in the public sphere thesis as it pertains to Death Cafés needs to be addressed, however. Chief among these is that Habermas conceptualizes the public sphere to be an ideal environment for political discourse, the components of which constitute his communicative action theory (that is, how validity claims, mutual consensus, intersubjective understanding function as communicative attributes for political empowerment). Schudson forwards the same condition, that "the more people participate as citizens in politics, the closer one comes to the idea of a public sphere" (1994: 147). Oreskes of the *New York Times* echoes the same sentiment in that the "first generation raised with television is a generation that participates less in democracy than any before it" (1988). Yet Death Café activities are not political in the conventional sense. Café attendees are not discussing empowerment through systems or geopolitical dominance. Instead, Café participants are seeking self-mastery and existential empowerment in spite of systems. However, Death Cafés do exhibit instances of political expression that reveal the character of a deliberative democracy "rooted in the intuitive ideal" where "the justification of the terms and conditions of association proceeds through public argument and reasoning among equal citizens" (Cohen 1997: 72).

Although Habermas's view that a colonized lifeworld within the public sphere implies the latter's transition away from a political function, the public sphere remains relevant for our discussion because Oldenburg's notion of the third place offers a different reading of the public sphere, where even in its apolitical function, such environments are still able to offer abundant cues and strategies for personal and community empowerment. Moreover, Oldenburg, unlike Habermas, did not see complete colonization of the public sphere/third place. For Oldenburg, such environments are alive and well, thriving in different degrees around the world, and are still able to generate the sovereign and autonomous communicative content that Habermas believes are needed for political and social change.

In spite of Habermas's desire to construct the public sphere as a site for the genesis of political change, Calhoun critiques Habermas for failing to "address the power relations, the networks of communication, the topography of issues, and the structure of influence of the public sphere except in very general terms of the existence of factions and parties" (Calhoun 1994: 38). The conceptualization of the public sphere as colonized and consequentially populated by passive nonactors is also an inconclusive perspective, a view that Oldenburg would likely contest. At this juncture and through cautious extrapolations that frame the Death Café as social movement, it appears that public spheres can remain in continuous transformation and thus function as social spaces that generate prototypical social movements for grievances of the time. They may be apolitical environments, but such a status in no way suggests they cannot transform into politicized environments in the future. Death Cafés are located in this fluid, liquid continuum.

Because Habermas views public spheres as colonized, he is critiqued for leaving out in his analysis the possibility for them to birth social movements even if they are apolitical. He overlooks the link between social movement participants who deliberately remain apolitical for now, but later, reorient their movement to politically contest the state. Thus, Death Cafés have the capacity to function as sites of political processes, but they can just as well function as birthplaces where apolitical social movements are born to address power relations and the many inequalities tied to mortality. Even this germinating process was alluded to by Calhoun himself: "Phenomena like nationalism, feminism, and gay, ethnic, or youth consciousness often involve crucial redefinitions of the issues and identities involved in political struggles" (1994: 34). That Death Cafés now have a global presence suggests that it is already a mass movement, albeit without the demonstrations inherent in many "out on the street" protests.

Before we transitioning to our discussion of the third place, we should heed Calhoun's reminder that the efficacy of public spheres lies "in the development of institutional bases," that is, tangible spatial environments (1994: 12). Although Habermas tends toward a dense, almost mechanical process of elaboration in describing the public sphere, Habermas at times spared himself theoretical labor and grounds his theory. For example, he provides historically rich insights into such physical spaces.

> Around the middle of the seventeenth century...tea—first to be popular— but also chocolate and coffee had become the common beverages of at least the well-to-do strata of the population...By the first decade of the eighteenth century London already had 3,000 of them, each with a core group of regulars. (Habermas 1991: 32).

In Lebert H. Weir's classic *Europe at Play*, the mid 1930s saw thousands of cafés throughout France. This amounted to an average of "one café to about every fifty people" (Weir 1937: 437–438). Similarly, John Gunther's *Twelve Cities* notes that Paris alone had 13,977 sidewalk cafés (Gunther 1967: 70). Coffee, an ideal stimulant for the requirements of the market and a budding capitalism, became an essential part of European life. Oldenburg, however, forwards a normative appreciation for the coffee phenomena:

Caffeine beverages encourage behavior different from that associated with alcoholic drinks. How much of the difference may be attributed to the chemicals themselves is difficult to ascertain; in either instance, behavior is largely the product of cultural learning and may vary widely from one society to the next. Yet there are definite patterns that cut across the world's cultures. In the Moslem world, where coffee drinking began, that beverage is the "wine of Apollo, the beverage of thought dream, and dialectic." Similar effects are noted in the Christian world. Coffee spurs the intellect; alcohol the emotions and the soma. Those drinking coffee are content to listen contemplatively to music, while those drinking alcohol are inclined to make music of their own. Dancing is commonly associated with the consumption of alcoholic beverages but not at all with coffee sipping. Reading material is widely digested in the world's coffeehouses but not in the bars. (1999: 184).

Insofar as how communicative dynamics unfold, Calhoun adds:

The conversation of these little circles branched out into affairs of state administration and politics. Journals of opinion were created, which linked the thousands of smaller circles in London and throughout the country. These were often based at particular coffee houses and replicated in their contents the style of convivial exchange. In France, salons, public institutions located in private homes, played a crucial role, bridging a literary public sphere dominated by aristocrats with the emergent bourgeois political public sphere. In Germany, table societies drew together especially academic but also other sorts of people. (1994: 12).

Furthermore, Habermas notes how public spheres such as cafés allowed an eroding aristocratic class to establish links with a burgeoning bourgeois stratum that included intellectuals and merchants, as well as new members of the middles class such as artisans and shopkeepers. Public spheres such as cafés and salons thus became mechanisms of social change in that access for members of the community was more informal. It also "embraced the wider strata of the middle class, including craftsmen and shopkeepers," with wealthy shopkeepers visiting "coffee house several times a day" and this "held true for the poor...as well" (Habermas 1991: 33). Such publics spheres ultimately served to convey how civil society articulated itself in ways that allowed the state authority to "correspond to its needs" (Habermas 1991: 74). Only in later iterations of the public sphere did it become apparent that the state and media had, according to Habermas, entered the purview of this last site of democratic expression, one that could still be salvaged through communicative action, a process that decolonizes juridified scripts pitched by the state and the market.

Unlike Oldenburg, Habermas neglects both the rhetorical and recreational aspects of communicative action. That too much emphasis has been granted to political and economic dynamics in Habermas's formulation of the public sphere (Garnham 1994: 360) behooves us to, at this juncture, enter a deeper discussion of Oldenburg's notion of the third place. The synchronicity between Oldenburg and Habermas is uncanny even though the former's work did not reference Habermas directly.

THE THIRD PLACE

Like Habermas, Ray Oldenburg's *The Great Good Place* (1999) identifies the significant relationship that third places have upon community life. More so than even Habermas, Oldenburg's notion of the third place is most apt for explaining the atmosphere, the "vibe," of Death Cafés. An urban sociologist with wonderful historical and cross-cultural insights into his rendering of this type of public space, Oldenburg's notion of the third place is discussed to remind readers that Death Café communicative dynamics can frequently be lighthearted.

As noted at the outset of this chapter, the third place is that configured and informal site of social interaction that welcomes informal communicative dynamics within its public. Both Oldenburg and Habermas envision the public setting as a site for contesting the juridified and regulatory orders of systemic authority. The third place is, as notes Oldenburg, "largely a world of its own making, fashioned by talk and quite independent of the institutional order of the larger society" (1999: 48). For Oldenburg, along with its ability to promote democratic practices at the community level, third places also perform the vital function of "uniting the neighborhood" (1999: xvii). Third places such as bars, hair salons, and coffeehouses, allow citizens to engage in talk and "let loose." Oldenburg concedes that the term is quite generic, but nonetheless sees the utility in employing it to describe "a variety of public places that host the regular, voluntary, informal, and happily anticipated gatherings of individuals beyond the realms of home and work" (1999: 16). Indeed, the home is not a third, but the "first place" where the conjugal family lives privately and informally. Work constitutes the "second place" as it is where public life is formalized. Both are unable to enhance community interaction.

The consequences of the Industrial Revolution were, for Oldenburg, a pivotal period insofar as community dynamics are concerned. For Oldenburg, the line between first and second places was blurred prior to industrial development in Western Europe and the United States. That is, work was often done from home be it through the skilled artisan or the farmer working the land. However, with the advent of industrial output, mass production, and mass consumption, the boundary between place of work and place of residence was demarcated. Consequently, this demarcation removed "productive work from the home and . . . morality, and spirit from family life" (1999: 16). Work and private environments thus became clearly distinct and in between these two spheres exists the third place. For Oldenburg, third places have tremendous staying power in spite of transformations to the family and work environments. Indeed, this community anchor point had been established "long before this separation, and so our term is a concession to the sweeping effects of the Industrial Revolution and its division of life into private and public spheres" (1999: 16).

Third places, however, are not to be essentialized as their presence and atmosphere reveal differing cultural predilections and sentiments toward such environments. Cultural, economic, and political dynamics across the present and across time configure the size, the dispersion, and the atmosphere of third places. Oldenburg's global travels and analyses have resulted in some interesting findings: third places in the United States have a very weak presence in urban life, hinting at our population's fear of public spaces. Oldenburg notes rather unflatteringly, "In newer American communities . . . third places are neither prominent nor prolific . . . one may encounter people rather pathetically trying to find some spot in which to relax and enjoy each others' company" (1999: 17). However, in Ireland, France, or Greece—indeed much of Europe—third places have an important function in the daily life of its urban residents. Oldenburg's examination of continental Europe's long chronology of relying on third places for community life makes us appreciate how cities like London and Paris have since welcomed yet another iteration of the third place in the guise of Death Cafés.

Oldenburg argued that third places have since a therapeutic effect upon residents of urban society and laments how little research has been undertaken on this area of social life. Although urban resources that reduce stress through rituals such as yoga and gym activities abound, the third place involves dynamics that are the "people's own remedy for stress, loneliness, and alienation" (1999: 20). Having traveled around the world to explore Vienna, Austria's coffeehouses, English pubs in London, cafés in France, the Italian *taberna*, and a variety of venues here in the United States, Oldenburg notes how third places function as neutral grounds in the community where people can be "most alive" and "most themselves" (1999: 20). In urban environments that discourage such forms of association, many "withdraw to privacy as turtles into their shells," and people become lonely "in the midst of many" (1999: 203). Oldenburg also incisively notes how third places "remain among the very few places where the generations still enjoy one another's company" (1999: xx). Oldenburg goes as far as proclaiming how "nothing contributes as much to one's sense of belonging to a community as much as 'membership' in a third place" (1999: xxiii).

Third places are sites of public life that counter notions of the city as being alienating places where, as urban sociologists like Lofland (1973) notes, we are forced to cope with strangers on a daily basis. At Death Cafés, however, the anxiety about a stranger-filled public is tamed as each Café event progresses. Friendships and camaraderie among strangers are fostered in ways that allow one to argue that Death Cafés bring strangers together and allow them the option of leaving, at the very least, as potential if not bona fide friends. Third places are where community is most "upbeat" and "cheerful," and where the art of conversation constitutes its main activity and is a "lively game" (1999: 20–29). For Oldenburg, the third place is the place where that "lone stranger . . . is most apt to become a regular" (1999: 35). Although Oldenburg discusses in much detail how cafés, book stores, and hair salons function as third places, it is the cafés, bars, and pubs of the neighborhood that tend to function as social lubricants to remove many interpersonal inhibitions. Successful third place cafés, bars, or pubs are deliberately cozy and have jovial environments that provide for its patrons what Oldenburg terms as "spiritual tonic" (1999). Most relevant for our understanding of the Death Café as a third place, is how the venues are just as effective in the process of "leveling" all patrons' social statuses so that "honest expression triumphs over sophistication" (1999: 125).

Oldenburg views the presence of leveling at third places as a model of how a healthy democratic society can interact communally. Third place leveling functions as a social lubricant by allowing those who live in poverty, for example, to have a social experience where daily life struggle is made to lose "much of its sting," simply because the "disadvantaged can be accepted as equals" (1999: 25); that is, a medical doctor might enjoy a beer with a custodian while a small business owner discusses the travails of business with a chaplain. In ideal situations, leveling is also good for business, as it does not formally engage in a politics of exclusion against certain types of patrons. Indeed, if a particular theme or polemic is to be addressed, leveling allows for communicative action to proceed. By functioning to be inclusive of all patrons through leveling, social status in third places become relatively muted and allows for the forwarding of Habermasian validity claims, activation of associated discourses, and the establishment of intersubjectivity and, ideally, mutual consensus.

> "Membership" in third place groups depends upon coming to terms with people who, on certain subjects... one doesn't agree with... Membership also means that sometimes, one's pet ideas don't go over with the group. They don't agree. Unlike that association based on ideology or "political correctness," or scapegoating, one's ideas don't "cost you" in third place gatherings... One intrudes an idea and the others may nod, or groan, or frown, or laugh but nothing is lost. It's all rather like a good classroom. (Oldenburg 1999: xxv).

Across the present and across time, cafés, bars, bookstores, and hair salons have functioned to offer the community an environment where people get to know one another. Drawing from his historical and cross-cultural examination of the third places in Western Europe and the United States, Oldenburg correlates these third places more explicitly in the context of two centuries' worth of urban development, which Oldenburg views critically. The view that urban development is somehow parasitic of community is not new. The discourse of urban planning and urban sociology frequently categorizes scholars with such views as "decline of community" theorists. Arguably, classics such as Gratz's wonderful work *The Living City* (1989) as well as Von Eckhardt's *Back to the Drawing Board* (1978), both of which address urban discontents and empowerment at the neighborhood level, fall into this category, as does Oldenburg's work.

Oldenburg is critical of the seeming ignorance urban residents have about urban stressors that bombard their lives. For Oldenburg, many thus fail to appreciate how "relieving stress can just as easily be built into an urban environment as those features which produce stress" (1999: 10). Many communities stand idly by when developers with their modernist orientations insert large and planned structures that are conducive to economism, but not community, into their neighborhoods. Even though Oldenburg's critique of modern environments without third places hints at his nostalgia, that Oldenburg considers the dearth of third places as unsuitable for *healthy* human habitation needs to be seriously considered. Indeed, Oldenburg views US urban environments as one that discourages human association. One consequence of this behavior is that it allows urban environments to continue their reproduction of alienating urban configurations:

> Without such places, the urban area fails to nourish the kinds of relationships and the diversity of human contact that are the essence of the city. Deprived of these settings, people remain lonely within their crowds. The only predictable social consequence of technological advancement is that they will grow ever more apart from one another... America does not rank well on the dimension of her informal public life and less well now than in the past. Increasingly, her citizens are encouraged to find their relaxation, entertainment, companionship, even safety, almost entirely within the privacy of homes that have become more a retreat from society than a connection to it. (1999: xxix).

Like Habermas, Oldenburg gives pride of place to conversation and communication. Although Habermas sees a trajectory for public sphere emancipation born from communicative action that attends to how some citizens' lifeworlds have been colonized, Oldenburg accommodates the recreational, even apolitical contexts of the third place:

> Nothing more clearly indicates a third place than that the talk there is good; that it is lively, scintillating, colorful, and engaging. The joys of association in third places may initially be marked by smiles and twinkling eyes, by handshaking and backslapping, but they proceed and are maintained in pleasurable and entertaining conversation.... Within its circles, the art of conversation is preserved against its decline in the larger spheres, and evidence of this claim is abundant....Even the sharper wits must refrain from dominating conversation, for all are there to hold forth as well as to listen (1999: 26–28).

In this regard, Oldenburg suggests that conversation and the character of the talk has the potential to create a powerful transcending effect upon third place communicators. In the context of Death Cafés, the surrender and catch episodes conveyed during communicative action constitute the elements of such transcendence.

Although Oldenburg frequently emphasizes how third places are social spaces where friendships are formed and maintained, he also identifies a few unwelcome personality types or groups that detract from third places, the first of which is the uncommunicative bore. To spot the "bores" of the third places, one need only observe the patron that speaks too loudly and too much—a means of compensating for their lack of wit. Boring patrons cause jovial patrons to feel impatient. Body language is first to articulate this state, as some may simply leave the group or find other means of creating an exit strategy. Bores, for Oldenburg, affect intragroup dynamics and relationships dramatically. Another group that has been criticized for detracting from third place environments is the "college crowd." Oldenburg is agitated by this demographic. However, Oldenburg ultimately concedes about his own complicity during his younger days, when his "gang discovered a marvelous place at the edge of our college town and presumed to take it over in great number" (1999: 131). A more charitable view can be found in the archetype of the "shy" person, a category of individuals not explicitly addressed by Oldenburg. One can surmise, however, that introverts at third places become the personal projects of an articulate extrovert and the shy person is invariably drawn out of his/her comfort zone.

The bore and college crowd, and even undergraduate students, were nowhere to be found at the Death Cafés presented in this work. Instead, there is a genuine desire by primarily the Baby Boomers that attend to converse, to ask, and to listen without what Childs describes as a "politics of conversion" (2003). Although leveling dynamics at Death Cafés exist by design (attributed to facilitator configuration of the environment), it also manifests as a very natural ethos in the collective of attendees. Death Café attendees know they are part of something unique, and that as a result, desire to share as well as listen to alternative and creative ways of conceptualizing, confronting, and coping with mortality.

The "problem" of bores and college students aside, Oldenburg quotes architect Victor Gruen, who observes that we construct "civic centers that are concentration camps for bureaucrats, who are thus prevented from mingling with common folks" (Gruen 1964; cited in Oldenburg 1999: 69). In a prescient observation, Gruen adds how these conditions "explain why they lose their touch with and understanding of the problems of the latter"

(Gruen 1964; cited in Oldenburg 1999: 69). Unlike Habermas who saw a bourgeois public sphere established by those who benefitted from the growth of the market, and thus now needed to have public environments where like-minded merchants, industrialists, and technocrats can convey information, Oldenburg notes that the increasingly prosperous middle class retreated or escaped from—invoking Fromm—the freedoms that did exist outside in the "world and its confusions" (1999: 26). The retreat in Oldenburg's generation was one of escaping into television, which for Oldenburg "really isn't interesting enough to garner all the blame heaped upon it" (1999: xxiii); for us today, such escapes take place through social media and online activities. Consequently, such an escape from community means that residents erroneously equate urban dynamics and stimuli with ill health, and private dynamics with good health, that the "causes of stress are social but the cures are individual" (1999: 10).

Like Habermas, Oldenburg also sees corporations colonizing the areas ideal for third places, without which no factories, chain restaurants, and large membership-driven stores—what he terms nonplaces—could exist. In the process, systemic forces turn the individual into a customer, shopper, client, or patient, "a body to be seated, an address to be billed, a car to be parked" (1999: 205). Compartmentalized residents, disciplined by consumerist architecture thus become constrained and constricted from self-actualization. The individual, disciplined, regulated, and controlled, is thus exposed to corporate stimuli where a "familiar logo beckons" by offering the "predictable and the familiar to the nation's nomads" yet "offers a real place to nobody" (1999: 205). Extending the critique of nonplaces into the televisual realm—and by implication a critique that applies to online activities as well—Oldenburg exhibits parallel concerns as Habermas about the effects of a colonized lifeworld upon a community's communicative action dynamics.

> Currently, Americans spend about 90 percent of their leisure time in their homes. Is the figure so high because home life is so attractive or is it because we have created a world beyond the home that no longer offers relaxed and inexpensive companionship with others, a commodity once as easily obtained as a stroll down the street? (1999: 214)?

Oldenburg recounts Pierre Salinger's positive experiences living in France:

The French, of course, have solved the problem of place. The Frenchman's daily life sits firmly on a tripod consisting of home, place of work, and another setting where friends are engaged during the midday and evening *aperitif* hours, if not earlier and later. In the United States the middle classes particularly are attempting a balancing act on a bipod consisting of home and work. That alienation, boredom, and stress are endemic among us is not surprising. For most of us, a third of life is either deficient or absent altogether, and the other two-thirds cannot be successfully integrated into a whole. (1999: 15).

In tandem with Habermas, Oldenburg forwards a solution on how to contest a mediated public sphere:

The best counter to the harmful and alien influence that the media too often represents are face-to-face groups in which people participate in discussion of what is important to them and how to preserve it. And here, perhaps, is where the media does its greatest damage. The delivered newspaper and the piped-in voices of radio and television encourage people to stay in their homes. Time spent in isolation is time lost to affiliation. (1999: 77).

Whereas Habermas viewed the public sphere as a site where democracy can begin to be revived through communicative action, Oldenburg envisions the solution beginning with the rejection of components of mediation such as television, radio, and news. Through public spheres such as a Death Café third place

people get to know one another and to like one another and then to care for one another. When people care for one another, they take an interest in their welfare; and *this is a vastly superior form of welfare than that obtained by governmental programs* (italics added). It is based on mutual consent, genuine empathy, and real understanding of people's situations. Nobody is a "case." (Oldenburg 1999: xxi).

In an observation that captures the dynamics of many Death Café public spheres:

Third place association is upbeat because of the freedom of expression that it encourages. It is freedom from the obligations of social roles and the styles and demeanor with which those roles must be played. Here, individuals may uncork that which other situations require them to bottle up. (Oldenburg 1999: 58).

Such concerns are not new, however. Aside from those articulated by our Death Café participants during my attendances, by the Cold War period Frankfurt School theorist Herbert Marcuse and his ilk of Critical Theory thinkers, of which Habermas is an intellectual scion of, were warning humanity about how ubiquitous advertisement and consumerism were turning people into "one-dimensional" beings that had lost all ability for independent thinking. Indeed, the role of technology in the process of turning citizens into one dimensional beings is hardly neutral, but in the final instance explicitly serves "the politics of domination" (Marcuse 1964: 80). Marcuse cites that one major consequence of this "institutional desublimation" where third places are erased from urban life is the "conquest of transcendence," a condition where superficiality prevails in ways that prevent consciousness raising and emancipation (1964: 79). Oldenburg shares these same sentiments and laments how

> our postwar residential areas are extremely hostile to strangers, outsiders, and new residents of the area...The city and the neighborhood suffer as well when there is a failure to integrate newcomers and enlist their good services to the betterment of community life...third places offer the great ease of association so important to community life. (1999: xviii).

Oldenburg and Habermas do not always theoretically synchronize their respective notions of third places and public spheres. For example, Oldenburg never explicitly addressed to what degree a venue is a third place if it is established with varied schedules, as in Betsy and Lisa's scheduling of Death Cafes to take place at different coffee shops, restaurants, and café-like environments during the year. Although other Death Café organizers are rooted to particular cafés, restaurants, or diners that allow for a contingent of people to engage in death talk, to what degree third place dynamics can continue to build community with this format, as in Betsy's more "mobile" Death Cafés, was not addressed. Indeed, Oldenburg views third places as rooted in the community where "regulars" can frequent their favorite third place establishment. This difference is significant because some Death Café configurations (as in those that take place at different sites) prevent "regulars" from grounding themselves in the community. The liberty I have taken with Oldenburg's formulations is to still conceive Death Cafés, even if they change venues, as bona fide third places. The key attributes of third places are all present (save its physical rootedness in, say a neighborhood block): it importantly remains a "neutral ground upon which people may gather" (1999: 22), allows people—and in the case of Death Cafés, strangers—to be themselves, privileges great conversation, builds solidarity and community, and encourages a leveling of status, a primary factor for why class, income, and occupational data were not disclosed by Café attendees who participated in this research.

Another key difference between Habermas's formulation of the public sphere and Oldenburg's third place is that, as earlier noted, the latter infused joy and recreation into third place environments. Habermas neglected to observe this type of communicative dynamic because his notion of the public sphere/third place was oriented toward the political. For Habermas, the public sphere's success is contingent upon communicative action geared toward encouraging citizens to engage in contestations against oppressive macro-level institutions. Only in such a manner could democracy complete itself as a project. While Habermas's public sphere ultimately served as a node for making clarion calls for mobilization, Oldenburg's formulation gave pride of place to being "present" within community establishments, even if those gathered did nothing else but convey memories from halcyon days. In this regard, Oldenburg was as critical of failing and/or eroding third places as Habermas was of a public sphere increasingly being colonized by social systems.

Both Habermas and Oldenburg would agree, however, that the main activity for third places must be conversation in, ideally, a cheerful and inclusive environment for its patrons. For Oldenburg, third places exhibit the pattern where every patron talks the right amount, for leveling dynamics would never allow any particular patron to monopolize the conversation for any extended length of time. Social status—muted within the third place—does not dictate who is spoken to and/or when one speaks. Third places are places that are welcoming, are informal, and emphasize happiness, humor and wit, exclusively relied-upon communication styles that engage patrons in "dramatic" conversations. Only through such dynamics can patrons escape the daily grind of life according to Oldenburg. In the United States, Oldenburg saw less promise, noting that "many public establishments reverberate with music played so loudly that enjoyable conversation is impossible" (1999: 30).

Most pertinent for our discussion of Death Café death talk is how both Habermas and Oldenburg consider public spheres/third places as environments that are indicative of a healthy democracy. Even third places can be envisioned as prototypical political environments in spite of it being rendered by Oldenburg as primarily a cathartic if not recreational social space for community life. Habermas almost shares in Oldenburg's alacrity but orients his gaze toward how members of public spheres can decolonize lifeworld colonization. Oldenburg accommodates these same dynamics but allows alternative attributes of group dynamics based on joy and recreation to surface, attributes that can include healthy banter without the perfunctory "requirement" to primarily engage in expressing validity claims, anticipating discourse responses, and repeating the same process each time a participant forwards a new argument. Oldenburg's third place is more playful than Habermas's public sphere. Yet foundationally, both were serious about how such public environments embodied and articulated democracy. Here, Habermas and Oldenburg's mining of history in their respective works reminds readers of the significance of public spheres and third places for social change.

Should public spheres/third places such as cafés contest the state too aggressively, Habermas provides a seventeenth-century account found in Emden's (1956) work *The People and the Constitution*:

> Already in the 1670s the government had found itself compelled to issue proclamations that confronted the dangers bred by the coffee-house discussions. The coffee houses were considered seedbeds of political unrest: "Men have assumed to themselves a liberty, not only in coffee-houses, but in other places and meetings, both public and private, to censure and defame the proceedings of the State, by speaking evil of things they understand not, and endeavoring to create and nourish universal jealousies and dissatisfaction in the minds of all His Majesties good subjects." (cited in Habermas 1991: 59).

For Oldenburg, this is not unprecedented. Citing similar responses by the state from throughout history to the present, from Scandinavian countries to Saudi Arabia, from Hungary to the Third Reich, and lest we forget, to the North Korea among others, governments can ill afford to allow coffeehouses or other types of third places to proliferate lest people would congregate to find "fault with the countries' rulers" (1999: xxiv). Oldenburg further adds that the process of "controlling local influences" has been ongoing for centuries (1999: 76). As such, Oldenburg is adamant that if third places "run counter to the type of political control exercised in totalitarian societies, so they are essential to the political processes of a democracy" (1999: 67).

Third places are political fora of great importance. In many countries the emergent solidarity of labor owed strictly to the profusion of cafés in which the workers discussed their common problems, realized their collective strength, and planned their strikes and other strategies. Though many credit an "enlightened" congress with the anti-segregation laws of the sixties, none of it would have happened but for prior assembly in black churches all over the South. (1999: xxiv).

And herein lies the utility of Oldenburg's elaboration: not only do third places at the very least have political inclinations, they are often politicized by a variety of disciplines that inform the human condition. He notes how "politics is not the only important subject discussed in third places. Philosophy, geography, urban development, psychology, history, and a great many others are entertained" in ways where urgent debate and communicative action behooves participants to "air their notions in front of critics" (1999: xxv). Oldenburg thus makes visible the dynamics of how communicative action decolonizes the lifeworld:

If Americans generally find it difficult to appreciate the political value of third places, it is partly because of the great freedom of association that Americans enjoy. In totalitarian societies, the leadership is keenly aware of the political potential of informal gathering places and actively discourages them. (Oldenburg 1999: 66).

In a closing amalgamation of Habermas and Oldenburg, one can envision how leveling at third places constitutes an important dynamic of communicative action, allowing for the validity claims and discourse responses to surface. The welcoming of communicative themes draws out the most democratic energies of community that can be made to challenge norm-free juridification from systems colonizing the lifeworld. This is a significant example of where and how democratic practices can continue beyond election cycles, and where it cannot continue if situated inside totalitarian systems. For example, in the United States it is not uncommon for bar patrons to gather together and lambast their current political leaders with tremendous vitriol. However, the same situation could never occur in the current North Korea. Oldenburg's orientation is that he takes some of the most taken for granted urban environments and assigns them an important community, if not political, status, one that points how democracy can unfold in informal urban settings. Habermas's efforts document the evolution of the public sphere in ways that reveal how within its confines the lifeworld was slowly and methodically colonized, and how communicative action could be harnessed to decolonize such a lifeworld.

The next chapter concludes my examination of the Death Café. Chapter 7 frames key concepts and narratives about mortality discussed in the context of the Death Café as a social movement. It also forwards the view that the ubiquity of risks in modern society is prompting actors such as Café participants to confront their mortality as a preemptive means for thriving in a world of risks. Doing so requires a reexamination of social movement literature, literature that harbors some important blinds spots about how movements need not contest the state to forward social change. By illustrating the Death Café as such a movement, I provide some theoretical considerations on how the movement's death identity, inculcated in the consciousness of Café participants, allows them to find fulfillment in life and living. It is this development, honed by repeated communicative action episodes around the United States and the world, that signal how participants of such a movement have begun the process of decolonizing their lifeworlds. Such a process is made possible by a collective death identity that is based on defogging the lens and decluttering the minds of those who dare confront their own death and dying.

CHAPTER 7

Decolonizing the Lifeworld of Death

The cremation of Gandhi (1948). Photographer unknown.

© The Author(s) 2017
J. Fong, *The Death Café Movement,*
DOI 10.1007/978-3-319-54256-0_7

In the process of establishing its social contours, the Death Café has evolved into an existential social movement. Matters related to one's existence and mortality are now confronted in ways that ensconce Death Cafés in local communities around the world. Through death talk's decolonization of the lifeworld, participants engage in a process of redefining and reassessing mortality on their own terms, revealing thematic concerns that people have about their finite existence, in an age where much denial about mortality obfuscates the process. Conceptualizing the Death Café as social movement is also possible for a variety of other reasons.

One key reason is that Café participants are in the process of collectively engaging with the theme of mortality by controlling how it is framed, a crucial task that allows for the visibility of the social movement and the continued conveyance of its message by movement participants, and emphatically, not by the system. For example, Death Café facilitators such as Betsy, Lisa, Karen, and Jon are versed with sharing healthy mortality themes through social media and online websites. The official Death Café webpage also promotes an underlying theme of mortality, reinforced by art contributed by visitors as well as a large interactive global map that shows where Death Cafés are taking place. Their mission statement articulates a community approach toward mortality and underscores the importance of a death identity: "At a Death Café people drink tea, eat cake and discuss death. Our aim is to increase awareness of death to help people make the most of their (finite) lives" (deathcafe.com).

Informative discussions on how social movements are framed can be found in the work of Hunt, Benford, and Snow (1994) as well as Snow and Soule (2010), all of whom derive their cues from Erving Goffman's classic work *Frame Analysis* (1974). For Snow and Soule (2010), a social movement's efficacious use of framing involves three crucial dynamics. The first is for activist-oriented actors to engage in diagnostic framing where problematic social issues are laid bare, defined clearly, and provided with potential solutions that are needed to resolve the issues. As a process, diagnostic framing "involves two signifying activities: the first is the problematization of life; the second is the attribution of blame or responsibility for the problematized conditions or state of affairs" (Snow and Soule 2010: 51). The second dynamic of framing involves prognostic framing, a process that gives structure to movement action strategies, a needed task for ensuring that the movement achieves success. Prognostic framing thus presents the types of action that the movement should pursue to remedy the problem (Snow and Soule 2010: 176).

Diagnostic and prognostic framing processes constitute the core of Death Café communicative action. Through these two ontological nodes, validity claims and discourse responses are formulated in ways that constitute death talk *in situ*.

The final dynamic of framing that helps us understand how the Death Café can be envisioned as a social movement is how Café attendees—but especially through our facilitators such as Betsy, Lisa, Jon, and Karen, along with other Café facilitators around the world—are engaged in motivational framing, a process of consciously and mindfully generating "solidary incentives and moral incentives" (Snow and Soule 2010: 137) so that participants can be inspired to engage in social change. Throughout this work, the contentions that have been employed to underscore such processes can be seen through Death Café communicative action, one that obviates the need to seize the state apparatus for influencing public policies for immediate, if not generational empowerment. In spite of this benevolent approach, Death Café communicative action and motivational framing still entail "the construction of vocabularies of motive that prods to action by, among other things, amplifying reasons for participation that override feared risks" (Snow and Soule 2010: 137). Motivation framing is often articulated toward the closing of a Death Café so that participants leave inspired to attend more Death Cafés if not start their own, a theme often voiced by Betsy and Lisa as well as other Café facilitators. This is death praxis, the process by which motivation framing aims to provide for its constituents some degree of transcendence and emancipation, practiced with the community as it confronts the symbiotic themes of life and death. Such motivational dynamics approximate some attributes of what Benford (1993a, 1993b) documented as types of motivation themes employed by activists of the nuclear disarmament movement: (1) the need to point to the severity of circumstances; (2) the necessity of conveying an urgent need for action; (3) the need for participants to be efficacious in their role as activists; that is, they have the power to effect change; and (4) that there are moral obligations to participate.

The aforementioned framing processes, along with corresponding discourses, conviviality, and humor that surface during Death Café gatherings are employed in ways that allow participants to experience what Doug McAdam describes as "cognitive liberation," noted in the classic work *Political Process and the Development of Black Insurgency* (1982: 48-51). For Kurzman, the profundity of such liberation takes root in an "oppressed people's ability to break out of pessimistic and quiescent patterns of thought and begin to do something about their situation" (1996: 154). That McAdam was able to identify cognitive liberation as catalytic for social movements suggests how surrender and catches and not escaping from freedoms (to author one's mortality) operate at Death Café gatherings. It is in this existentializing process where the group inspires the individual to author a personal view on one's path toward end of life that makes the Death Café a unique social movement that somewhat defies conclusive categorization.

Finally, we can conceptualize the Death Café as a social movement because it has an ethos based on action for community death talk as a means toward an authentic, good life and death, a process still calibrating its reflexivity into a sharper narrative. In this regard, Death Cafés' promotion of accepting mortality by decluttering life, thereby allowing for an ostensibly more sincere approach toward managing action for life and living *and* death and dying, constitutes sentiments of a death identity: that if we keep our mortality close, death and dying can thus be prepared for metaphysically, logistically, and even legalistically. For Café attendees, death and dying will also be able to instruct us on how to live life to its fullest. And it reminds participants that it may be prudent, in certain instances, to contest medical micromanagement of mortality upon a dying person's body. Harboring such an ethos, the Death Café as a movement is thus not exclusively ideational and metaphysical but promotes logistical and situational awareness of one's corporeal existence. A glimpse in how some American citizens have been able to achieve this goal can be seen in the increasing acceptance of assisted dying (Dugan 2015).

The most recent manifestation of such acceptance can be seen in the passage of California's End of Life Option Act in Fall of 2015, proposed by those who view death as a process and moment that can be dignified. States such as Oregon, Washington, and Texas already have their death with dignity legislations while other states are fighting for this option through political processes. The important cases of Brittany Maynard and Betsy Davis come to mind. Brittany employed Oregon's Death with Dignity Law to end her life after being diagnosed with terminal brain cancer. In an article published by *CNN* after her passing on November 2, 2014, she wrote:

I've had the medication for weeks. I am not suicidal. If I were, I would have consumed that medication long ago. I do not want to die. But I am dying. And I want to die on my own terms... I would not tell anyone else that he or she should choose death with dignity. My question is: Who has the right to tell me that I don't deserve this choice? That I deserve to suffer for weeks or months in tremendous amounts of physical and emotional pain? Why should anyone have the right to make that choice for me? (Maynard 2014).

Brittany continues:

> Having this choice at the end of my life has become incredibly important. It has given me a sense of peace during a tumultuous time that otherwise would be dominated by fear, uncertainty and pain. Now, I'm able to move forward in my remaining days or weeks I have on this beautiful Earth, to seek joy and love and to spend time traveling to outdoor wonders of nature with those I love. And I know that I have a safety net...
>
> I hope for the sake of my fellow American citizens...I hope that you would at least be given the same choice and that no one tries to take it from you. When my suffering becomes too great, I can say to all those I love, "I love you; come be by my side, and come say goodbye as I pass into whatever's next." I will die upstairs in my bedroom with my husband, mother, stepfather and best friend by my side and pass peacefully. I can't imagine trying to rob anyone else of that choice. (Maynard 2014).

Less than a year after California passed its End of Life Option Act, Betsy Davis, afflicted with Lou Gehrig's disease, gathered her family and friends for a farewell party in Ojai, California. According to Betsy's sister, Kelly Davis, "What she really wanted was for everyone to reconnect. I think she knew what she was doing—she was creating a support group" (Bever 2016). Betsy's friend, Niels Alpert, noted how "she knew she would rather take control of her final destiny before she...was totally helpless." He further added: "She was very happy to see her best friends and most beloved family members, so that aspect was joyful. Of course, underneath that, we were all feeling a deep sense of pain and grief." At the invitation to her own farewell party, Betsy wrote:

> First, you are all very brave for sending me off on my journey...Thank you so much for traveling the physical and emotional distance for me. These circumstances are unlike any party you have attended before, requiring emotional stamina, centeredness, and openness. I strongly encourage you all to connect with every person at the party—this will not only benefit you but me as well.

She continued:

> There are no rules. Wear what you want. Speak your mind. Dance, hop, chant, sing, pray . . . but do not cry in front of me. Okay, one rule. But it is important to me that our last interactions in this dimension are joyful and light. If you need to cry, there will be designated crying areas . . . or just find a corner. One of the symptoms of ALS is uncontrollable laughing/crying. So, in effect, I'm not crying because of you, but merely because my neurons are having a meltdown. However, if I laugh, it probably is because of you. (Bever 2016).

If every human being understood end of life *objectively* as one of corporeality through a cessation of vital functions, then the drive for collective inspiration and empowerment through a death identity becomes a moot point. However, the presence of Death Cafés point to a greater need by people to confront what constitutes or is beyond the objective. For Anthony Giddens, an objective view of death is but a myopic view of mortality. The cases of Brittany Maynard and Betsy Davis, along with data presented in this work, point to how community and people who contest systemic control of mortality are doing so from not an objective starting point, but from subjective and intersubjective dynamics that can accommodate the liminalities of meanings and generated profundities that emerge from confronting mortality.

> In a purely biological sense, death is relatively unproblematic—the cessation of the physiological functions of an organism. Kierkegaard points out that, in contrast to biological death, "subjective death" is an "absolute uncertainty" . . . The existential problem is how to approach subjective death . . . for if we cannot understand "subjective death," then death is no more or less than the transition from one being to non-being; and the fear of non-being becomes one of the primal anxieties . . . (Giddens 1991: 49).

The cases of Maynard and Davis notwithstanding, through death talk seen at our Death Cafés, participants are primarily subverting systemic rendering of their lives not so much in a revolutionary manner but more so as a transcendental and transformational approach that requires a sociological imagination of death, a process undertaken by Death Café participants very much ahead of schedule. Giddens eloquently describes this process:

> Thinking back to the past, to the first experience of death of another person, allows one to begin to ferret out hidden feelings about death. Looking

ahead in this case involves contemplating the years of life which the person believes remain, and imagining the setting of one's own future death. An imaginary confrontation with death allows the question to be posed all over again: "What to do?" (Giddens 1991: 74)?

Thus, to see the Death Café movement as somewhat subversive is not inaccurate: attendees gather to contest the oversimplification and cheapening of what is a significant social experience in the human condition. In the process, they identify distortions that are parasitic upon the lucidity needed for confronting our mortality as well as how to outmaneuvering them. As can be seen by our Café participants, many attendees view their own death and dying experience as one of collective assembly that—in spite of its inflections through culture, philosophy, spirituality, and religiosity—celebrates community and self-empowerment by only minimally accommodating systemic renderings of mortality.

Beyond these conditions the Death Café need not have any other purpose for there can be no corporeal victory over mortality. Confronting this facticity, Café participants are embarked on a movement that declutters, exhibiting raw sensibilities toward truths for those who dare to confront them. These raw truths occupy large swathes of the human condition between the antipodes of birth and death. Allaying one's fear of death and dying, along with its implications—the potential aloneness imposed on the dying self and the potential state of self-extinction, or its converse—Café participants appear to be aware of how the search for systemic answers yields little depth. These issues, confronted by Café participants through the inflections of culture, rationality, spirituality, and religiosity, henceforth assist their acceptance of death and dying as a means to decolonize the lifeworld. The Death Café lifeworld is that vital public sphere and third place where life actions can hint at some sort of sovereign control over one's horizon of mortality. Without searching for these horizons, Café participants are fully aware in their own way that juridified and norm-free systems will establish control of one's life and death experiences.

Is the Death Café Movement a "New" Social Movement?

Many scholars of social movements would classify the Death Café as a new social movement (NSM), with Alberto Melucci (1980) originating the term (see also Boyte 1977; Touraine 1971, 1977, 1981, 1985; Habermas

1981; Hunt, Benford, and Snow 1994; Melucci 1980, 1985, 1989, 1994, 1996; Jasper 1997; Lee 2007). It is certainly a "new" social movement chronologically in that it was founded by Bernard Crettaz in the first decade of the twenty-first century, and that it crossed over to the United Kingdom, dispersed throughout Western Europe and the United States, and now has spread to the rest of the globe. NSM scholars would also contend that the Death Café movement also exhibits many attributes that set it apart from social movements prior to the Civil Rights, where catalysts for civil disobedience or protest primarily emerged from discontents related to labor issues. Touraine described this period as one where "industrial values prevailed over the notion of post-industrial society" (1985: 780). But a crisis of industrial values soon took hold, ushering a new panoply of social angst that questioned the meaning of existence in ways that allow for "personal development corresponding to external change" (Melucci 1989: 62). Indeed, during the 1970s, a large number of organized movements surfaced to convey their angst against the "machine of mass culture" (1989: 89).

In Habermas's much underappreciated eponymous article, NSMs exhibit attributes of struggle that do not place them within the arenas and discontents of material reproduction (1981: 33). Echoing other scholars examining NSMs, Habermas concurs that such movements focus on discontents that arise about community, ecology, identities based on ethnic, racial, religious, and gender rights, peace concerns, and lifestyles—the diacritica of the human experience. More importantly for Habermas, these discontents emanate from *outside* of state institutions: Rosa Parks and Cesar Chavez were not politicians. However, because the aforementioned issues harbor the ability to "colonize the lifeworld" when seized and distorted by those with power and money within systems (1981: 35), a devolution of legitimation as perceived by the grass roots takes place.

> The objectives, attitudes, and behavior prevalent in youthful protest groups can at first be grasped as reactions to specific problem situations perceived with great sensitivity: "green" problems. The large industrial intervention in ecological balances, the scarcity of non-renewable natural resources, and the demographic development present industrially developed societies with serious problems. Yet these challenges... require technical and economic solutions that must... be planned globally and implemented by administrative means. (Habermas 1981: 35).

The term postmodernity is thus often employed to signify the opening up of new historical spaces for collective expressions and agitations that no longer relate to labor, the majority, or the center. Postmodernity, or its alternative moniker, poststructuralism, is a highly problematic way of essentializing a large chunk of time that presumably discerns it from modernity. In the case of examining social movements, a postmodern perspective suggests that NSMs embody a collective awareness that there are no more "centers of gravity" through socially constructed discourse that can attend to all of humanity. In such a context, there is "widespread skepticism about providential reason, coupled with the recognition that science and technology are double-edged, creating new parameters of risk and danger as well as offering beneficent possibilities for humankind" (1991: 27–28). Giddens, for example, argues how the term postmodernity is used to signify an era where many in society have conceded to the incontrovertible fact of uncertainty and its associated diacritica. In such a human condition, we have come to accept—often grudgingly—that "nothing can be known with any certainty, since all preexisting 'foundations' of epistemology have been shown to be unreliable," that history has not conclusively ushered in "progress," thereby inspiring NSMs to construct new realities for empowerment (1990: 46). Postmodern epistemology views "history" as "devoid of teleology," where "no version of 'progress' can plausibly be defended; and that a new social and political agenda has come into being with the increasing prominence of ecological concerns and perhaps of new social movements generally" (Giddens 1990: 46).

However, in whichever way we want to conceptualize the different permutations of modernity, its collapse is signaled by the crisis of the welfare state and modernity in general (Habermas 1986). In the wake of modernity, postmodern discourses relied on social construction and deconstructions to strip away the layers of meaning that generate discourses taken to be as fact. No longer is there facticity: material consequences can be redefined, reread, and deconstructed to the nth degree. Consequently, humans have been cast adrift in a universe of fluid semantics, symbolisms and simulacra. However such a view underscores the compelling argument that the atmospheric deconstruction of language *apart* from its material consequences makes postmodern thought detrimental for the formation of social movements. For Giddens, that we even reference a postmodern age "is a mistake which hampers an accurate understanding of its nature and implications" (1990: 51). My work adopts Giddens's critique toward postmodernity, namely, that "to speak of post-modernity as superseding modernity appears to invoke that very thing which is declared (now) to be impossible: giving some coherence to history and pinpointing our place in it" (1990: 46). Not willing to abandon the project of the Enlightenment, Giddens notes how epistemic and ontologic trajectories remain decipherable in modernity. Rather than seeking alternative discourses that "take us 'beyond modernity,'" Giddens argues how the cues of late capitalism can nonetheless "provide a fuller understanding of the reflexivity inherent in modernity itself," for modernity is not only "unsettling because of the circularity of reason, but because the nature of that circularity is ultimately puzzling" (1990: 49). Thus, the capacity for a reflexive modernity to check on itself *vis-à-vis* the quality of its material *and* existential consequences establishes the ethos for social change and the process for generating social movements.

Although the European tradition tended toward explaining social movement activity and formation through structural factors while the American variant assigned less explanatory power to them, both continental discourses concede that NSM dynamics exhibited resistances to the failed utopianisms sloganeered by modernity. Indeed, during the Civil Rights period until the end of the Cold War, "the most notable development in the social movement sectors since the early 1970s has been an expansion of the grassroots citizen politics" (Lee 2007: 32). That the Death Café began in Europe and has spread across the Atlantic (and now throughout the world) suggests that grassroots NSMs such as the Death Café, whether in the United States, Europe, or Asia, have the potential to create an identity that exhibits striking similarities in its movement configuration, dynamics, and conceptualizations of space and time. For Lee these similarities are seen in how NSMs are "situated in neighborhoods and communities" where "grassroots citizen action consist of locally initiated informal groups...encompassing quite heterogeneous political outlooks, issues...that traverse virtually all movement concerns of the present time" (Lee 2007: 3).

NSM scholars make their case by noting how the proliferation of these movements are occurring at a time when state ideology and political parties are often viewed as illegitimate actors, unable to rectify the cultural discontents and diverse needs of the populace. Examining the rise of peace, student, antinuclear, minority, animal rights, alternative medicine, and ecology movements, to name but a few categorizations, Larana et al. (1994) affirm the view that a shift to identity movements is indicative of how class issues based on labor movements have waned. Not unlike many

Frankfurt School thinkers, NSM activists and those who researched them saw "an era of growing anti-modernism and reenchantment of the life-world, expressed through disaffection with technology, industrialism, bureaucracy, and utilitarian rationalism" (Lee 2007: 10). Furthermore,

> The belief in technological progress dwindled rapidly toward the mid-70s in the experience of worldwide recessions, oil crisis, farm bankruptcies, bank failures, unemployment, inflation, and decrease in the living standard for the majority of the working class, low class of the working poor, and the urban "underclass." (Lee 2007: 10).

Of the many scholars addressing NSMs, Melucci's expansive view of the global dimensions of NSMs is noteworthy (1994). In a process he terms as the "planetarization of the system," an analog of globalization dynamics, Melucci notes how digital information in the context of globalization also proliferates these NSMs. There are few obstacles in the digital information era that can stop the fast circulation of information around the world. Although the Internet is but less than three decades old, its ability to destroy spatiality by rendering all distance equidistant, its ability to nullify extended communicative response times, renders localized experiences as simultaneously global as well. That NSMs are now part and parcel to this fast proliferation of information hints at the Death Café's potential as a global movement to create a shared humanity that can be experienced around the planet. Such social movements often outmaneuver techno-cratic hegemony by promoting communicative and leveling dynamics for their members to express themselves. For Melucci, the proliferation of movement themes is actually made stronger by stable and coherent trans-national informational flows. Thus, many antecedents of communicative action, that is, the need to establish "trust, credibility, shared beliefs, and values" in ways that "can only arise through regular social interactions in particular cultural settings" can now be secured through global flows of information (Jasper 1997: 25). Indeed, one can appreciate this format through Karen's End of Life University and its hosting of online Death Cafés. Sharing the sentiments of Habermas and Oldenburg, Laraña et al. (1994) argue that the proliferation of such movements imply a "demo-cratization dynamic" of daily life, through civil as opposed political chan-nels of society.

For Melucci, the democratization dynamic in NSMs include the reap-propriation of cultural and symbolic issues from systems that have expropriated them, a process that is characterized by identity rather than economic discontents, the latter of which galvanized working-class movements from the mid-nineteenth century in Europe and the United States (1985, 1989; see also Johnston et al. 1994). The authors similarly stress how NSMs harnesses a social base that "transcends class structure" (Johnston et al. 1994: 6). Melucci himself notes how his thinking on the issue ultimately allowed him to "gradually" abandon "the concept of class relationships" (1994: 103). Similarly, Hunt, Benford, and Snow argue that NSMs "transcend traditional class divisions and corresponding _struggles for control of state and economic institutions. Instead they concentrate on transformations of civil society and life worlds" (1994: 188). Jasper adds to this formulation in his important work *The Art of Moral Protest* a normative appreciation of how morality infuses NSMs, arguing that moral protest also "spans not only state lines, but social class boundaries" and that moral protest "is not a recent fad, no mere child of an affluent society" (1997: 4). Lee articulates similar views where NSMs are seen to be opening a new movement front that serves as an "alternative to the class politics of redistribution." No longer can workers—the key agent of social change from a variety of Marxian views—serve as a "macro agent of emancipation" (2007: 7). Because the Death Café promotes a normative view of personalizing and/or authoring one's living and dying trajectories, it constitutes a form of moral protest against juridifying and norm-free systems. Moreover, because death and dying means the end of physicality, class sentiments are ineffectual in framing a key crescendo of the human condition since notions of class implies keeping up appearances through material acquisition and display of adornment and of aesthetics, a "labor" of denial.

The Death Café's nonclass orientation toward mortality is not the only main attribute that allows it to be framed as an NSM. Habermas argues that NSMs uniqueness stem from their emphasis on issues that pertain to quality of life, "individual self-realization," and "participation" (1981: 33), and that their resistances are "directed toward abstractions that are forced upon the lifeworld" and thus must be "addressed within the lifeworld" (1981: 36). Habermas notes how such movement manifestations are acceptable because of modern society's "culturally impoverished and unilaterally rationalized praxis of everyday life" (1981: 36).

Thus, ascribed characteristics such as sex, age, skin color, even neighborhood and religion, contribute to the establishment and delimitation of communities, the creation of sub-culturally protected communications groups which further the search for personal and collective identity... This is all intended to promote the revitalization of buried possibilities for expression and communication. (Habermas 1981: 36).

Habermas envisions NSMs as being able to "limit the particular dynamic of the economic and political administrative system of action" that have encroached into the lifeworld (1981: 37), a process that is inimically shaped by "power and money" (Lee 2007: 50). Lee adds that NSMs are much more able than labor-based movements to address "interest, issues, and needs relating more directly to everyday life and values" (Lee 2007: 3). Elsewhere, Lee notes that celebrating "creativity, autonomy, freedom, identity, meaning" in the lifeworld through NSMs inspires movement members to be defiant against sociocultural domination (Lee 2007: 23). Indeed, for Lee, the "decentered politics of NSMs" allow for an "enlarging and reconfiguring" of that most precious and incomplete site of democracy for Habermas, the public sphere (Lee 2007: 40).

Alain Touraine, progenitor of the term postindustrial society, wrote extensively on issues that are tackled by NSMs (see Touraine 1971, 1977, 1981, 1985). Whereas Habermas saw the system encroaching into the lifeworld through a variety of institutions and mediated organs of the state, Touraine oriented his critique specifically to those who control technology in ways that enable them control over people's lives. Thus, the technocracy—the stratum of technical experts that are embedded in the market and government—became the target of Touraine's critique. His more specific implication of the technocracy is useful because one of the main critiques exhibited by our sample of Café participants was directed toward the medical establishment's technological power over the human body. Where Habermas saw communicative action that is able to decolonize the lifeworld, Touraine saw NSMs emanating from the lifeworld contesting the hegemony of technocracy. For Jasper, Touraine's vision and his emphasis for a sociology of action can be employed to "fight technocracy...just as the labor movement had opposed industrial capitalism" (Jasper 1997: 71). Jasper is himself Habermasian in this regard, conceding to the existence of a technocratic class that behooves NSM activists to protect "private life from colonization by technocrats" (1997: 72).

THE CATALYST OF RISKS

Giddens (1990, 1991, 1998, 1999) and Ulrich Beck (1992) illuminate a set of conditions that contextualizes the proliferation of NSMs: the many risks that are often *manufactured* in ways that control an uncritical population, generated by the juggernaut that is modernity. Whereas Fromm saw people escaping freedoms from within the psyche, due to fears of responsibility and accountability, Giddens and Beck provide the conditions from within *and* without that compel members of society to confront the risks. For Beck, the risks are primarily external. In the classic *Risk Society* (1992), Beck examines the legacy of capitalism and its employment of instrumental rationality to construct norm-free macro-level institutions of cultural production. Such a process, Beck argues, compels the "human imagination" to stand "in awe" of the ever-increasing destructive forces unleashed by an unbridled modernity, one that has now taken on the iteration of globalization. He also adds that such processes of modernization have generated a "growing critique" against it which manifests as public discourse (1992: 20). Observing its globalized proliferation, it can be inferred that such a public discourse is also a *global* public discourse "no longer tied to their place of origin—the industrial plant." More incisively, Beck argues that globalization has created a sort of stratified risk distribution system where any actor in society can be located. A manufactured risk society, then, frames the modern human condition. Beck also notes that one's consciousness of risk, or risk awareness, is determined by one's orientation to science, an orientation that frequently implicates it. Thus, like Giddens, Beck also implicates the sciences. Most importantly, however, is Beck's observation that scientific hegemony has frequently been challenged by social movements that have confronted technocracy's power over life. In this regard, Beck notes with alacrity that "techno-economic development is losing its cultural consensus" (1992: 203), an observation that points to why Death Cafés are popular: they generate consensus about mortality that attempts to unfetter their links to techno-economic micromanagement and control of death.

Underscoring Giddens's concept of reflexivity, Beck notes how "the sciences are now being confronted with their own objectivized past and present—with themselves as product and producer of reality and of problems which they are to analyze and overcome" (1992: 156). As more and more tangible risks are generated, Giddens, like Beck, envisions an overwhelming power in the technocracy to edit modernity, propelling it toward, for better or worse, social change. In the classics the *Consequences of Modernity* (1990) and *Modernity and Self Identity* (1991), Giddens argues that the numerous changes to the human condition brought on by industrialization has generated a social world "replete with risk and dangers, to which the term 'crisis'" serves "not merely as an interruption" to social life, "but as a more or less continuous state of affairs" (1991: 13). Such crises, whether actual or exaggerated, embed themselves in the sociological imagination of the populace, jeopardizing the trust a person or a group has toward their social systems.

For Giddens, the notion of risk and trust intimately intertwine. Giddens (1990) argues how trusting a system implies that one's relationship to others and to institutions is based on how such systems can potentially minimize risk. Thus, in an insightful observation, Giddens's late capitalist society is one where the prevalence of risk—in all its tangible and psychic manifestations—have to be managed by institutions such as stock-market investment firms and organizations that oversee physically dangerous sports. Yet conversely (and crucially), a flawed or failed system can through its malfunctioning or maldeveloped institutions, generate new kinds of risks it is unable to ameliorate. It is within such a volatile context that the character of science, progress, and modernity, along with discontents toward their notions of utopianism, are critiqued by NSMs.

Giddens's conceptualization of a runaway juggernaut modernity illuminates another trajectory not fully elaborated by Habermas: that modernity will *colonize future lifeworlds* as well. This process thereby generates and ensconces existential, cultural, and political anxieties into the social actor's future. Consequently, a risk society not only manufactures vulnerabilities for a population, but more rather members of the population are anxious and angst-ridden because of the "risk calculation themselves," one that entails the labor of "screening out 'unlikely' contingencies, thus reducing life-planning to manageable proportions" (Giddens 1991: 182). Elsewhere he emphasizes how "in conditions of modernity, for lay actors as well as for experts in specific fields, thinking in terms of risk and risk assessment is a more or less ever-present exercise' (1991: 124). Thus, citizens of postindustrial era must not only contend with how technocratic management of society, often through the market if not the state, distorts our relationship to time and space by manufacturing risks. Citizens must also contend with how such a process simultaneously accommodates the management of their lives. People are also constrained by their panoptic relationship to modernity's manufactured risks, frequently constrained by their demands and implications upon their publics and upon life overall. The process renders people vulnerable to their biographies evaporating into the "indefinite spans of time-space" in what Giddens terms disembedding, or the "lifting out of social relations from local contexts and their rearticulation across indefinite tracts of time" (Giddens 1991: 18). Such a process is managed by modernity's expert systems, or what Giddens terms as "systems of technical accomplishment or professional expertise that organise large areas of material and social environments in which we live today" (1990: 27). His insight on this matter is worth quoting in length:

> Most laypersons consult "professionals"—lawyers, architects, doctors, and so forth—only in a periodic or irregular fashion. But the systems in which the knowledge of experts is integrated influence many aspects of what we do in a continuous way. Simply by sitting in my house, I am involved in an expert system, or a series of such systems, in which I place my reliance. I have no particular fear in going upstairs in the dwelling, even though I know that in principle the structure might collapse... When I go out of the house and get into a car, I enter settings which are thoroughly permeated by expert knowledge-involving the design and construction of automobiles, highways, intersections, traffic lights, and many other items. Everyone knows that driving a car is a dangerous activity, entailing the risk of accident. In choosing to go out in the car, I accept that risk, but rely upon the aforesaid expertise to guarantee that it is minimised as far as possible. (Giddens 1990: 27).

Expert systems deploy modes of technical knowledge hegemonically. By amalgamating this process with Habermas's notion of juridification, one can envision how technocratic control is indeed secured by distanced regulatory and legalistic language. And insofar as their dominance relates to how mortality is experienced in anticipated or unanticipated ways, they constitute key themes that underpin death talk critiques by Death Café participants.

Our risk society, replete with uncertainties and anxieties, compels citizens to organize and seek answers and meaning about the modern human condition. However, surrounded by different attributes of risk, the anxieties generated necessitate the need to adopt a "calculative attitude to the open possibilities for action, positive and negative" (Giddens 1991: 28). By seeking more empowerment through communities, the turn toward more intimate settings that offer perceptively less risks is indicative of "trust lapses," a legitimation crisis that signals the increasing cynicism and lack of faith people have toward systems of control. These trust lapses are part and parcel to factors that generate a variety of NSMs that confront issues pertinent to the human experience *beyond* the material culture offered by the market. For Giddens, the people's trust in a system is of great importance. As "consciously taken decisions," but more often as a "generalized attitude of mind" that function to relate an actor to systemic imperatives, trust in systems is a "determining element in whether or not an individual is actively and recurrently plagued with anxieties" (1991: 182–183). Giddens continues:

> No one can show that it is not "rational" to worry constantly over the possibility of ecological catastrophe, nuclear war or the ravaging of humanity... If most successfully bracket out such possibilities and get on with their day-to-day activities, this is no doubt partly because they assess the actual element of risk involved as very small. But it is also because the risks in question are given over to fate—one aspect of the return of *fortuna* in late modernity. (1991: 183).

For Giddens, a risk-ladened society is constituted by citizens concerned about their safety, about their futures, and about control of their bodies, among other things. It is within these attributes of modernity that Death Café narratives, death talk, and a death identity are generated. Noting that we now live in a world that is seen as a "fraught and dangerous one," Giddens sees a population skeptical of the view that the "emergence of modernity would lead to the formation of a happier and more secure social order" (1990: 10). By making such an observation, Giddens creates ample room for NSM movements to operate against. However, he cautions that the backdrop of living in a world of risk configured by hyper time and technological changes, in turn, often generate new risks themselves. It is not surprising then that NSMs are attending to the consequences such dynamics have upon notions of community, inequality, and discontents.

Because social systems in the modern age manufacture risks, when citizens are unable to fully control it, they must either run from it or confront it collectively through social movements. Only then can citizens possess a "systematic way of dealing with hazards and insecurities induced and introduced by modernisation itself" (Beck 1992: 21). Beck harbors a charitable view of NSMs, noting how its "criticism of science, technology and progress—does not stand in contradiction of modernity, but is rather an expression of reflexive modernization beyond the outlines of industrial society" (1992: 11). In an incisive view that may explain the popularity and spread of the Death Café movement, Beck notes how such new movements "raise questions that are not answered by the risk technicians at all, and the technicians answer questions which miss the point of what was really asked and what feeds public anxiety" (1992: 30). He continues:

> It may be said that social movements and citizens' groups are formed in relation to modernization risks and risk situations . . . aroused in the form of a desire for a 'life of one's own' (in material, temporal and spatial terms, and in structuring social relationships) . . . In this way *new social movements* come into existence again and again . . . In this sense . . . the new social movements (ecology, peace, feminism) are expressions of the new risk situations in the risk society. On the other, they result from the search for social and personal identities and commitments in detraditionalized culture. (Beck 1992: 90).

Pertinent to our discussion as well is how the Death Café, in its expression as an NSM, is understood in the literature to infrequently contest social systems in ways that destabilize or destroy them. By implication this may suggest they are less assertive than other more radicalized movements based on class-oriented praxis. Instead, NSMs manifest in ways that have "little direct conflict with institutions" (Gusfield 1994: 66). Melucci's insights parallel Gusfield's in that NSMs are seen not to promote actions "designed to achieve outcomes in the political system," since they tend to raise challenges that "recasts the language and cultural codes that organize information" (1994: 102). Lee similarly notes how NSMs and their supporters generally "opt for tactics that appeal to the bystander public" and that they will rarely "initiate disruptive tactics that would interfere with the daily routines of life" (2007: 14).

I would like to add a somewhat more complex rendering of how Death Cafés function as NSMs; that is, in spite of the many rich conceptualizations that scholars argue characterize NSMs, the Death Café movement as "new" is arguably and exponentially less so if we observe its unit of analysis, one that Café participants confront, analyze, and interrogate: mortality. Death Cafés' central focus on the theme of death connects it to all people that have ever lived back before recorded time—that is, back into "deep time" when the natural calendrical cycle of seasons, full moons, solstices, eclipses, and the vagaries of the natural environment held sway in framing the mortality of people. Through the unit of analysis that is mortality, the Death Café can be seen as simultaneously an *old, new,* and *future* social movement simply because death and dying have been an integral part of the human experience since time immemorial. It compels the social actor to confront their epistemic and ontologic place in existence and, for many, beyond existence or beyond time itself. The Death Café as NSM is thus an atavism that currently arises in a world where the promises of faith *and* science to understand the meaning of death appears fatigued and unsatisfactory. Conversely, during yesteryear, thanatolgically oriented groups communicatively cohered because of their fatigue with certain strains of faith, a process that led to the formation of alternative practices of new religious beliefs. As it stands, a more appropriate designation for the Death Café is that it is a modern existential death movement that emphasizes transcendence dynamics.

In spite of the diacritica that reveals the contours of NSMs as a distinct category of social movements, not all scholars are willing, at the outset, to concede to such a fine discernment. For example, Marks and McAdam are not convinced with the "old" versus "new" distinction to designate social movements, noting that the distinction is "simply untenable" (1996: 268). For Marks and McAdam, there is "little in the value goals, tactics, or organisational forms of the NSMs to suggest that they represent a qualitatively new type of social movement" (1996: 268). For detractors, NSMs are simply social movements that are adapting to the discontents of a historical period. However, their critiques adopt a structural view of movement formation, a sociological imagination that is once again grounded in the historical unfolding of particular discontents, and whether resources or opportunities in the system specific to their generation avail themselves for harnessing by activists. That said, Marks and McAdam correctly remind us about the complexity of social movements: that there are "new" features in some old movements and that there are "old" features in NSMs (1996: 268).

We must remember that the polemics about what constitutes a social movement is best relegated behind the more important question of what social movements define as "success." Gamson's important work *The Strategy of Social Protest* (1975) provides a rather Habermasian qualification, evoking the latter's *Legitimation Crisis* to assess a social movement's efficacy: that even if certain aims are not realized through the state, policy changes, or even political parties, it is enough that the social movement be perceived as legitimate, a status that appears to be bestowed upon the Death Café, given its growing popularity. If we indulge those who see

NSMs as not categorically new, and indulge in the designation of the Death Café as a modern existential movement that has always existed in different atavisms through time, then we allow the movement's participants to secure a great degree of legitimacy because they are but current nomads in a long chronology where others have offered alternative readings about how mortality constitutes a foundational experience of the human condition. As we shall see, such a view is at odds with many other variants of social movement theories because it does not factor in a need to bring in public policy change that can presumably rectify social inequalities, and in extreme circumstances, foster revolutionary changes in the state.

RESOURCE MOBILIZATION AND POLITICAL OPPORTUNITY VIEWS

In addition to the rich body of NSM literature are the important resource mobilization and political process theories, the latter of which frequently referred to political opportunity theory. Both discourses found textual exposition between the 1970s and 1990s alongside nascent NSM elaborations. Key thinkers in the resource mobilization school conveyed their arguments through works such as Eisinger's "The Conditions of Protest Behavior in American Cities" (1973), McCarthy and Zald's works *The Trend of Social Movements in America* (1973) and "Resource Mobilisation and Social Movements" (1977), Tilly's *From Mobilization to Revolution* (1978), and Gamson's earlier mentioned *The Strategy of Social Protest* (1975), to name but a few. However, this discourse assigned primarily structural factors to explain the birth, maintenance, and momentum of social movements. Although the aforementioned scholars primarily examine the politicized contexts that influence social movements, and less frequently a social movement's more sanguine or apolitical orientations and practices, their insights deserve mention.

Resource mobilization theory argues that social movement efficacy results from careful acquisition and management of not only financial resources, but resources from social capital and cultural capital contexts. Resource mobilization theory emphasizes that collective action is dependent on the "ability of associations to mobilize resources and to conduct the organization on the basis of planned and rational action" (Johnston et al. 1994: 4–5). The popular but overextended resource mobilization theory thus argues that connections to journalists, politicians, or key political entrepreneurs—along with the mother's milk of politics, money, and other movement necessities such as workers and staff, etc., are resources needed to prosecute a successful social movement. Also included are:

> Labor, facilities, preexisting networks, elite support, and communication media on one hand and, on the other, structural linkages with the established political process, occupational structure, socioeconomic growth, and other organizations that control resources... also... social network, mass media, elite support, information, and even legitimation in the eyes of the public. (Lee 2007: 17–20).

Since the central argument forwarded by resource mobilization proponents is that collective indignation and anger are not enough to generate social change, its utility in identifying units of analyses that are tangible and intangible in equipping movement dynamics made it a popular paradigm for analyzing a variety of social movement conditions. For example, Tilly (1978) and McCarthy and Zald's (1973, 1977) writings assert how such an orientation creates room for observing rational agency and instrumental rationality, dynamics that allow not only groups but individuals to act strategically as they pursue amelioration of their discontents. For Marks and McAdam, social movements and revolutions are thought to "emerge and develop in response to changes that rendered institutionalised political systems increasingly vulnerable or receptive to challenge... Thus a close causal relationship was posited between institutionalised and movement politics" (Marks and McAdam 1996: 250).

Because resource mobilization theory accounts for material consequences via tangible and intangible assets that benefit a social movement, assessing their dynamics is comparatively straightforward: quantify such resources and the movement with the most toys wins, so to speak. In this regard, resource mobilization theory has some merit due to its reality checks about the logistical prospects of collective behavior. Essentially, the paradigm argues that idealism cannot alone ensure wins for movements, and that cultural capital, social capital, and material culture are pivotal for ensuring success. For Kitschelt, however, this is a problematic assumption for the perspective concentrates too much "on those internal variables of movement mobilization... e.g., incentive structure in membership recruitment, internal organization, specification of goals and skills in forming coalitions with allies" (Kitschelt 1986: 59). In the process, resource mobilization theory overlooks the normative and ideological dimensions of movement formation as well as how it develops mass appeal and strategies for mobilization (Lee 2007). Resource mobilization theory is also poor at illuminating the link between the historical nature of grievances and identity formation (Johnston et al. 1994). Furthermore, because any tangible and intangible component of a social movement could be construed as a resource, the perspective risks "becoming tautological, making the entire social world into resources," where "even moral support, public opinion, psychological states, and favorable symbolism have been considered resources" (Jasper 1997: 31).

Another major body of research that attends to how opportunities benefit social movement dynamics is political process theory, alternatively referred to as political opportunity theory. Political opportunity, in essence, is a theoretical view of social movements that posits how "activists do not choose goals, strategies, and tactics in a vacuum" but within political contexts that set "the grievances around which activists mobilize, advantaging some claims and disadvantaging others"; that is, "prospects for advancing particular claims, mobilizing supporters, and affecting influence are context-dependent" (Meyer 2004: 126). Although the notion of political opportunity had been addressed in classics such as Martin Lipset's *Political Man* (1963) and Peter Eisinger's 1973 article "The Conditions of Protest Behavior in American Cities," the best elaborations in my view come from McAdam (1982) and Sidney Tarrow's classic work *Power in Movement* (1998). Both McAdam and Tarrow share the view that political mobilization constitutes a process where citizens mobilize in civil society to hold sections, if not the entire state system, accountable for social inequalities—but only when the timing is right. For Lipset, it is in democratic systems that such processes find their fullest expressions for determining the legitimacy of social institutions. Along with the empowerment afforded by cognitive liberation, McAdam includes the availability of political opportunities as another key ingredient in his formulation: in short, activists strike when opportunities open up in the political system to do so. In the process McAdam illuminates the important interaction between the more amorphous faculties of perception and consciousness, and its ability to time its insertion into favorable political conditions.

McAdam defines political opportunity as "any broad social change process that significantly undermines the calculations and assumptions on which the political establishment is structured," thus causing "a significant expansion in political opportunity for single or multiple challengers" (1982: ix).

Examining the African American struggle with such a lens, he notes how the efficacy in managing a social movement's organization is an important requirement so as to position the movement for seizing political opportunities as they emerge. A fascinating interplay that surfaces in the wake of a state in crisis, combined with an agitated citizenry through their respective social movements, is captured by McAdam:

> Most movements confront an elite divided in its reaction to the insurgent challenge. Some components of the elite usually perceive the movement as a threat and seek through their actions to neutralize or destroy it. Others see in it an opportunity to advance their interests and thus extend cautious support to insurgents. (1982: 57).

Indeed, political opportunities, along with good organization, consciousness raising, timing, and framing, allowed established Civil Rights organizations to identify the

> unique framing opportunity which the Cold War afforded them. By drawing a stark parallel between Jim Crow policies in the U.S. and the suppression of freedom in the Soviet bloc, established leaders sought to prod a reluctant federal establishment into action by framing civil rights reform as a tool in America's struggle against communism. (McAdam 1982: xxii).

Most significant for our discussion of how political opportunity explains Death Café dynamics, McAdam, further elaborates how the nuances of political opportunity can surface through, among other factors, "w*idespread demographic shifts* [italics added]" (1982: ix). McAdam's highlight of demographic factors is exponentially important for this work's inclusion of Baby Boomers as the primary agents of social change in the Death Café movement. Along with Habermas's (1981) similar acknowledgement of the importance of demographic factors, we can now appreciate why Baby Boomers are ideally timed in their participation with Death Cafés. They are entering the later stages of their lifecycle in vast numbers and desire to find a generational community, a process that can solidify a generational solidarity with close to 80 million of people in the United States alone. As a demographic, Boomers are poised to determine for the Death Café movement and its scions whether there is a need for a politicized mortality trajectory that can coexist alongside its existential and transformative orientations, a scenario that will be revisited toward the conclusion of the chapter.

In this regard, and perhaps in this regard alone, political opportunity's accommodation of demographic shifts makes it a useful perspective for explaining the rise of Death Cafés and their primarily Baby Boomers actors. However, the political opportunity view is not without some shortcomings and these will be discussed after examining some of the core tenets of the view.

For Meyer and Minkoff, the utility of political opportunity is its ability to "predict variance in the periodicity, style, and content of activist claims over time… and across institutional contexts" (2004: 1458). Keen not to present political opportunity theory as a deterministic panacea for social action, Meyer and Minkoff caution that a "polity that provides openness to one kind of participation may be closed to others" (2004: 1463). They also concede that "we know less about *how* opportunities translate into collective action" (Meyer and Minkoff 2004: 1463). Eisinger (1973) and later Koopmans (1996) explicitly employ a political opportunity view, conceptualizing the opportune porousness of a system as important for predicting whether social movements form and are able to maintain their momentum against establishments being challenged.

Other important thinkers and proponents of the political opportunity such as Tarrow (1998) defines political opportunity as the "consistent—but not necessarily formal or permanent—dimensions of the political environment that provide incentives for collective action by affecting people's expectations for success or failure" (1998: 76–77). Tarrow summarizes its essence in *Power in Movement* (1998:77–81) in ways that also suggest how a more "open" or "closed" system propels or limits social movement gains, respectively:

1. Increasing access to the system, for people "do not often attack well-fortified opponents when opportunities are closed" (77).
2. Shifting political alignments, which in democratic systems is signified by electoral instability (78).
3. Divided elites stemming from conflict within and between them, dynamics that "also encourage outbreaks of contention" (79).
4. Influential allies that can support and/or legitimate activists' concerns and "act as friends in court, as guarantors against repression, or as acceptable negotiators on their behalf" (79).
5. Limited repression and facilitation, so that the movement has room to grow and persist in its actions (80).

6. Low state strength—stronger and more centralized states are generally harder to "crack" and offer fewer entry points for movement contestation (81).

Goldstone (2004: 347) provides additional factors derived from Tarrow's work:

7. Ineffective and illegitimate state repression—states that engage in inconsistent or excessive repression often increase movement success by showing themselves to be ineffective or illegitimate. The skill and mode of state repression is, thus, important to movement outcomes.
8. International conditions and allies that support movement actors and their goals.

For Kitschelt, political opportunities and its structures are "comprised of specific configurations of resources, institutional arrangements and historical precedents for social mobilization, which facilitate the development of protest movements in some instances and constrain them in others" (1986: 57). More recently Nepstad (2011: 6–7) identifies political opportunities derived from her amalgamation of ideas from McAdam (1982), Bunce (1999), Bunch and Wolchik (2006), Hale (2006), Huntington (1991), and Jasper (1997) as consisting of

1. shifts in international alliances and agreements;
2. newly called elections;
3. succession crisis following the retirement of a long-standing ruler;
4. inspiration from successful uprising in other nations;
5. public outrage generated by moral shocks, such as the assassination of a leading opposition figure.

Tarrow, like many proponents of the view, tows the conventional political opportunity line: actors are seen to mobilize primarily to contest the state. Even if the political entrepreneur is a professional malcontent, all wait for that right moment to strike (Tarrow 1989, 1998). The process need not be based on objective conditions, however. Kurzman (1996) notes how it is enough for activists to *perceive* that there are forthcoming opportunities for them to forward their social movement aims. Gamson and Meyer (1996) are less optimistic, noting that the failure of many movements is due to activists being unrealistic and idealistic about what constitutes opportunities. Other scholars have adopted the above criteria with additional formulations (see Kitschelt 1986; Clemens 1997; Esman 1994; Costain 1992; Jenskins and Klandermans 1995; Kriesi 1996; Kriesi et al. 1992, 1995; McAdam, McCarthy and Zald 1996; and Rucht 1996). For activists to forward social change—especially if it revolves around public policy changes—the structure of political opportunities and the strength of the social movement organization are the key determinants of their success (McAdam 1982; Kurzman 1996). Tarrow affirms such a view and goes as far to note that people only participate in social movements if opportunities are ideal.

One of the main critiques against the political opportunity view is that the theory lacks consensus as to what constitutes favorable opportunities for activists to exploit, and more importantly whether "favorable opportunity structures" function as the primary factor in determining movement emergence or success (Goldstone 2004: 346). Another critique is how political opportunity theory places less emphasis on the role of strategy and strategizing as major factors in achieving social movement goals. Nepstad, through a relational theory of political power, argues that strategy and strategizing are significant factors, alongside political opportunities, that strengthen social movements.

In her critique of political opportunity theory, Nepstad notes how it is not enough for the social movement to simply "activate" when political conditions are ideal. More importantly for Nepstad, effective strategy and strategizing are just as crucial in the process of ushering social change when political opportunities arise. Nepstad concedes, however, that once a social movement erupts onto the political scene, "its chances of successfully overthrowing the state are shaped, to some degree, by structural conditions" (2011: 6). However, she invokes the political views of Hannah Arendt (1970) to forward a relational perspective: that "rulers have no intrinsic power" on their own, and that it is the citizens who "possess various types of power that they may either grant to rulers or withhold" (Arendt 1970; Nepstad 2011: 8), and that "any theory of revolutionary success or failure must therefore include an assessment of both structural conditions and revolutionary strategy" (2011: 7).

There are also few suggestions about how political opportunity can explain processes by which social movements form to confront sanctioned or metaphysical topics that manifest in the lifeworld. Instead, it assigns catalytic status of movement formation to, say, demographic shifts in a population that ostensibly will generate enough collective indignation to monitor dynamics of the state, in hopes of forcing it to concede to movement demands. When those dynamics are opportune, the movement takes action. However, this is a state-centric rendering of social movements. Indeed, much of the body of literature on social movements—even those illuminating the merits of NSMs—adopts the view that social movements exist to force public policy and/or systemic change within the social system being contested. Even if the activists are ensconced in their social movements or if they function as lobbies, or even if they constitute the political parties that aim to support a politician sympathetic to the movement, social movement literature tends to view these aforementioned factors as one that challenges the political apparatus or requires it for legitimation (Kriesi et al. 1995). Even Nepstad's excellent analysis of nonviolent social movements envisions a binary (and tense) relationship between the grass roots and the political system, where even nonviolent social movements are seen to engage in the "removal of an existing regime or ruler" (2011: xiii).

The view of the democratic state as one to be challenged for social change is a major, albeit assumed, trajectory in the social movement literature. Yet as noted by Habermas, the state is comparatively non-existent when elections are not in play to illuminate social problems and their amelioration; that is, other macro-level institutions control the generating of narratives on social issues. The perspectives of Death Café participants suggest that they view the trinity as primarily the operative agents that shapes our lives and deaths just as intimately, if not more so, than organs of the state. The trinity also house anonymous authorities in that we are rarely aware of particular individuals or groups that convey social narratives on mortality. Moreover, they are also authoritarian: orientations toward mortality are meted out in ways where recipients receive shock value and regulatory and legalistic language about mortality. As Habermas presciently notes, renderings of the lifeworld from nonstate macro-level institutions tend to be norm-free in nature, lacking depth or ethics beyond the immediacy demanded by systemic imperatives to mechanically "process" members of the population.

In spite of the blind spots in the social movement literature, promising analyses of the Death Café can still be had through political opportunity theory, even though the aim of the Death Café is not (yet) an exclusively politicized one that demands state concessions for empowerment. That said, political opportunity theory does not exhaustively explain all aspects of the Death Café movement beyond demographics since the theory also depends on structural conditions for their explanatory power (that is, degree of repression and/or porousness of political systems that vary across the present and across time).

THE MANUFACTURING OF RISKY "OTHERS"

The aforementioned social movement theories fail to address how NSMs can descend into a dynamic that expresses divisive identity politics. Such an omission is unfortunate: a death identity as assembled throughout my work is not cultural in the sense that it represents one shared belief system that can be compared to other shared belief systems. Mortality is a facticity of the human condition since time immemorial as well as across the present *and* into the future. In this regard, death remains a crucial experience of the human condition that affects many symbolic systems operating in society. As can be seen in our participants' experiences with the Death Café, not all NSMs—if we envision the Death Café movement as such—will contribute to a neotribalist politics of conversion and exclusion, a process that has frequently fragmented potentially healthy human relations, leaving sectarian tensions in its wake (Childs 2003). Moreover, the Death Café's popularity suggests that not all NSMs rely on a historical sense of victimhood to formulate empowerment for mortality, where only in its wake will the social actor be reassembled as a survivor, if at all. The subtext of a Death Café death identity is that participants communicatively conceptualize and support one another as survivor.

As elaborated by Giddens, we live in a modern era of uniquely high risks and mistrust of our social systems. Yet the identity politics that inform some social movements, especially those that draw on a sense of perennial vulnerability, only serves to exacerbate social demarcations even further: the components of risk for certain groups must now include "other" groups as stressors that coexist alongside the oppressive tendencies of technocratic systems. In the context of the United States, cultural walls are transformed into fortresses and political correctness is then employed to hyper-sensitize discourse and *constrain* free communicative action and deliberative democracy: a wrong choice of a word, a wrong inflection, or lilt in speech about how certain groups or issues are represented, further distorted and melodramatized by the media, sends constituents of the offended cultural group into a defensive frenzy. To what extent such a process has stunted our ability to dialogically resolve conflict at the grass roots remains to be seen.

The idea of celebrating diversity is actually pitched in this context to hide the fact that although integrationist policies since the 1970s in the United States have succeeded institutionally, generating *affective* solidarity to unite us as a people with a shared humanity has failed. The sloganeering and celebration of diversity instead aestheticize diversity, rendering it as a form, or even formula (e.g., there are x% of this group at our place of employment, or there are y% of this group, n% of that group, and z% of this group at our schools). To view multicultural groups in terms of content and not form might require the acknowledgement that certain groups may not politically or existentially agree with one another, and that such disharmony likely resulted in cultural tensions or even confrontations in the past. Thus, the aggressor/victim binary rears its head in many groups' respective cultural discourses for the sake of empowerment and disempowerment, one that must activate the notion of "us" versus "them."

A critical discourse of democracy has yet to explicitly ask *why* the multicultural community is so frequently idealized in the first place. This should not be surprising, however, for if one were to critically ask why multiculturalism exists, one is forced to confront the fact we can "see" (but only aesthetically) diversity today due how different cultural groups tend to cohere with members of their own group, a process born from voluntary segregation. In such instances, people are actually manufacturing their own risks through a lens that view *other* cultural groups as progenitors of risk. Nonetheless, a celebration of diversity stays clear of existential content and relies on aesthetic validations instead. Only then can the idea of multiculturalism and diversity remain idealized. Examples can be seen in coverage of festivals, cultural attire, etc., while ignoring the root cause of why people voluntarily segregate into cultural comfort zones in the first place.

Take, for example, San Francisco's iconic Chinatown, a frequently visited community by tourists from around the world: One would be hard-pressed to find a tourist who realizes that the earliest nineteenth-century Chinatowns in the United States all had their starts as impoverished and downtrodden ghettoes, populated by immigrant labor that was shunned and exposed to violence and institutional discrimination by the mainstream American society. Yet nicely tucked in their ethnic enclaves, they nonetheless express their Chinese aesthetics through simulacra and other forms, serving as a beacon that diversity is there for all to "see." And consider how elite segments of the population already enable voluntary segregation along class lines in that the wealthy can voluntarily segregate themselves inside gated communities, this in spite of the fact that the main driving motivation behind such voluntary segregation is that the wealthy doubt the motives of those "others" with less wealth than them. That we allow such divisive class sentiments to be a lived lifeworld experience hints at the consistent allowances we make for other voluntarily segregated groups to not engage with one another based on their identified preferences. It was not long ago that we allowed institutions to segregate Americans for us, as in the period of racial apartheid under Jim Crow. Seeing that there are accountability and legitimation problems with such institutionalized processes, we have nonetheless allowed many misinformed individuals and groups in the grass roots to continue the tradition on their own accord.

It should be emphasized, however, that this is not solely an American polemic. One of the most prominent leaders of the twenty-first century, German chancellor Angela Merkel, noted in 2015 that multiculturalism in Germany is a "lie" in spite of her open-door refugee policy for a country smaller than the state of Montana, one which has already attended to over one million refugees in 2015 alone. Such a liberal policy from her center-right government has "attracted praise from all over the world" (Noack 2015). It should be emphatically noted that Merkel was aware that there are *limits* to multiculturalism as a theme, noting how "multiculturalism leads to parallel societies and therefore remains a 'life lie.'" At the end of 2014 in the German city of Karlsruhe, Merkel echoed similar sentiments: "Of course the tendency had been to say, 'Let's adopt the multicultural concept and live happily side by side, and be happy to be living with each other.' But this concept has failed, and failed utterly" (Noack 2015). In contrast, in the United States politicians continue to skirt the issue, focusing instead on acknowledging the aesthetics, or the *form*, of diversity, over the historical dis*contents*—where they exist—of group identity and group interaction. The celebration of a society progressing toward acceptance of diversity rarely articulates how such allophilia cannot be an end in itself. For Childs (2003), it must instead be but a means toward the destination of a shared humanity, a "transcommunality" based on an ethics of respect.

EPILOGUE

One of the more sublime aspects of the human experience is that still unsolvable mystery of why and what follows our corporeal, tangible existence. The questions that attend to such a theme have led much of the human experience down spiritual and philosophical paths, paths that continue into the dynamic age of consumption. Yet within the framework of a technological age that for most instances has provided a myriad of solutions for social problems, it has also subjugated nature for its own sense of comfort, a process that now edges systematically toward micro-management of mortality. Yet the *meaningful* unknown that is our mortality remains on distant horizons. Like mariners, we have cast ourselves adrift, to be moved in some epochs by winds of faith, in others, by machines spawned by science. On the shore, however, are those whose hopes and dreams seek access to similar horizons by giving pride of place to a process that celebrates sovereignty and autonomy. The Death Café, a novel concept for community gatherings that examines living through mortality themes, offers many of us insight into the significance that modern beings continue to place on the issue of death and dying. Death Café attendees are analogously mariners that are exploring these horizons.

What can we learn from the Death Café experience? That as a social movement it is at times a critique against our risk society and in others a celebration of having transcended it. This volatile mixture is surprisingly symbiotic. By communicatively closing the distance between fear and acceptance of our mortality, the paths by which participants sacralize their mortality includes an overall acceptance of one another's sensibilities on death and dying, and through one another's contribution of cues that can offer doses of emancipation for life and living. In spite of being in a community of strangers, Death Café participants thus "trust in the existential anchoring of reality...and to some degree in a cognitive sense" (Giddens 1991: 35). As noted in my work, such a development stems from Habermasian communicative action dynamics—albeit in milder form—that take place in a primarily apolitical space, a process that for Giddens ensures ontological security. Consulting and sometimes debating their way through the theme of mortality, Café attendees have generated varying degrees of ontological security that carries "the individual through transitions, crises and circumstances of high risk" that affect us all (Giddens 1991: 38).

As can be seen in the transcriptions and Wordle canvases of our participants, we are reminded about the collective, people aspect of mortality where a community is nearby to confront it. In this process, accommodations are made for its raw, symbolic, and emancipatory dimensions. That Death Cafés are proliferating suggests that there is an inability in our major institutions to remove risks or provide satisfactory security in the lifeworld. In response, Giddens identifies a most useful orientation toward mortality through Janette Rainwater's *Self-Therapy* (1989) where she advocates a "dialog with time" as a means to contest its distortions by modernity. Rainwater's views on time add greatly to the views shared by LePoidevin and Melville at the outset of Chapter 5. Time —in a Western sense—is released in our consciousness to frame life and death, to give some sort of linearity to the human condition in life that can be romanticized into a journey. Yet our chronology is never our own if our lifeworld is colonized because other frameworks of time are imposed upon us. Rainwater was Habermasian in her advocacy to reappropriate time for the protagonist as a means toward lifeworld decolonization of mortality.

Although time has no tangible manifestation, the circumstantial evidence of its presence surfaces in each Café attendee's Wordle canvas, a canvas that contains the components of an individuation process that holds its dialog with time. Through this process, the actor engages in what Rainwater terms as autobiographical thinking, one that our study shows includes thematic reflections on many implications of mortality such as coping mechanisms for death and dying, anxieties, legalities, the notion of liberation through death, death as authenticity and truth, how one can envision and prepare for a good death through death talk, if there is an afterlife, how death is experienced through culture, and how we can use death to contest society's imperatives. For Rainwater, through autobiographical thinking we begin "developing a sense of one's life history" as a means of "escaping the thrall of the past and opening oneself out to the future" (cited in Giddens 1991: 72). Giddens affirms Rainwater's view, adding how "holding a dialog with time is the very basis of self-realisation, because it is the essential condition of achieving satisfaction at any given moment—of living life to the full" (1991: 77). No longer is the body a passive object, but a reflexive, thinking, action system highly capable of praxis all the way toward end of life.

For Giddens, a dialog with time makes room for reflection and allows for "a process of self-questioning about how the individual handles the time of her lifespan. Thinking about time in a positive way—as allowing for life to be lived, rather than consisting of a finite quantity that is running out—allows one to avoid a 'helpless-hopeless' attitude" (1991: 73). Given the colonization of the current lifeworlds as well as our future lifeworlds, citizens engaged in a dialog with time will need to identify "stressful events (actual events in the past and possible ones to be faced in the future) and coming to terms with their implications" (1991: 73). Although such identification is derived off discrete experientials, it nonetheless provides biographical continuity to the human in the process of being. Indeed, many citizens today still live in colonized lifeworlds that behoove decolonization. But since confronting death and dying are conceivably lifetime processes, one that can be nourished by strangers and their discursivities through dialog, Café participants' dialog with time through death talk serves to embed Café actors within the dynamism of living. This is done so in ways that minimizes concerns about, or creates awareness of, the possible risks to one's existence, which ultimately reaches its crescendo at death.

Engaging in risk assessments to check on a system of techno-experts that operate our media, market, and medical establishments, Death Café attendees are essentially decolonizing their present *and* future. Café participants do not desire to hand over their sovereignty on death and dying to experts, for this implies they have escaped from their freedom to self-personalize their life paths. Café attendees must open death and dying up and unpack its belongings for modernity has sequestered death and tucked it into systems, a process of "removing basic aspects of life experiences...from regularities of day-to-day life" (Giddens 1991: 156). Such a process is analogously seen in the sequestration of madness, criminality, and sexuality. Indeed, Giddens did not spare the hospital from critical assessment, noting that in spite of its employment of advanced medical technology and expertise, they are nonetheless "like prisons and asylums" in that they have "similar consequences in terms of the concealment from general view of certain crucial life experiences—sickness and death" (1991: 161). Yet in spite of such systemic control, Giddens argues that ontological security can still be found in the populace outside such systems, a state that can inspire the opening of the self out to the great unknown. The

surrender and catch moments that reveal new openings for self-actualization, one that underscores a developing death identity, does not
take place in a social vacuum.

Given such contexts, I would like for us to consider how living and
dying in the present age can be enhanced by community, perhaps even
more so than in premodern periods where religiosity and belief systems
authored for individuals the entire universal framework to live under
until their final moments. Ironically, they may have experienced greater
existential fear should their convictions falter, in spite of the likelihood
of being surrounded by loved ones when there was an abeyance of
warfare or natural disasters. We are less certain today as universal
frameworks are but sloganeered ideas with no center. Yet the Death
Café introduction of a death identity runs counter to the uncertainties
of mortality in spite of the cultural fragmentations and associated risks
of late modernity. This is because participants focus instead on our
shared humanity beyond socially constructed categories that many
others reify.

The Death Café as a modern existential movement may remain,
arguably, one of the few movements that allow a context of differences
to transcend into a context of *no* differences, thus enabling for the
actor a potential rebirth into emancipation, a rebirth into the existence
and mortality that we all share. The Death Café requires little
resources for its continued mobilization and operation other than a
venue for death talk to take place, with good food and drinks functioning as additional social lubricants for fostering community. It
remains noninstrumental in its rationality and macro-organizational
manifestations are unnecessary. Thus, as identity politics carve out
sectarian lifeworlds, death talk and its corresponding death identity
unites them to articulate how a good death can be conveyed—in all
of its permutations—as a *quality of life* issue. Indeed, the cross-cultural
and global dispersion of Death Cafés prompted Jon Underwood during his interview by Karen Wyatt to remark that people are "ready" for
Death Cafes.

In closing, countering the maldevelopments in the human condition of
late modernity are the raw responses of community that accept our shared
human condition of mortality. The reality checks on a less than impressive
technocratic utopia, expressed through dying yet inspiring people like
Brittany Maynard and Betsy Davis, and through all of the wonderful
people constituting this research, as well as those attendees at Death

Cafés in the United States and around the world, have taught us that there is a global community that is amenable to the notion of becoming one's own author in life and death. In the process, they have provided cues for one another, from the bottom-up, from the grass roots. Indeed, we have been shown how the decluttering process can be expressed and conveyed at the third place that is the Death Café. And perhaps most importantly, the Death Café experience reminds us that death and dying can simultaneously include society in the public sphere as well as within the dying individual, for society was there all along to provide cues and memories, along with freedoms *and* constraints for those who dared to hold a dialog with time, a continuum that will end for us at some point in what can hopefully be a fulfilling life chronology.

Holding a dialog with time through community, contemplating how a world of risk affects mortality, communicating with community the various trajectories of emancipation now and near death, allows freedom to be operative in a variety of decolonizing lifeworld environments. Whether we believe our last day on earth is but the birthday of eternity, famously stated by the stoic Roman philosopher Seneca, is but one of the many horizons of our mortality. Yet the Death Café's ultimate instruction for us to return from these horizons to live is best captured by legendary British football manager Brian Clough's remarks after a life-saving surgery: "Don't send me flowers when I'm dead. If you like me, send them while I'm alive."

REFERENCES

Alexy, Robert. 1996. "Jurgen Habermas's Theory of Legal Discourse." *Cardozo Law Review* 17(4–5): 1027–1034.

Anastaplo, Goerge. 1986. "Education, Television, and Political Discourse in America." Center Magazine July—August: 21.

Arendt, Hannah. 1970. *On Violence*. New York: Harcourt, Brace and World.

Ariès, Phillipe. 1974. *Western Attitudes Toward Death: From the Middle Ages to the Present*. Baltimore: The Johns Hopkins University Press.

Ariès, Phillipe. 1981. *The Hour of Our Death*. New York: Alfred A. Knopf, Inc.

Backhaus, Gary, and George Psathas. 2007. *The Sociology of Radical Commitment: Kurt H. Wolff's Existential Turn*. Lanham: Lexington Books.

Bauman, Zygmunt. 2000. *Liquid Modernity*. Cambridge: Polity.

Bauman, Zygmunt. 2004. *Wasted Lives: Modernity and its Outcasts*. Cambridge: Cambridge University Press.

Beck, Ulrich. 1992. *Risk Society: Towards a New Modernity*. London: Sage Publications.

Benford, Robert D. 1993a. "'You Could be the Hundredth Monkey': Collective Action Frames and Vocabularies of Motive Within the Nuclear Disarmament Movement." *Sociological Quarterly* 34(2) 195–216.

Benford, Robert D. 1993b. "Frame Disputes within the Nuclear Disarmament Movement." *Social Forces* 71: 677–701.

Berelson, B., and P. Lazersfeld. 1948. *The Analysis of Communication Content*. Chicago: University of Chicago Press.

Bever, Lindsey. 2016. "A Terminally Ill Woman Had One Rule at Her End-of-Life Party: No Crying." *The Washington Post*. Website accessed on August 29, 2016. https://www.washingtonpost.com/news/inspired-life/wp/2016/08/16/a-terminally-ill-woman-had-one-rule-at-her-end-of-life-party-no-crying/

© The Author(s) 2017
J. Fong, *The Death Café Movement*,
DOI 10.1007/978-3-319-54256-0

Boyte, Harry C. 1977. "The Populist Challenge: Anatomy of an Emergent Movement." *Socialist Review* 32: 39–81.

Bunce, Valerie. 1989. "The Polish Crisis of 1980–1981 and Theories of Revolution." In *Revolution in the World System*, edited by Terry Boswell, 167–188. Greenwood: New York.

Bunce, Valerie, and Sharon Wolchik. 2006. "Favorable Conditions and Electoral Revolutions." *Journal of Democracy* 17(4): 5–18.

Burawoy, M. 2005. "For Public Sociology." *American Sociological Review* 70: 4–28.

Butler, Katy. 2013. *Knocking on Heaven's Door: The Path to a Better Way of Death.* New York, NY: Scribner.

Calhoun, Craig. 1994. *Habermas and the Public Sphere.* Cambridge: MIT Press.

Childs, John Brown. 2003. *Transcommunality: Fro the Politics of Conversion to the Ethics of Respect.* Philadelphia: Temple of University Press.

Chriss, James J. 1998. "Review Essay of Jürgen Habermas's Between Facts and Norms." *Sociology & Criminology Faculty Publications.* Paper 100.

Clemens, Elisabeth. 1997. *The People's Lobby: Organizational Innovation and the Rise of Interest Group Politics in the United States, 1890-1925.* Chicago: University of Chicago Press.

Cohen, J. 1997. "Deliberations and Democratic Legitimacy." In *Deliberative Democracy: Essays on Reason and Politics*, edited by James Bohman and William Rehg, 67–92. Boston: MIT Press.

Corr, Charles A. 1992. "A Task-based Approach to Coping with Dying." *Omega— Journal of Death and Dying* 23: 81–94.

Corr, Charles A., Clyde M. Nabe, and Donna M. Corr. 2006. *Death and Dying, Life and Living* (5th). Belmont, CA: Thomson Wadsworth.

Corr, Charles A. 2015. "Teaching about Life and Living in Courses on Death and Dying." *Omega—Journal of Death and Dying* 73(2): 174–87.

Costain, Anne N. 1992. *Inviting Women's Rebellion; A Political Process Interpretation of the Women's Movement.* Baltimore, MD: Johns Hopkins University Press.

Craig, Jenkins J., and Bert Klandermans. 1995. "The Politics of Social Protest." In *The Politics of Social Protest: Comparative Perspectives on States and Social Movements*, edited by J. Craig Jenkins and Bert Klandermans, 1–13. Minneapolis, MN: University of Minnesota Press.

Dallas, Mary Elizabeth. 2016. "Many of Oldest Old Say They're at Peace with Dying: Study Finds Most People over 95 are Simply Grateful for Every Day." http://HealthDay.com. WEBSITE accessed on August 11, 2016. https://con sumer.healthday.com/senior-citizen-information-31/misc-death-and-dying-news-172/waiting-to-die-with-no-one-to-talk-to-about-it-709587.html.

Deathcafe.com. "Welcome to the Death Café." WEBSITE accessed on December 19, 2015. http://deathcafe.com/

DeLong, Lisa Solis. 2011. *Blood Brothers: A Memoir of Faith and Loss While Raising Two Sons with Cancer.* Mustang, OK: Tate Publishing & Enterprise.

DeSpelder, Lynne Ann, and Albert Lee Strickland. 2009. *The Last Dance: Encountering Death and Dying.* New York: McGraw-Hill Higher Education.

Doležalová, Markéta. 2012. "Milada Horáková (1901–1950)". *Institute for the Study of Totalitarian Regimes.* WEBSITE accessed on July 24, 2013. http://www.ustrcr.cz/en/milada-horakova-en.

Doug, McAdam, John D. McCarthy, and Mayer Zald. 1996. "Introduction: Opportunities, Mobilizing Structures, and Framing—Toward a Synthetic Comparative Perspective on Social Movements." In *Comparative Perspectives on Social Movements,* edited by IDEM, 1–20. Cambridge: Cambridge University Press.

Dugan, Andrew. 2015. "In U.S., Support Up for Doctor-Assisted Suicide." http://Gallup.com. WEBSITE accessed on October 11, 2015. http://www.gallup.com/poll/183425/support-doctor-assisted-suicide.aspx.

Economist Intelligence Unit. 2015. *The 2015 Quality of Death Index: Ranking Palliative Care Across the World.* Singapore: Lien Foundation Lien Foundation.

Eley, Geoff. 1994. "Nations, Publics, and Political Cultures: Placing Habermas in the Nineteenth Century." In *Habermas and the Public Sphere,* edited by Craig Calhoun, 289–339. Cambridge: MIT Press.

Emden, Cecil S. 1956. *The People and the Constitution.* Oxford: Clarendon.

Enrique, Laraña, Hank Johnston, and Joseph R. Gusfield. 1994. *New Social Movements: From Ideology to Identity.* Philadelphia: Temple University Press.

Esinger, Peter K. 1973. "The Conditions of Protest Behavior in American Cities." *American Political Science Review* 81: 11–28.

Esman, Milton J. 1994. *Ethnic Politics.* Ithaca, NY: Cornell University Press.

Fong, Jack. 2014. "The Role of Solitude in Transcending Social Crises–New Possibilities for Existential Sociology." In *A Handbook of Solitude: Psychological Perspectives on Social Isolation,* edited by Robert Coplan and Julie Bowker, 499–516. Hoboken, NJ: Wiley-Blackwell Publishers.

Fong, Jack. 2017. "Sentiments and Perspectives of Academics about Massive Open Online Courses (MOOCs)." *Journal of Excellence in College Teaching* forthcoming in 2017. 28(1): 49–76.

Frank, Arthur. 2000. "Notes on Habermas: Lifeworld and System." University of Calgary, Dept. of Sociology. WEBSITE accessed on June 11, 2014. http://people.ucalgary.ca/~frank/habermas.html.

Fromm, Erich. 1969. *Escape from Freedom.* New York: Henry Holt and Company, LLC.

Fromm, Erich. 2012. *To Have or To Be.* London: Bloomsbury Publishing.

Gamson, William. 1975. *The Strategy of Social Protest*. Homewood: Dorsey Press.

Gamson, William, and David Meyer. 1996. "The Framing of Political Opportunity." In *Comparative Perspectives on Social Movements: Political Opportunities, Mobilizing Structures, and Cultural Framings*, edited by Doug McAdam, John D. McCarthy and Mayer N. Zald, 275–279. Cambridge: Cambridge University Press.

Garnham, Nicolas. 1994. "The Media and the Public Sphere." In *Habermas and the Public Sphere*, edited by Craig Calhoun, 359–376. Cambridge: MIT Press.

Gerbner, George. 1980. "Death in Prime Time: Notes on the Symbolic Functions of Dying in the Mass Media." *Annals of the American Academy of Political and Social Science* 447 ((January)): 64–70.

Giddens, Anthony. 1990. *Consequences of Modernity*. Cambridge: Polity Press.

Giddens, Anthony. 1991. *Modernity and Self-Identity. Self and Society in Late Modern Age*. Cambridge: Cambridge University Press.

Giddens, Anthony, and Christopher Pierson. 1998. *Conversations with Anthony Giddens: Making Sense of Modernity*. Cambridge: Polity.

Godway, Eleanor. 2007. "Surrender and Catch and the Question of Reason: Kurt Wolff and John Macmurray." In *The Sociology of Radical Commitment: Kurt H. Wolff's Existential Turn*, edited by Gary Backhaus and George Psathas, 77–91. Lanham: Lexington Books.

Goffman, Erving. 1974. *Frame Analysis*. New York: Harper & Row.

Goldstone, Jack. 2004. "More Social Movements or Fewer? Beyond Political Opportunity Structures to Relational Fields." *Theory and Society* 33(3/4): 333–365.

Gordon, Joy. 2007. "Kurt Wolff's Work and its Place in Twentieth Century Social Thought." In *The Sociology of Radical Commitment: Kurt H. Wolff's Existential Turn*, edited by Gary Backhaus and George Psathas, 64–69. Lanham: Lexington Books.

Grady, Hugh H., and Susan Wells. 1985/1986. "Toward a Rhetoric of Intersubjectivity: Introducing Jürgen Habermas." *Journal of Advanced Composition* 6: 33–47.

Gratz, Roberta Brandes. 1989. *The Living City*. Hoboken, NJ: Wiley-Blackwell Publishers.

Gruen, Victor. 1964. *The Heart of Our Cities*. New York: Simon & Schuster.

Guinness, Molly. 2010. "Never Say Die? Far from it in Paris Death Café." *Independent*. WEBSITE accessed on December 11, 2014. http://www.inde pendent.co.uk/news/world/europe/never-say-die-far-from-it-in-paris-death-caf233-2121850.html.

Gunther, John. 1967. *Twelve Cities*. New York: Harper & Row.

Habermas, Jürgen. 1967. *Toward a Rational Society: Student Protest, Science and Politics*. Boston: Beacon Press.

Habermas, Jürgen. 1971. *Knowledge and Human Interests*. Boston: Beacon Press.

Habermas, Jürgen. 1975. *Legitimation Crisis*. Boston: Beacon Press.

Habermas, Jürgen. 1981. "New Social Movement." *Telos* 49: 33–37.

Habermas, Jürgen. 1983. *Moral Consciousness and Communicative Action*. Cambridge: MIT Press.

Habermas, Jürgen. 1984. *The Theory of Communicative Action, Volume 1: Reason and the Rationalization of Society*. Boston: Beacon Press.

Habermas, Jürgen. 1986. "The New Obscurity: The Crisis of the Welfare State and the Exhaustion of Utopian Energies." *Philosophy & Social Criticism* 11: 1–18.

Habermas, Jürgen. 1987. *The Theory of Communicative Action, Volume 2: Lifeworld and System: A Critique of Functional Reason*. Boston: Beacon Press.

Habermas, Jürgen. 1991. *The Structural Transformation of the Public Sphere: An Inquiry into a Category of Bourgeois Society*. Cambridge: MIT Press.

Habermas, Jürgen. 1994. *Justification and Application: Remarks on Discourse Ethics*. Cambridge: MIT Press.

Habermas, Jürgen. 1996. *Between Facts and Norms*. Cambridge: MIT Press.

Habermas, Jürgen. 2000. *The Philosophical Discourse of Modernity: Twelve Lectures*. Cambridge: MIT Press.

Hale, Henry. 2006. "Democracy or Autocracy on the March? The Color Revolutions as Nomal Dynamics of Patronal Presidentialism." *Communist and Post-Communist Studies* 39(3): 305–329.

Hanspeter, Kriesi, Ruud Koopmans, Jan W. Duyvendak, and Marco G. Giugni. 1999. "Risk and Responsibility." *Modern Law Review* 62(1): 1–10.

Hochschild, Arlie. 1989. *The Second Shift*. New York: Avon.

Horkheimer, Max, and Theodor W. Adorno. 1972. *Dialectic of Enlightenment*. New York: Continuum.

Huntington, Samuel. 1991. *The Third Wave: Democratization in the Late Twentieth Century*. Norman: University of Oklahoma Press.

Illich, Ivan. 1976. *Medical Nemesis: The Expropriation of Health*. New York: Pantheon Books.

Imber, John. 2007. "Kurt H. Wolff and Sociology." In *The Sociology of Radical Commitment: Kurt H. Wolff's Existential Turn*, edited by Gary Backhaus and George Psathas, 69–75. Lanham: Lexington Books.

Inglehart, Ronald. 2008. "Changing Values among Western Publics from 1970 to 2006." *West European Politics* 31(1–2): 130–146.

Jasper, James M. 1997. *The Art of Moral Protest: Culture, Biography, and Creativity in Social Movements*. Chicago: The University of Chicago Press.

Johnston, Hank, Enrique Laraña, and Joseph R. Gusfield. 1994. "Identities, Grievances, and New Social Movements." In *New Social Movements: From Ideology to Identity*, edited by Enrique Laraña, Hank Johnston and Joseph R. Gusfield, 3–35. Philadelphia: Temple University Press.

Jütten, Timo. 2013. "Habermas and Markets." *Constellations* 20(4): 587–603.

Kalberg, Stephen. 2007. "Kurt Wolff's Epistemology of the Heart." In *The Sociology of Radical Commitment: Kurt H. Wolff's Existential Turn*, edited by Gary Backhaus and George Psathas, 78–80. Lanham, MD: Lexington Books.

Keeter, Scott, Cliff Zukin, Molly Andolina, and Krista Jenkins. 2002. "The Civic and Political Health of the Nation: A Generational Report." *Center for Information & Research on Civic Learning & Engagement*. Funded by the Pew Charitable Trust.

Kellner, Douglas. 2000. "Jean Baudrillard." In *The Blackwell Companion to Major Social Theorists*, edited by G. Ritzer, 731–753. Malden, MA: Blackwell.

Kemmis, Stephen, and McTaggart Robin. 2007. "Participatory Action Research: Communicative Action and the Public Sphere.." In *Strategies of Qualitative Inquiry*, edited by Norman K. Denzin and Yvonna S. Lincoln, 271–330. Thousand Oaks: Sage Publications.

Kim, Hesook Suzie, and Inger Margrethe Holter. 1995. "Critical Theory for Science of Nursing Practice." In *In Search of Nursing Science*, edited by A. Omery, C. E. Kasper, and G. Page, 205–219. Thousand Oaks: Sage Publications.

Kitschelt, Herbert. 1986. "Political Opportunity Structures and Political Protest: Anti-Nuclear Movements in Four Democracies." *British Journal of Political Science* 16: 57–85.

Koestler, A. 1966. *Dialogue with Death*. New York: McMillan.

Koopmans, Ruud. 1996. "New Social Movements and Changes in Political Participation in Western Europe." *West European Politics* 19: 28–50.

Krey, Peter. 2002. "The Life-World and the Two Systems." *Scholardarity*. WEBSITE accessed on November 28, 2015. http://www.scholardarity.com/?s=krey+life-world+two+systems.

Kriesi, Hanspeter, Ruud Koopmans, Jan W. Duyvendak, and Marco G. Giugni. 1992. "New Social Movements and Political Opportunities in Western Europe." *European Journal of Political Research* 22: 219–244.

Kriesi, Hanspeter, Ruud Koopmans, Jan W. Duyvendak, and Marco G. Giugni. 1995. *The Politics of New Social Movements in Western Europe: A Comparative Analysis*. Minneapolis, MN: University of Minnesota Press University of Minnesota Press.

Kriesi, Hanspeter. 1996. "The Organizational Structure of New Social Movements in a Political Context." In *Comparative Perspectives on Social Movements*, edited by Doug McAdam, John D. McCarthy, and Mayer Zald, 152–184. Cambridge: Cambridge University Press.

Krippendorf, K., and M. A. Bock. 2009. *The Content Analysis Reader*. Thousand Oaks: Sage.

Kurzman, Charles. 1996. "Structural Opportunity and Perceived Opportunity in Social-Movement Theory: The Iranian Revolution of 1979." *American Sociological Review* 61 (February): 153–170.

Laraña, Enrique, Hank Johnston, Joseph R. Gusfield. 1994. *New Social Movements: From Ideology to Identity*. Philadelphia: Temple University Press.

Lee, Su H. 2007. *Debating New Social Movements*. Lanham: University Press of America, Inc.

Legaciesofwar.org. 2016. "Secret War in Laos." WEBSITE accessed on January 9, 2016 http://legaciesofwar.org/about-laos/secret-war-laos/

Lelyveld, Nita. 2013. "Passing Thoughts at L.A.'s First Death Cafe." *Los Angeles Times*. WEBSITE accessed September 23, 2014: http://www.latimes.com/la-me-beat-death-cafe-20130415-dto,0,7928516.htmlstory.

Lipset, Seymour Martin. 1963. *Political Man*. New York: Anchor Books.

Lofland, Lyn H. 1973. *A World of Strangers: Order and Action in Urban Public Space*. Prospect Heights: Waveland Press, Inc.

Lofland, Lyn H. 1979. *The Craft of Dying: The Modern Face of Death*. Thousand Oaks: Sage Publications.

Manovich, L. 2010. "What is Visualization?" *Poetess Archive Journal* 2(1): 1–32.

Marcuse, Herbert. 1964. *One Dimensional Man*. Boston: Beacon Press.

Marks, Gary, and McAdam Doug. 1996. "Social Movement and the Changing Structure of Political Opportunity in the European Union." *West European Politics* 19(2): 249–278.

Maynard, Brittany. 2014. "My Right to Death with Dignity at 29." *CNN*. Website accessed December 22, 2015. http://www.cnn.com/2014/10/07/opinion/maynard-assisted-suicide-cancer-dignity/

McAdam, Doug. 1982. *Political Process and the Development of Black Insurgency, 1930–1970*. Chicago: University of Chicago Press.

McCarthy, John D., and Mayer N. Zald. 1973. *The Trend of Social Movements in America: Professionalization and Resource Mobilization*. Morristown, N.J: General Learning Press.

McCarthy, John D., and Mayer N. Zald. 1977. "Resource Mobilization and Social Movements: A Partial Theory." *American Journal of Sociology* 82: 1212–1241.

Melucci, Alberto. 1980. "The New Social Movements: A Theoretical Approach." *Social Science Information* 19: 199–226.

Melucci, Alberto. 1985. "The Symbolic Challenge of Contemporary Movements." *Social Research* 52: 789–816.

Melucci, Alberto. 1989. *Nomads of the Present: Social Movements and Individual Needs in Contemporary Society*. Philadelphia: Temple University Press.

Melucci, Alberto. 1994. "A Strange Kind of Newness: What's 'New' in New Social Movements?" In *New Social Movements: From Ideology to Identity*, edited by Enrique Larana, Hank Gusfield and Joseph R. Gusfield, 101–130. Philadelphia: Temple University Press.

Melucci, Alberto. 1996. *Challenging Codes: Collective Action in the Information Age*. Cambridge: Cambridge University Press.

Meyer, David S. 2004. "Protest and Political Opportunities." *Annual Review of Sociology* 30: 125–145.

Meyer, David S., and Debra C. Minkoff. 2004. "Conceptualizing Political Opportunity." *Social Forces* 82(4): 1457–1492.

Mezirow, Jack. 2003. "Transformative Learning as Discourse." *Journal of Transformative Education* 1(1): 58–63.

Miles, Lizzy, and Charles A. Corr. 2017. "Death Café: What Is It and What We Can Learn from It." *Omega—Journal of Death and Dying.* 75(2):151–165.

Mills, Kelley, T. 2012. "Letters of Milada Horáková" Center for History and New Media. WEBSITE accessed on April 22, 2014. http://chnm.gmu.edu/wwh/d/25/wwh.html.

Mitford, Jessica. 1963. *The American Way of Death.* New York City: Simon and Schuster.

Neimeyer, Robert A., Richard P. Moser, and Joachim Wittkowski. 2003. "Assessing Attitudes Toward Dying and Death: Psychometric Considerations." *Omega—Journal of Dying* 47(1): 45–76.

Nepstad, Sharon Erickson. 2011. *Nonviolent Revolutions: Civil Resistance in the Late 20th Century.* Oxford: Oxford University Press.

Niemi, Jari I. 2005. "Habermas and Validity Claims." *International Journal of Philosophical Studies* 12(2): 227–244.

Nietzsche, F. 2006a. *Human, All too Human.* Objective Systems Pty Ltd ACN.

Nietzsche, F. 2006b. *Thus Spoke Zarathustra.* Cambridge, UK: Cambridge University Press.

Noack, Rick. 2015. "Multiculturalism is a Sham, Says Angela Merkel." *Washington Post.* WEBSITE accessed on August 17, 2016. https://www.washingtonpost.com/news/worldviews/wp/2015/12/14/angela-merkel-multiculturalism-is-a-sham/.

Oldenburg, Ray. 1999. *The Great Good Place.* New York: Marlowe & Company.

Omery, Anna, Christine E. Kasper, and Gayle Page. 1995. *In Search of Nursing Science.* Thousand Oaks: Sage Publications.

Oreskes, Michael. 1988. "The Nation; An American Habit: Shunning the Ballot Box". *New York Times.* WESBITE accessed on March 11, 2014. http://www.nytimes.com/1988/01/31/weekinreview/the-nation-an-american-habit-shunning-the-ballot-box.html.

Oxley, Peter. 2006. *Cosmic Time.* BBC

Pettypiece, Shannon. 2013. "Death Dinners at Baby Boomers' Tables Take on Dying Taboo." *Bloomberg.* WEBSITE accessed on September 24, 2013: http://finance.yahoo.com/news/death-dinners-baby-boomers-tables040100216.html#.

Rainwater, Janette. 1989. *Self-Therapy: A Guide to Becoming Your Own Therapist.* Toronto, ON: Harpers Collins.

Reay, Diane. 2013. "Universities and the Reproduction of Inequality." In *A Manifesto for the Public University*, edited by J. Holmwood, 112–126. London: Bloomsbury Academic.

Rinpoche, Soygal. 2012. *The Tibetan Book of Living and Dying*. San Francisco: Harper.

Ritzer, George. 2003. *Contemporary Sociological Theory and Its Classical Roots.* Boston: McGraw Hill.

Ritzer, George. 2010. *Enchanting a Disenchanted World: Continuity and Change in the Cathedrals of Consumption.* Thousand Oaks: Sage Publications.

Ross, Kubler. 1969. *On Death and Dying: What the Dying Have to Teach Doctors, Nurses, Clergy, and Their Own Families.* New York: Scribner.

Rossato-Bennett, Michael. 2014. *Alive Inside* New York: Projector Media, Shelly & Donald Rubin Foundation. Projector Media, Shelly & Donald Rubin Foundation.

Rucht, Dieter. 1996. "The Impact of National Contexts on Social Movement Structures: A Cross-Movement and Cross-National Perspective." In *Comparative Perspectives on Social Movements*, edited by Doug McAdam, John D. McCarthy and Mayer Zald, 185–204. Cambridge: Cambridge University Press.

Schudson, Michael. 1994. "Was There Ever a Public Sphere? If So, When? Reflections on the American Case." In *Habermas and the Public Sphere*, edited by Craig Calhoun, 143–163. Cambridge: MIT Press.

Sheets-Johnstone, Maxine. 2002. "Size Power, Death: Constituents in the Making of Human Morality." *Journal of Consciousness Studies* 9(2): 49–67.

Slaughter, Shiela, and Gary Rhoades. 2004. *Academic Capitalism and the New Economy: Markets, State, and Higher Education.* Baltimore: The John Hopkins Press.

Slocum, Joshua, and Lisa Carlson. 2011. *Final Rights: Reclaiming the American Way of Death.* Hinesburg, VT: Upper Access Inc., Book Publishers.

Smith, Ronald G. E. 1996. *The Death Care Industries in the United States.* London: McFarland & Company, Inc., Publishers.

Snow, David A., and Sarah A. Soule. 2010. *A Primer on Social Movements.* New York: W. W. Norton & Company.

Stahl, Titus. 2013. "Habermas and the Project of Immanent Critique." *Constellations* 20(4): 533–552.

Stehr, Nico. 2007. "How I Came to Sociology and Who I Am: A Conversation with Kurt H. Wolff." In *The Sociology of Radical Commitment: Kurt H. Wolff's Existential Turn*, edited by Gary Backhaus and George Psathas, 37–61. Lanham: Lexington Books.

Szczelkun, Stefan. 1999. "Summary of the Theory of Communicative Action." *Royal College of Art, London.* WEBSITE accessed on June 8, 2016. http://www.csudh.edu/dearhabermas/publsbm01.htm.

Tarrow, Sidney. 1989. *Democracy and Disorder: Protest and Politics in Italy, 1965–1975*. Oxford: Clarendon.

Tarrow, Sidney. 1998. *Power in Movement: Social Movements, Collective Action, and Politics*. Cambridge: Cambridge University Press.

Tilly, Charles. 1978. *From Mobilisation to Revolution*. Reading, MA: Addison-Wesley.

Tiryakian, Edward. 1962. *Sociologism and Existentialism: Two Perspectives on the Individual and Society*. New Jersey: Prentice Hall.

Tolle, Eckhart. 2008. *A New Earth: Awakening to Your Life's Purpose*. London: Penguin.

Touraine, Alain. 1985. "An Introduction to the Study of Social Movements." *Social Research* 52(4): 749–787.

Viegas, F. B., M. Wattenberg, and J. Feinberg. 2009. "Participatory Visualization with Wordle." *Visualization and Computer Graphics, IEEE Transactions* 15(6): 1–8.

Virilio, Paul. 2000. *The Information Bomb*. London: Verso.

Von Eckhart, Wolf. 1978. *Back to the Drawing Board*. Washington, D.C.: New Republic Books.

Warren, Mark E. 1993. "Can Participatory Democracy Produce Better Selves? Psychological Dimensions of Habermas's Discursive Model of Democracy." *Political Sociology* 14(2): 209–234.

Weir, L. H. 1937. *Europe at Play*. New York: A.S. Barnes & Company.

Willmott, Hugh. 2000. "Death. So What? Sociology, Sequestration and Emancipation." *Sociological Review* 48(4): 649–665.

Wolff, Kurt. 1976. *Surrender and Catch: Experience and Inquiry Today*. Dordrecht, Holland: D. Reidel Publishing Company.

Wolff, Kurt H. 1962. "Surrender and Religion." *Journal for the Scientific Study of Religion* 2(1): 36–50.

Wolff, Kurt H. 1974. *Trying Sociology*. New York: John Wiley & Sons.

Yetim, Fahri. 2005. "A Discourse-Based Meta-Communication Model for Collective Sense-Making." Paper presented at The Language Acton Perspective on Communication Modelling, Kiruna, Sweden, June 19–20, 2005.

INDEX

© The Author(s) 2017
J. Fong, *The Death Café Movement*,
DOI 10.1007/978-3-319-54256-0

273

CPSIA information can be obtained
at www.ICGtesting.com
Printed in the USA
LVOW13*2211121217

559535LV00004B/4/P